Contents

Introduction

The first book in the *Innovations* series was originally created to provide intermediate to high-intermediate students with interesting models of natural spoken English to motivate them beyond the intermediate plateau. *Innovations* has now been updated and expanded into a full series (*Elementary, Pre-intermediate, Intermediate, Upper-intermediate* – with the *Advanced* level in preparation), for teachers looking for a fresh approach to young adult and adult learning.
It is based on a language-rich, lexical and grammatical syllabus that stems from the kinds of conversations that learners want to have.

So what's so innovative about *Innovations*?

Innovations Elementary, like the rest of the series, aims to promote understanding of natural spoken English and maximise students' ability to speak English with confidence. It does this not only by providing students with plenty of opportunities to use language in personal, creative and communicative contexts, but more importantly, it also provides a spoken model of English.

The language presented in the *Innovations* series is English commonly used in everyday life by fluent speakers. The series syllabus is designed to meet students' communicative needs and is therefore compatible with the objectives and can-do statements of the Common European Framework (CEF). At all levels, the prime objective of *Innovations* is to promote communication. As a result, the starting point for the syllabus is not the usual list of tense-based structures, but rather the typical conversations students strive towards in English. What is then presented and practised is the language (both vocabulary and grammar) that will help students be able to have those conversations. At elementary level, this means exposing students to more grammar than many other elementary coursebooks and introducing different tenses at an earlier stage in the book. However, these tenses are presented in simple ways within limited, but natural contexts. The focus remains on learning typical dialogues rather than presenting all aspects of the grammar in one go.

How does *Innovations Elementary* fit in with the rest of the series?

At elementary level, students learn to use some of the most common questions that they may be asked and a limited number of typical replies. In doing so, they cover a lot of basic grammar and vocabulary in specific contexts. The listening texts provide examples of how this language works within conversations and prepare students for *Pre-intermediate*, where students meet some of the same questions and answers, but within extended conversations. The reading sections in *Elementary* also help to introduce some basic vocabulary and collocations that are developed further through more topic-based units in *Pre-intermediate* and then *Intermediate*. Through this constant recycling and expanding of their English, the series aims to provide students with a very solid base in the conversations they will most need and want to have.

Innovations Elementary aims to take students to the level of the Cambridge KET exam and beyond A2 in the CEF.

Organisation

Innovations Elementary is divided into 24 units. Each unit is further divided into two double-page spreads, each providing a self-contained lesson of 60–90 minutes, though teachers may wish to vary the order in which they teach these elements.

The first double-page spread focuses on typical questions students need to ask and answer in basic communication. The unit title generally points to the main questions which are presented and around which conversations develop. The grammar and vocabulary in these sections are tightly focused on providing the language needed to answer the questions. The listening texts provide models of simple conversations that include some of the language already presented. Students practise these longer conversations and are then guided towards personalising them.

The second two pages focus on a reading text. The reading sections contain a broad variety of texts and tasks to develop students' receptive reading skills. They touch on topics related to the first part of the unit. The texts are carefully graded to allow students and teachers to get the maximum benefit from them. The majority are also recorded on the audio CDs / cassettes. Within these sections, topic vocabulary and useful lexis from the texts are focused on and aspects of grammar are presented and practised.

The final exercises in the unit generally focus on pronunciation. These exercises practise features of spoken English such as word stress, sentence stress and linking, but mainly present and practise individual sounds with the help of phonetic symbols to aid students in their self-study.

Writing sections are contained in all the odd-numbered units of the Workbook, while the even-numbered units contain exercises on key words and linkers in writing (*because, after, but, if* etc.). The writing section provides one or two simple models of the kind of texts required in the KET and PET exams. Students are then given the task of writing similar texts using the model as a guide.

There are five **Review** units with exercises to test and revise what students have learnt.

The **Tapescript** at the back of the Coursebook features all the conversations, listening texts and most pronunciation exercises that appear on the audio CDs / cassettes.

The **Grammar Commentary** at the back of the Coursebook provides students with useful advice and information about learning the grammar presented in the course. It also gives plenty of extra examples of how grammar is used in communication.

The **Pronunciation Introduction** links in with the pronunciation sections in the Coursebook. The first page provides general advice about how to work on pronunciation and has a list of phonetic symbols. The next two pages provide photos, diagrams and descriptions of how to produce the individual sounds. This section can be used as a tool in class and also as a reference for self-study.

The **Expression Organiser** at the back of the Coursebook allows students to record and translate some of the most important expressions in each unit.

Other components

The Coursebook is complemented by a set of three audio CDs / two audio tapes, a Workbook, this Teacher's Book and a separate, photocopiable Teacher's Resource Book. There is also support in the form of a website with useful links and the test-creating CD-ROM Exam View, Pro.

- **Audio CDs / cassettes**

  The audio CDs / cassettes contain recordings of all the conversations, reading texts, pronunciation exercises and those lexical exercises where stress and intonation are particularly important.

- **Workbook**

  The Workbook can be used for self-study, but any of the exercises may be done either in class or as homework. In addition, the Workbook contains writing tasks. The Workbook closely follows the contents of the Coursebook to provide the full support and revision students need at this level. There are also some additional language exercises to expand students' vocabulary and language notes that teach students useful items of grammar and lexis. Teachers may choose to use the Workbook in class or decide that there is sufficient exercise material in the Coursebook. If teachers choose not to use the Workbook as part of the course, it is a good idea to recommend it to students as additional practice.

  It is a good idea to set units as homework AFTER the corresponding units have been covered in class. In fact, you could even wait until you have finished Unit 2 in class before giving Unit 1 in the Workbook as homework. That way, the Workbook serves to consolidate what students have studied already and is a great form of revision for them. Probably the best way to use the Workbook is to simply tell students

to try _____ unit at home, to check _____ at the back of the book and to ask you in the next class if they have any problems. You might want to tell the class to try to do two or three exercises from each unit every day, rather than trying to do the whole thing in one big block the day before the next class.

- **The Teacher's Resource Book**

  The Teacher's Resource Book provides 40 photocopiable activities and games that closely support the material in the Coursebook. They are probably best used as revision in the lessons after you have finished a particular Coursebook unit. They offer a fun, interactive way of going back over what students have studied to see how well they have internalised and can now use, their new language.

- **Exam View, Pro**

  This unique CD-ROM contains a bank of test items for each unit that teachers can customise. It is simple, quick to use and provides unit-by-unit tests for those teachers who require them. Again, this affords teachers another way of revising the material that has been covered in class.

- **Web materials**

  This material can be found on the publisher's website http://elt.thomson.com. It consists of a special selection of websites that expand upon the topics and content of each unit, along with exercises for students to complete.

Getting the most out of Innovations

This Teacher's Book provides plenty of detailed advice on how to get the most out of *Elementary Innovations*. However, the following section contains some general points about teaching elementary students and using the special features of the Coursebook.

Teaching Elementary students

What knowledge does the material assume?

Elementary students have some very basic knowledge of English that they may have picked up from studying a basic course, from studying at school or simply from exposure to English in the global culture. This Coursebook assumes students have at least a passive knowledge of numbers, days of the week and the names of months, plus some basic verbs such as *is, are, have, say*, etc, pronouns (*I, you, he*, etc.) and possibly quite a few nouns. They may even know one or two typical questions such as *What's your name?* or *What's your job?* as well as stock responses such as *I don't know* or *I don't speak English*. When they produce English, however, it is restricted to statements such as *Me go, You want coffee?*, etc., and strings of nouns and lots of gesture. Certainly in multi-lingual classes, this kind of knowledge is needed to do the course.

However, in monolingual classes, with the support of translation by the teacher and pre-teaching through techniques such as TPR (see below), *Innovations Elementary* could be used at a lower level.

The input elementary students don't need – and the input they do!

Many coursebooks take the view that because elementary students make lots of mistakes and can't produce grammar accurately, they cannot understand grammar. As a result, the main focus is often to teach grammar rules and forms in a simplified way, which often restricts how the grammar can be used in communication. However, we strongly believe that while students certainly do (and will continue to) make mistakes, this doesn't mean that they can't understand concepts such as the past, present and future or that they can't produce a variety of limited structures early on in an elementary course. In fact, in terms of their longer-term development, it is essential that students are exposed to a variety of structures and normal conversation if they are to develop the ability to master the language at pre-intermediate level and beyond.

The problem with the traditional elementary syllabus

Traditionally, elementary books systematically work through the main tenses and their different forms. A number of problems emerge from this approach. The first and most important is that conversations don't work in this way in real life. Therefore, by implication, the conversations and practice activities presented in such material are not natural. This is not only a problem from the point of view of learning, but it also makes life difficult for students as real language users because they don't get sufficient exposure or repetition of the

conversations they will need to produce outside the classroom. The first example of the verb *went* in many elementary coursebooks comes between page 50 and 60, whilst in many books *going to + verb* may not appear until near the end of a hundred-hour course. As a result, elementary students frequently get frustrated because it may be a whole year of classes before they learn to ask in English, *Did you have a nice weekend?* or *What are you going to do after university?*

At the same time, there is also a question as to whether the 'simplified' grammar really is simple! The use of auxiliaries in questions, negatives, short answers and question tags is an area which is different to many languages and experience suggests it takes students a long time to master. Because of this, books – and particularly elementary books – obsessively focus on this area of *difficulty*. The materials, however communicative they may be, become exercises in transformations and mathematics. What becomes important is getting the right auxiliary in the question and reply rather than any real exchange taking place:

Did you have a nice weekend?
> Yes, I did.

Have you been to Spain?
> Yes, I have.

The truth is, most of the time we don't even use auxiliaries in our replies. Elementary students can function perfectly well and *correctly* by just saying *Yes* or *No* and then focussing on the typical follow-up comments and questions.

Negatives are obviously important, but they are much less common than positive structures. Furthermore, they are common in quite a number of typical expressions:

I don't know.
I don't like it.
I don't remember.
I'm not sure.
I didn't go.
I didn't do anything.
I didn't hear you.

Many negatives could be learnt as *expressions* before they are learnt as grammar. The same is true of question formation and, in fact, pretty much all grammar. Indeed, this is effectively how we learn our first language – hearing lots of examples of typical language, in typically narrow contexts before generating rules from which we can produce original statements. *Elementary Innovations* aims to follow this model of teaching and learning. It provides lots of models of a wider variety of structures than are normally found in elementary coursebooks.

As a result, we feel that it is best for teachers *not* to introduce supplementary grammar exercises on top of those that are in the book. If you wish to supplement, we

suggest extra practice and role-plays (such as those you will find in the Teacher's Resource Book), exercises from the Workbook, graded readers or elementary vocabulary exercises.

What if students ask me questions about grammar? What if they get things wrong?

Students at this level WILL make lots of mistakes. They will try and say things that are beyond their grammatical capabilities. This is inevitable at elementary level! Don't worry! You should not expect students to be either accurate or fluent by the end of this course any more than you should expect it with any elementary course. Correct students lightly. Give them the whole expression they want to say when they try to extend themselves and get them to repeat these in English. If you can, write these expressions on the board so students have a record of them.

When students ask a question about grammar, it's probably best to treat it like a question about vocabulary – even if it is about a grammar word. Explain it in the shortest way; translate it if you can or give one or two other examples, perhaps a very basic explanation of concept / meaning, and move on. Don't give long grammar rules or try to give subtle rules differentiating one form from another. Wherever possible, just correct and say *That's just the way we say it*. Don't introduce remedial practice activities of grammar points just because your students get something wrong.

Explanations and extra grammar practice will NOT mean your students stop making mistakes, especially when speaking. They are often *more* likely to cause worry and confusion. They may also cause frustration, because they take time away from students learning and practising genuine communication.

Correcting students

These are the techniques we personally use in our classes. The techniques depend on the stage of the class.

a. Presenting and drilling language
If you are drilling a new word or expression and a student gets something wrong (usually missing a word), repeat the whole expression first and then ask the student to repeat it. If they make the same mistake again, say the word correctly and get the student to repeat it. Then, say the rest of the expression from the mistaken word to the end of the expression and get the student to repeat. Finally, say the whole expression. For example:

T: I need to go to the bank.
S: I need to go bank.
T: to the
S: to the
T: to the bank.
S: to the bank.
T: I need to go to the bank.
S: I need to go to the bank.

In the above example, be careful you don't emphasise 'to the' too strongly. Try to use the weak form /tə ðə/ that students are likely to hear.

b. Monitoring students as they do a written task
When students have tried to copy a model, but have written it down incorrectly, point to the model(s), showing them the correct pattern. Then point to theirs, (you may have to do this twice). The students will usually correct themselves. If they can't, just tell them or write it for them and highlight the pattern again.

c. Monitoring students as they do a speaking task
During a controlled speaking practice, note students' mistakes with form and pronunciation as you monitor. Don't interrupt students too much at this point (if at all), but instead deal with the mistakes on the board when the activity is finshed. Rather than simply write mistakes on the board, write the expressions correctly on the board but with the mistakes gapped. For example:

I need to _____ to _____ bank.

With pronunciation errors, point to the word / expression on the board and ask students to say it. Then re-model the word / expression and get them to say it again. You could help students with particular sounds by using some of the tips in the pronunciation sections or refer students directly to the guide.

d. Monitoring students as they do freer practice
When students are involved in freer practice, it is important that you only correct language that has already been presented. When students produce new language in free practice, it is important not to interrupt their fluency.

You may occasionally need to take part in freer practices with students in their pairs. If you do so, be careful not to let the activity drag on too long. Encourage students to say what they want to say as best they can (including using their mother tongue) and then provide the model in English. At the end of a speaking activity, you can summarise for the other students orally what you heard said. Sometimes, tell the class what certain students tried to say and give them better ways of saying it on the board. For example:

"Samir said *I no want live London. Is people, people, people*. I know what he means, but we say: *I don't want to live in London. It's too crowded*. (Write these two sentences on the board.) *Crowded* means *people, people, people*. Samir, *crowded* in Arabic?"

In this way, the student sees they have communicated what they wanted to say and the correction is done in a positive way. If students ask why we say 'don't' or 'too', I would say *because that is how we say it*. At this point in their learning, the meaning of the whole expression is clear enough and that's what students should be focussing on at this stage.

Does the different content of *Elementary Innovations* require a different methodology?

No! All the exercise types you will see are common to many other courses and all of the activities are common to many language classes. For most teachers the following activities and techniques will probably be familiar. You may even consider some as positively old-fashioned! However, we believe they are the most effective methods for dealing with language at elementary level.

1. Translation and L1

For all elementary students, translation is a natural part of learning a foreign language. They will often record words they learn in class by writing the English and a translation. They will want to say things in English, but be completely unable to find the words, so they will use a bilingual dictionary, translating from their language to English. As teachers we should not discourage translation, but rather encourage the RIGHT kind of translation and use L1 to make learning easier.

When students translate or you translate for them, most nouns at this level are likely to have a single direct translation. It is still a good idea to encourage translation of the verbs and / or adjectives that typically go with the nouns as well. This is important because collocations often don't translate directly. For instance, in one language you might *see TV* rather than *watch TV*. For this reason there are a number of exercises in the book that ask students to translate whole expressions and collocations, rather than single words.

a. Multi-lingual classes and translation

Even if your students don't share a common language or you don't speak their language, translation exercises can still be effective in the class. You can get students to translate expressions onto a separate clean piece of paper, writing only in their language. In pairs, Student A can then point to one of the expressions in Student B's language and Student B can try to say it in English. Alternatively, you can get students to try to translate the expressions back into English from their own first language and then compare what they have written with the original sentences in English. This is an activity they could also do at home.

Often you may have pairs of students with a common language who can first discuss and translate expressions together and then test each other. You will often see students struggling or arguing about a translation, which may suggest you need to re-teach an expression.

b. Monolingual classes and translation

Teachers of monolingual classes often worry about their students using too much of their own language (L1) in the class and in certain cases may ban it. Students should repeat expressions in English and when they practise. They should also always use

English in controlled exercises. However, using L1 can sometimes be very useful and much more efficient. You can check students have understood by asking for translations; you can explain vocabulary using translation (see the section on pre-teaching below); you can let students do some of the freer speaking activities in L1 first and then translate some things for the students into English. Students could then repeat the task in English.

We would also advise you to use L1 for instructions, at least in your early classes or the first time students meet a particular task type.

2. Pre-teaching language

Any exercise in any coursebook is a small test. Exercises assume students know a few of the words and can work out the others either by using a dictionary, working with another student, by guessing from context, or by a process of deduction. With more difficult exercises and texts or with weaker groups, you may want to pre-teach some language, *before* you do the exercise in the book. Such whole-class teaching can sometimes also be more dynamic and interactive, and can provide a change of pace and focus in the class, which many students appreciate.

Suggestions about when and how to pre-teach language appear in the detailed lesson notes. However, the following is an overview of techniques.

a. Total Physical Response (TPR) – also known as acting out!

This is a particularly effective method of teaching words and expressions. The class needs to be able to stand up and have enough space to move around in. The teacher mimes a verb and says the word / expression, e.g. *watch TV*. All the students then do the same mime. The teacher does another mime and says the word. The students copy. This is repeated for four or five words. The teacher then calls out the different words presented and the students do the mimes. The teacher then presents perhaps another four words in the same way as before.

After testing the students on each verb two or three times, the teacher then mimes and asks students to say the word / expression. The teacher should correct and drill pronunciation if necessary. The students then test each other. Student A says the verb and Student B acts. After doing this, do the exercise in the Coursebook, where students get the written form and sometimes new collocations.

b. Drawings and photos

Many words can be simply drawn using outlines and stick men. In some cases, you might want to copy and enlarge the pictures provided in the Coursebook. It's also possible to find images on the Internet through a search. For each word or expression use a separate sheet of paper and make the drawing big enough for the whole class to see. Show students the picture and say the word. Students then repeat it chorally and individually. Stick the picture on the board. Show the class the next picture and say the word and so on. Check students have remembered the other words by pointing to the pictures on the board and eliciting the words taught. Students will then be exposed to the written form of the word / collocation when they do the exercise in the Coursebook.

c. Translation

The teacher says the word or expression in L1 and then in English. Students repeat it in English chorally and then individually. The teacher says the next expression in L1 and translates it into English and so on. Again, from time to time, re-cap the earlier expressions and re-teach if necessary. You might want to write the words or expressions on sheets of paper or an OHP transparency to give students a visual reminder as well and then just point to them when re-capping / testing students.

d. Conversation building

The first half of each unit focuses on simple questions and answers, building towards conversation. Usually the exercises in the book teach various ways of asking the same question and the listening puts them into a slightly longer context. You can start by teaching one version of the whole conversation. Teach the first line of the conversation using a picture, mime or translation as above. Drill it in English and as you get students to say it individually, reply with the next line of the conversation. Write the first line of the conversation on the board and elicit the next line from the students. They may tell you in English or in L1. If you can, use one of these ideas, drill the correct English and then get students to say the two-line conversation in pairs. Write up the next line on the board and in the same way elicit the third line of the conversation, drill it and elicit the 4th line. Then get students to practise all four lines of the conversation. Write up lines 3 and 4 and, if students are able, continue the process, to a maximum of eight lines. Once the whole conversation is on the board, give students a minute or two to finish writing it all down and to try to remember it. Then get students to practise in pairs from memory.

After doing this, you could continue with the unit in the book. The material will reinforce the original conversation you have taught by providing alternative answers and often additional comments and vocabulary. Equally, the initial conversation you've taught can provide additional support and context before starting the unit.

e. Learning by heart

Learning by heart has often been seen as anti-creative and anti-communicative. However, the basis of most creative activity, whether it be music, art or acting is frequently simple drills, memorization and repetition. It's the confidence learning in this way that actually allows a musician or actor to express feeling. Furthermore, for many people learning lists offers a clear target and proof of success and is therefore highly satisfying. The problem is less in the activity itself and more in the nature of the language we ask students to learn. For learning by heart to be successful, students should be provided with language that they can use immediately.

Learning lists of single words is unlikely to lead to great success because many basic words are relatively empty in meaning on their own and therefore easy to forget. *Take, have, get, go, put,* etc. only take on meaning when put in context, and those collocations vary from language to language.

When giving collocations, expressions or phrases to learn by heart, make sure you choose the ones that students will be most likely to hear or say. For example, it would be easy to give an example of *can* as *I can read*. However, in reality when would we tell someone *I can read*? In reality, *I can read* is neither the best example for *can* nor for *read*. Learning *Can you help me?* or *Are you reading this?* or *Did you read that thing about X in the paper this morning?* is more likely to lead to greater fluency.

Learning by heart can be used to 'pre-teach' language by simply giving students lists of language from a unit *in advance* for them to translate and learn. You could use the Expressions Organiser at the back of the Coursebook or alternatively use the language strips which head each unit. If you can, provide your own translations for the students. Students can try and learn the expressions at home before starting on the unit. The exercises you do in class become a learning check and more time can be devoted to spoken practice and using the language. This kind of pre-teaching is particularly useful for students who do not share the Roman alphabet and they may have more problems writing down language quickly in class or be less able to recognise words which have common roots in other languages.

Dealing with the main activity types in *Elementary Innovations*

1. Listening texts

Most of the listening texts in *Elementary Innovations* are preceded by vocabulary and / or grammar exercises that pre-teach some of the language students will hear. Some of the early tasks require students to simply hear and tick the language they have previously been taught. In some cases, students have to answer simple questions to begin with or take brief notes. These are generally quite achievable for low-level students and promote student confidence.

When you do a listening task in class, students may complain that they haven't understood anything. What they usually mean is that they didn't understand *everything*. It's therefore not a good idea to play the recording again immediately, before students discuss what they *did* hear. As a teacher, you can write some of their ideas on the board, perhaps indicating with a question mark things you know aren't quite right, but at this stage leaving it open. You can then play the listening again for students to re-check their ideas or move on to the second, more detailed exercise.

After the second listening get students to compare their ideas before dealing with them on the board as a class. Comparing answers is particularly relevant with listening texts as it reflects outside-of-class reality. Think of a situation you may have been in – that of being with a friend in a foreign country where neither of you speaks the local language fluently. You ask a local person for directions. After that person leaves, the first thing you do is ask your friend if they understood what had been said. Sometimes this leads to confirmation, whilst at other times it produces uncertainty. However, it is usually followed by both of you reconstructing part of what you heard. This might then help you if you ask another person for the same directions.

The final **Listen again** task requires students to complete gaps in the text using word recognition. In the earlier units, students are given the support of having the words in a box. You could get students to cover the box, if you want to test them more. In later units, the conversations are just gapped. Again, after playing the conversations, get students to check in pairs. Go through the answers by playing the recording, stopping it after each answer and eliciting it from students. Write the answers up on the board so the students can copy them. Drill vocabulary as you go through and explain / check new words. In the Teacher's Book there is advice on difficult words and how to teach them.

Some instructions ask students to look through the tapescript at the back of the book to find expressions or examples of grammar. You may wish to play the recording as they do this so that students can see the relationship between sound and the written word.

This process may mean students hear a listening three or four times during a lesson. This is a necessary thing at this level. Students don't usually find it boring; they find it reassuring and helpful.

2. Reading texts

There is a reading text on the second double-page spread of each unit. These texts are linked thematically to the title of the unit. All the texts have been written by the authors for use in class. They provide examples of different kinds of texts, e.g. e-mails, stories, articles, etc. All the texts recycle and expand on language taught in the course.

In the earlier units, there are generally simple gist tasks, often involving matching short texts to pictures or vocabulary. You may want to get students to label and talk about the pictures before they read. We often pre-teach vocabulary before students read the text. Again, you could ask students to test each

other or think of related language using a bilingual dictionary or by asking you.

All of the texts are recorded on the CDs / cassettes. This introduces flexibility in your lesson in two ways. Firstly, you can do the reading as a listening, following the procedures above. Alternatively, you can play the recording as the students read for the first time. In terms of class management, this is helpful, because it ensures all the students do the task at the same time and at the same speed. It is also useful for the students because it encourages quicker reading. After the first task, make sure students compare their answers. As they do this, you could get them to close their books or cover the text. The best test of comprehension is how well students recall a text. They naturally explain the text in their own words rather than just repeating what's in the text.

There is usually a second, more detailed comprehension task, often a vocabulary check or recall activity, which requires students to focus on specific language. Let students look at the task for one or two minutes to see if there are any problem words or if they know any of the answers already. You could do this as a class, by asking quickly if anyone knows the answer, but not confirming it at this stage. Then get students to read the text again before doing the task again. With stronger groups, get students to cover the text; with weaker groups, let them refer to the text.

3. Role plays and free-speaking tasks

Both the listening and reading texts are generally followed by a freer speaking task, where students give their personal opinions, tell a personal story or do a role-play based on the text. In the earlier units, these are obviously much more restricted. You can do these exercises in pairs or as a whole class. If you do them as a whole class, DON'T ask one student after the next round the room. This creates a very predictable and dull routine, which can kill the class. Try to ask different people, moving from one part of the room to another, more or less at random. You may not have time to talk to everyone. It doesn't matter.

4. Pronunciation and dictation

In each unit, there are one or two pronunciation sections. These focus on presenting individual sounds and phonetic symbols, word and sentence stress, and features of connected speech such as linking. However, all these sections have the added purpose of revising language that has been taught in this and previous units.

The pronunciation activities generally ask students to produce individual sounds, then to listen to and produce the sounds in single words, then in short sentences. To help learners produce the sounds, there is a guide at the back of the Coursebook with photos and diagrams showing the position the tongue and lips take for each sound. The tapescript also has the single words in phonetic script and you could start with these and get students to try and guess the words before hearing them. There are additional suggestions in this Teacher's Book on how to help students with their pronunciation. There are models of the sounds, words and sentences on the recording or you may prefer to model them yourself.

As you go through the single words, elicit the collocations and expressions used in the unit. This helps to recycle and revise language. For this reason, the pronunciation sections generally come at the end of a spread or a unit. However, you may wish to use these sections at other points in the lesson. For example, you could use them at the beginning of a lesson as a warmer and as a way to preview the unit or you could use them at any time when the particular issue of pronunciation arises.

In the later units, the pronunciation sections usually finish with a dictation of six or eight sentences, featuring key sounds. These sentences are again generally revising language. You can use these sentences in a number of ways:

- Let students listen while looking at the sentences in the tapescript. Then get them to practise saying them.

- Play the recording and get students to repeat the sentences.

- Play the recording as a dictation and get students to write down each sentence after they hear it. Pause the recording after each sentence and play the recording again until students have all the sentences written down.

- Play all the sentences through once without stopping and then put students in pairs to reconstruct the sentences from the words they heard. The aim is that they work together and produce grammatically correct and coherent sentences, rather than producing an exact copy of the sentence on the recording. This technique is known as 'dictogloss'.

- Get students to mark sentence stress and word stress on the sentences in the tapescript and then listen and check their answers.

Other common features

1. The language strips

The language strip at the top of each unit heading contains some of the more complicated language that students will encounter in the unit. At this level, it's best to ignore the language strip until after you have finished the unit. In a subsequent lesson, you can refer students back to the language strip, tell them to read through them and underline anything they don't understand. They then compare what they have underlined in pairs or groups and help each other out. This gives you the chance to monitor and see if there are any bits of language you still need to go over.

With stronger classes, you might want to begin a unit by doing a similar procedure. Tell students this is all language they'll meet in the unit, get them to read through it, underline new expressions and compare in pairs. Carry out the same procedure as outlined above.

With weaker classes, of course, you may just want to ignore the strips altogether!

2. The Real English notes

There are Real English notes throughout the Coursebook. They refer to a particular piece of language (word, expression or grammatical structure) that appears in one of the activities or texts. The notes contain many features of everyday English that traditional coursebooks often overlook and so it is important to draw students' attention to the explanations and extra examples. If you want to exploit them further, add more examples of your own or ask a few related questions for students to discuss in pairs.

3. Photographs

Photographs play an important role throughout the Coursebook. They are often there to help you explain some of the words students may ask about. Also, many exercises ask students specifically to match photographs and text, (e.g. pages 14 and 15), to role-play situations depicted in them, (e.g. pages 68 and 69), or to respond to them personally. Ideas about how to use photos like this are given in the detailed unit-by-unit notes or in the Coursebook instructions.

4. Review units

There is a review after every six units. Review units give students the chance to consolidate language they have studied. These reviews have been written to use in class time and have a number of speaking activities. However, you may want to set some of the exercises as homework. Two of these exercises are *Look back and check* and *What can you remember?* where students recall information they have learned and repeat previous activities. Repeating activities, perhaps unsurprisingly, often leads to better student performance the second time around. You may want to ask students to do activities like these more regularly as a quick way to help them revise. The review units also contain a *Vocabulary builder* page to develop students' vocabulary in areas already studied, an extra *Listening* to recycle much of the language and conversations already looked at and some extra work on *Pronunciation*, looking at the different ways in which certain letters are pronounced within different words.

Unit overview

General topic
Introducing yourself and other people.
Talking about people you know.

Conversation
Three people introduce themselves and others.

Reading
People I know

Language input
- Useful expressions: *My surname's Dellar, Do you live here? How are you?*
- Countries: *Brazil, Spain,* etc.
- Possessive ('s): *My friend's name is Barbara.*
- Adverbs of frequency: *People sometimes call me Andy.*
- Common expressions for when you meet: *shake hands, hug each other,* etc.
- The verb *to be: This is my brother.*

Language strip
As this is the first unit in the book and will probably be your first lesson with a new class, it's best to deal with the language in the **Language strip** as it comes up in various activities.

Conversation

1 Hello

Start the lesson by telling students your name, like this: *Hello. I'm ... .*

Then ask some individual students: *What's your name?* If students reply in full sentences (*My name is X ...*), discourage them! The normal way to answer in English is just with your first name. When you have done this with three or four students, tell students to listen. Say the whole sentence: *Hello. I'm [your name]. What's your name?* and get the class to repeat together. Then get individuals to say the sentences. Reply with: *[your name]. Hi.* and perhaps shake their hand.

When you have done this three of four times, ask students to have the same conversation in pairs. If possible, get the students to stand up and walk round the class having the same conversation with some different people.

Ask students to write down the conversation on a piece of paper and then compare it with what's in the book. If you want to, play the brief conversation between the two characters shown in the photograph and tell students to listen to *how* they say the words.

2 Names

If you can, translate the expressions in red for the students. Tell students what your full name is and then ask one or two students what their full names are to check understanding.

You may like to show what *surname* is by bringing a photo of your family in, or drawing a picture of a family. Point to each person in the picture and say their surname, e.g. *Dellar.* Then say it's their *surname.* Then say the first names of each person, e.g. *Hugh Dellar.*

Tell the class to write four sentences that are true for them, using the words in red. As they're writing, go round and check that they've understood the task.

Depending on where your students are from, they may have two surnames or two middle names. Explain or ask which are which.

Next, get one student to read out the questions in the practice and get another student to answer. Do this twice and then ask students to repeat in pairs or by walking around and talking to some different students. As they do so, go round and listen to their pronunciation, correcting and remodelling for them if they need it. Do this with each pair rather than the whole group, unless you hear something everybody has trouble with. In that case, deal with it at the end of the activity as a class, maybe remodelling it and drilling it.

3 Using vocabulary: countries

You could introduce this by repeating the conversation from **1 Hello** and then continuing it with the question: *Where are you from?* For example:

A: *Hello. I'm Phil. What's your name?*

B: *Andreas. Hi.*

A: *Where are you from, Andreas?*

If the student can't answer, either translate the question or show the student a picture of your country or your country's flag and say: *I'm from X. Where are you from?* Give them the correct word for their country in English if they don't know it and get them to repeat it. Then say: *Here are some more countries. Match the flags to the countries.* Hold up the book and show them how to do the exercise. Say: *Brazil – This? This? This ... ?* until you point to the correct flag and students stop you. Students can work in pairs to do the rest of the exercise.

When most students have finished, play the tape and students check answers. Go through the answers on the board. Ask the students: *Number 1? Number 2?* and correct their pronunciation if necessary, getting all the students to repeat the words.

Answers

1. Poland	2. Spain	3. Japan	4. South Africa
5. Italy	6. Mexico	7. Brazil	8. Switzerland

At the end, draw a question mark on the board and the reply: *Brazil*. Elicit the question: *Where are you from?* Ask students to repeat the question together and then individually. As each person repeats the question, you can reply and add: *What about you?* Point to the conversation in the book and ask students to practise the conversation in pairs.

You could get students up and moving round the room, practising the conversation with different people, but starting with: *Hi. I'm ... . What's your name?* and moving on to: *Where are you from?* Demonstrate with one student before you ask other students to do the same.

Finally, put students in pairs and ask them to write down as many other names of countries in English as they can. Give them five minutes and then elicit ideas from the class – write the names of the countries on the board. Mark the stress on the country names by underlining the stressed syllable or putting a big dot above it. Drill the names and then get individual students to repeat.

4 | Listening: *Do you know my sister?*

Point to the book and the cassette / CD player and tell students they are going to listen. They will hear people say their names and where they're from. Tell them to listen and write down what they hear in the gaps. Say: *Complete the sentences in the book. For example: I'm Peter. I'm from Brazil ... ? Germany ... ? Poland ... ? Where? Listen.*

Play the conversations, pausing briefly after each one. Give students a minute or two to compare their answers in pairs. Ask what they have. If the whole group between them can provide the answers, don't play the conversations again, unless the class really wants you to.

Answers
1. Switzerland, Yuka 2. Brazil, Italy 3. Japan, Leanne

5 | Listen again

Tell the class they are going to hear Conversation 3 again, between Hiro, a man, and Brenda and Leanne, two women. This time they should listen and complete the conversation with the words in the box. Read the words in the box as a class before listening to check they understand everything.

Play the conversation and then give the students a minute to compare their answers with a partner.

You may want to elicit the answers immediately or you may want to play the conversation one more time and stop after each gap. Students then call out their answers. Write them on the board.

Answers		
1. how	5. think	9. live
2. what	6. works	10. the weekend
3. too	7. nice	
4. my sister	8. sorry	

Go through any new language. For example:
- The *weekend* is Saturday and Sunday. In Britain, most people don't work on these days.

- *Hi* is another way that friends say *Hello* to each other. Go through the **Real English** note and drill *Hiya* and *Hi*.
- We say *Oh really* to show we're interested. Drill it, making sure students sound interested.
- *Hull* is a city in the north-east of England.

6 | Useful expressions

Tell the students to translate 1–8 into their language and write their translations in the book. If you share the same L1 as the class, check the translations or with weaker students, simply tell them.

If any of the weaker students have problems translating any of the expressions, it may mean you need to explain them again or ask other students who share the same first language to translate for them.

Next, ask students to read Conversation 3 in pairs. They can change roles once they finish. As they do so, go round and listen to their pronunciation, correcting and remodelling for them if they need it. Do this with each pair rather than the whole group, unless you hear something everybody has trouble with. In that case, deal with the problem at the end of the activity as a class by remodelling it and drilling it.

If you haven't done so already, tell students to read the **Real English** note, then drill the new words as a class,

7 | Let me introduce you.

Act out when to use this expression. Ask one student what their name is and then say:
Oh, OK. A. Let me introduce you to B. A, this is B.

Go through the new language:
- *Brother, sister* – draw a family tree and say *my mother, my father, me, my brother; he's a boy, my sister; she's a girl*.
- *Flatmate* – draw a picture of a flat in a house with two bedrooms and two people in. Say: *This is me. This is my flatmate. We live in the same flat.*
- *Husband / wife* – show them a wedding ring and say *The man – husband. The woman – wife*.
- *Cousin* – explain using the drawing of the family tree.

Tell the students to write the names of real people in as many of the gaps as they can. As they're writing, go round and check that they've understood and are writing sensible things down. If students are struggling, model by telling them about people in your life, ideally using some photos as you say: *OK. This is my friend, Rick. This is my brother, Colin,* etc.

Once most students have finished writing, tell them they have two minutes to try to learn the words in red. They then close their books and work in pairs to ask each other questions like those in the examples. Make sure they read the two examples before you ask them to practise. You might want to ask one or two students some questions using the words in red to model the activity for the group.

Explain *'s* in *friend's name* or *brother's name*. Say the *'s* means *the name of my friend / brother*, and read **Grammar note** G1 on page 136 together.

If any students ask about *I haven't got a brother*, tell them it's the same as *I don't have a brother*. Both are correct. (In this course, we use *haven't got* more often as it's more common in British English.)

Get students ask each other the questions. Go round and listen to their pronunciation, correcting and remodelling things for them if they need it.

If you are finishing your class here, ask students to bring photographs of their friends and family to the next class.

Reading

If you are starting a new lesson, begin with a bit of revision. You could tell the class to show their photos to a partner and say: *This is my friend, Rachel. This is my wife, Melissa* and so on. Round up with a couple of corrections or by correcting and writing on the board any new language students try to say.

Alternatively, write this on the board:
_____ ? (name)
_____ ? (country)

Elicit the two missing questions. Write: *What's your name?* and *Where are you from?* on the board and then tell students to walk around asking other students these questions. As they do so, go round and listen to their pronunciation, correcting and remodelling things for them if they need it.

1 Using grammar: *always ... never*

Look at the activity and tell the class to translate the grammar words into their L1. If you need to explain, point to the frequency line and maybe say:

always – every day, a lot
usually – most days
never – not at any time

Tell the class the person in the picture is one of the writers of the book and that they're going to hear him talk about his name. First, though, they should try to decide how they think he'll finish the sentences. Give them 4 or 5 minutes and then let them compare in pairs before playing the recording. Play it once and let students compare answers again. You may want to elicit the answers immediately or you may want to play the conversation one more time and stop after each answer. Students then call out their answers. Write them on the board.

Answers

1. usually
2. sometimes, usually
3. always
4. always, never
5. hardly ever, sometimes
6. usually, sometimes
7. usually, sometimes

Go through any new language. For example:
• *Andy* is short for Andrew. Ask if any of your students' names are short for anything.
• *Old friends* are people you've known for a long time, from when you were very young until now.
• *My love* is usually used between husbands and wives or boyfriends and girlfriends.
• *Dad* is a normal way of saying 'father'. Older people often say it. Children usually say *Daddy*. Go through the **Real English** note.

Give students a few minutes to write some similar sentences about what people call them. Tell them to try to use the grammar words in their sentences. You could help them by first telling them what people in YOUR life sometimes / usually / always call you. As they're writing, go round and check that they've understood and are writing sensible things down.

Then put the students in pairs and ask them to compare what they've written. Finish with a couple of corrections or by writing on the board anything new you heard students trying to say.

Tell the students to read **Grammar note** G2 on page 136. Tell them to also read the **Real English** note if they haven't done so already.

2 Meeting people

Tell students to look at the photos and act them out. Drill the expressions as they do so. Ask them to read the questions and examples and then give some examples of things you, yourself do / don't do. Make sure you use adverbs of frequency as you do this. You might need to give the class a couple of minutes to prepare. Then get them to tell a partner their answers. Round up with a couple of corrections or by correcting any new language the students have used on the board.

3 Using grammar: *be*

Students should have met the verb *be* before, but even if they haven't, the sentences in this activity are all ones they've met before and so can be treated as revision.

Tell the students you're going to do some grammar. Look at the activity and tell the class to complete **1–8** using the correct form of the verb. You might want to do the first one as a class to model the activity. Give students 4–5 minutes and then let them compare in pairs before checking the answers.

Answers

1. is   2. am, am   3. are   4. are, Are   5. is
6. are   7. is   8. is

As you elicit the answers, write them on the board. It's best not to try to explain the answers at this stage. Just say: *This is how we say it.*

You should just point out and say again: *I – am / You – are / It – is / They – are.* You can then tell the students to read **Grammar note** G3 on page 136.

4 While you read

Start by telling the class that the man in the family photo is Gerry and he's Scottish. Tell the students they're going to read what Gerry says about some photos. Ask the students to read the text on page 11 and decide which descriptions go with which photos. Make sure students understand that some of the descriptions don't match the photos.

Do the text as a listening, reading or both. (See **Introduction** for procedure).

After students finish reading / listening, get them to discuss their answers in pairs. Round up by asking the class how they knew the answers. They will probably use single words like *wife*, *children*, etc. Try to rephrase these ideas into whole sentences, so say things like: *Yes, OK. This is his wife. So this is A. What's her name? Can you remember?*

Answers

1. C   2. A   4. B

As you get the answer for 1, you might mention *kids* is an everyday way of saying *children* and tell the class to read the Real English note on this. You could ask a couple of students if they have any kids and help them with their answers.

At this stage, don't deal with any unknown vocabulary. Wait until after **5 Word check**.

5 | Word check

Tell the class you're going to look at some of the new language from the text. Ask them to try to complete 1–8 from memory, without looking at the text. As students try the activity, go round, monitor and check for any problem words.

You might need to explain:
- *Edinburgh* /ɛdinbrə/ is a city in Scotland.
- *City centre* – draw a picture of a circle. Say: *city*. Draw a smaller circle in the middle and say: *city centre*.
- *Smiles* – act this out.
- *Birmingham* is a big city in England.

After a few minutes, have students compare their ideas in pairs. You could also tell them to go back to the text to check their ideas. Tell them to underline the expressions in the text. Then elicit answers from the class, writing them on the board as you do so.

Answers

1. capital   2. from   3. met   4. phone   5. says
6. for   7. own   8. born

As you go through the answers, drill pronunciation where relevant. Go through any new language.

For example:
- The *capital* is the number one city in a country. Check by asking: *What's the capital of this country?*
- *Met* is the past tense of *meet*.
- *Phone you* – act this out.
- *Go for a coffee* means to go to a café. You could add *go for a drink* (beer / wine) and *go for a walk*.
- *On my own* – with nobody. Draw a house and one person in it. Say: *I live on my own*.
- *I was born* – in the past. Tell them where you were born and when. Maybe ask some other students where they were born to check they understand. Don't worry about explaining it's the past simple passive!

6 | Speaking

Tell the students to read the questions and to think about their answers. You might want to drill the questions. If you want to, let students ask YOU some of these questions first. Use the language from the exercise in your answers.

Now let students ask each other the questions, either in pairs or walking around the class, talking to some different people. You could finish with a couple of corrections or by correcting anything new you heard students trying to say on the board.

Homework

You could tell the class to do **Unit 1** in the **Workbook** for homework or you could wait until you've done **Unit 2** in class as well.

Alternatively, ask the class to draw or photocopy some pictures of important people in their life and to try to write a few sentences about them. Tell them to use Gerry's text to help them.

Collect the writing next lesson and correct it. Correct any mistakes with things already studied in class and give students better ways of saying new things that they're trying to say.

Unit overview

General topic
Talking about where you are from.

Conversation
Three different conversations about where people are from.

Reading
My home town

Language input
- Countries and cities: *Milan's in Italy.*
- Ways of travelling: *by bus, by car, on foot*
- *Is it far from here?*: typical answers
- Pronunciation: stressed sounds and sentence stress
- Grammar: questions with *is* and *are*

Language strip
At this early stage of the book, it's best it's best to deal with the language in the **Language strip** as it comes up in various activities. You could always come back to it later as revision. Alternatively, tell students to learn the expressions for homework.

Lead in
Do one of the following:
- Ask students to quickly draw five faces of people close to them in their lives. Tell them to write underneath each picture *my friend, my sister, my gran*, etc. but not their names. Students then swap pictures with their partners and ask each other: *What's your friend's name? What's your mum's name?* etc. They reply by saying: *Oh, this is Danny. This is Charlotte*, etc.
- Get students to repeat the conversation they studied in **Unit 1**. Demonstrate the conversation with one student first. Students then practise in pairs. When they have finished, repeat the conversation with another student. This time, continue the conversation by asking: *Whereabouts?* Students will probably not know this question. You can teach it by drawing the outline of the student's country and putting question marks in different places and saying: *Here? Here? Here? – Whereabouts?* Drill the question *Whereabouts?* and then repeat the whole conversation with another student. Then ask students to practise the conversation in pairs again.

Conversation

1 Using vocabulary: countries and cities

Show students the book and point to the exercise. Tell them to match the countries to the cities, pointing from the countries to the cities. Do the first one with the students. For example, England: *The city in England?*

pointing at a–h. Wait for a student to answer Birmingham and then tell everyone to do the rest.

When most students have finished, get them to compare in pairs. Then check the answers.

> **Answers**
>
> 1. e.   2. a.   3. g.   4. b.   5. h.   6. c.   7. d.   8. f.

You could ask students to test each other. Student A says the city and Student B closes the book and says the country.

2 Whereabouts?

Tell the class to cover **1: Using vocabulary**. Show them what you mean by doing it yourself. Then get them to fill in the gaps in the conversation. Students then listen to the recording and check their answers.

You could also do this as a class activity without using the tape. Elicit the answers from the class and write them on the board. As you go through each conversation, drill the following expressions:
Where are you from?
Oh really?
Whereabouts?

Go through any new language. For example:
- *Whereabouts?* means where exactly.
- *In the north* – draw a map of the country you're in and four compass arrows. Also ask students for *east* and *west* by pointing to the other compass points.

> **Answers**
>
> 1. France   2. Milan   3. Japan   4. Birmingham

Weaker classes could then just read out the conversations in pairs. As they do so, go round and listen to their pronunciation, correcting and remodelling things for them if they need it.

Next, ask students to have new conversations using the other countries and cities from **1: Using vocabulary**. Demonstrate how to do this with another student.

In multi-lingual classes, ask students to circulate and have similar conversations with the other people in the class.

The **Teacher's Resource Book** also has an activity to practise this conversation for any class.

3 Listening: *Whereabouts? Is it far?*

Point to the book and the cassette / CD player and tell students they are going to listen to three conversations of people talking about where they are from.

With weaker groups, write up the names of six countries on the board, including the three on the recording. Then say: *Listen. Which countries do you hear?* With stronger groups, tell them to listen and to try to write down the countries they hear.

Play the conversations once all the way through. Give students a minute or two to compare their answers in pairs. Ask them: *Where are the people from? Whereabouts? What else did you hear?*

Round up what they have and if the class can provide the answers, don't play the conversations again, unless the class really wants you to. If students don't have all the answers, play the conversations again, pausing after each conversation.

> **Answers**
> 1. Victor is from Cuzco in Peru – in South America. It's the second city. It's about an hour by plane from the capital. Mei is from Singapore.
> 2. Maria is from Valencia in Spain. Bart is from a small town in Belgium called Leuven. It's about half an hour by car from the capital, Brussels.
> 3. Artur is from Warsaw, the capital of Poland. June is from Bow in east London. It's twenty minutes away by underground, half an hour by bus.

4 Listen again

Tell the class they are going to hear Conversation 3 again, between June, a woman, and Artur, a man. This time you want them to listen and complete the conversation with the words in the box. You might want to let them read the words in the box before they listen to see if they understand everything.

Play the conversation and then give the students a minute to compare their ideas with a partner.

You may want to elicit the answers immediately or play the conversation one more time and stop after each gap. Students then call out their answers. Write them on the board.

> **Answers**
> 1. really   2. the capital   3. Whereabouts
> 4. from here   5. It's   6. by bus

Go through any new language. For example:
- *Is it far from here?* Draw the country you're in. Mark a city and then draw lines to other places. Say and answer the question for each place.
- Give examples of the *underground* from the country you're in or draw a picture of a train under the ground.
- *Half an hour* is the normal way to say thirty minutes. You could ask how to say 15 minutes – *quarter of an hour.*

You could also drill:
Oh really?
Oh wow!
Is it far from here?

Next, ask students to read out the conversation in pairs. They can change roles when they finish. As they do so, go round and listen to their pronunciation, correcting and remodelling things for them if they need it. Do this with each pair rather than as a class, unless you hear something everybody has trouble with. In that case, deal with it at the end of the activity as a class, remodelling it and drilling it.

5 Using vocabulary: ways of travelling

Point to the activity in the book and say: *Match the words to the pictures.* Students can do this individually or you could do it as a class. Go through the answers and drill the words chorally and individually.

> **Answers**
> 1. A.   2. B.   3. F.   4. C.   5. E.   6. A.

Don't try to explain why we say *on foot*; we just do. After checking the answers, ask one or two students which way of travelling they prefer. You could also point out that the big road in C is *a motorway* (*freeway / highway* in the US). Write this on the board.

6 Is it far from here?

Explain, or translate the following:
a quarter of an hour = 15 minutes
two and a half hours = 2 hours 30 minutes

Point to the activity title and say: *Is it far from here?* Then say the first sentence: *It's ten minutes by train* and repeat the question. Wait for a student to say: *No, not really.* Repeat with the second question. Then tell the class to do the others on their own.

When most students have finished, get them to compare in pairs. Then check the answers.

> **Answers**
> 2. Yes
> 3. No, not really
> 4. Yes
> 5. No, not really
> 6. Yes
> 7. Yes
> 8. No, not really
> 9. Yes
> 10. No, not really

Again, drill some of the more difficult expressions:
two and a half hours
about an hour and a quarter
about a quarter of an hour

You could use the answers to do a substitution drill. You repeat the question and different students answer using the ten different answers.

To practise this new language, ask four or five students: *Is your house far from here?* Help them articulate their answers using the pattern they've just looked at. Then ask students to ask and answer in pairs. You could then get students up and moving round the room, having the conversations with different people.

The **Teacher's Resource Book** has an activity to practise this and the other questions students have learnt in this unit.

7 Pronunciation: stressed sounds

This activity introduces a feature that is commonly used throughout *Elementary* and *Pre-Intermediate Innovations* – the use of capital letters in the **Tapescript** to highlight stressed sounds in words and sentences.

Put the students in pairs and tell them to practise saying the countries. Then either drill them or play the recording. Make sure students understand the capital letters show main stress. You could clap your hands, bang your foot or thump a desk to demonstrate stress in these words.

Play the next part of the recording and tell the class to underline or mark with a big dot the stressed sounds (syllables) in the nationalities. Tell them to check their answers on page 121. Drill the words using the answers. Next, get students to ask and answer the three questions in pairs. If you want to, let students ask you some of these questions first. Expand slightly upon your answers if you can. For example:
Students: Do you know any English people?
Teacher: Yes, I have a friend called Rob. He's from Carlisle in the north-west of England.

For homework, ask students to try to learn the conversation in **4 Listen again**, and then test them next lesson. Alternatively, get them to write their own conversation with Artur, giving responses that are true for them.

Reading

If you are starting a new lesson, begin with a bit of revision. Ask students to repeat as much of the conversation in **4 Listen again** as they can from memory. Alternatively, ask them to walk around the class asking some different students *Is your house far from here?* Round up with a couple of corrections or by correcting any new language the students have produced on the board.

1 Describing places

Point to the exercise in the book and tell students to read the text and decide which descriptions go with each photo. Tell them to listen and read at the same time. Play the recording.

Alternatively, ask students to cover the text and do the task as a listening. Students will need to compare their ideas in pairs after one listening and then listen again.

After students finish reading / listening, get them to discuss their answers in pairs. Round up as a class and ask the class how they knew the answers. They will probably use single words, *sea, mountains*, etc. Try to rephrase these ideas in whole sentences. Say things like: *Yes, OK. This picture here is Luleå. It's by the sea. And this is Pokhara. It's in the mountains. It's a small town.*

If students don't volunteer these short answers, you can just say these words and point to the relevant part of the pictures. Make sure you check they understand why each answer is the correct answer. Use the photos to point out things mentioned in the descriptions.

Answers

1. F. 2. E. 3. C. 4. A. 5. D. 6. B.

Next, ask one or two students which place sounds nice, and which place they like. Ask them why. They will probably say one or two words like *modern* or *quiet* which you can then rephrase into whole sentences like *Yes, it's a very modern city* or *It's a village. It's very quiet.* If you can translate, let the students explain why in their own language, translate it for them and then get the student to repeat in English. Write some of these things on the board in whole sentences.

At this point, you could also tell the class which places sound nice to you and explain why, using some language from 1–6. In pairs, students then ask each other the question *Which of the places sound nice to you?* If you have a small class, ask the class. At this stage, don't deal with any unknown vocabulary. Wait until after the Word check.

2 Word check

Read the words in the boxes together. Go through any new language. For example:

* *Crowded* means too many people. Very bad! I don't like it. Act having to push your way through a big crowd.
* A *village* is smaller than a town, (which is smaller than a city). Ask students if they are from a city, town or village. Ask how many people live there to check understanding.
* *Public transport* is the buses, trains and underground in a town or city. Ask students if they think they have good or bad public transport.
* Ask what the *second city* in their country is.

Ask the students to complete **1–5** and then **6–10** using the words in the boxes. You might want to do the first one as a class to model the activity.

After a few minutes, have students compare their answers in pairs. Tell them to go back to the text to check their ideas and underline the expressions in the text. Check the answers as a class, writing them on the board as you do so. As you go through the answers, drill pronunciation where relevant.

Answers

1. crowded
2. nice
3. village
4. public transport
5. town
6. sea
7. city
8. north
9. second
10. place

3 Using grammar: questions with is and are

Look at the activity and tell the class to complete 1–8 by adding *is* or *are* in each gap. Give them 4 or 5 minutes and then let them compare in pairs before checking the answers.

As you elicit the answers, write them on the board and drill the questions. You could also ask the class *Why?* when they call out answers. Point out and repeat *are you*, *is it*, *are they* etc.

You might need to explain *population* – how many people live there. Ask students what the population is in their country. Then tell the students to read **Grammar note** G4 on page 136.

Next, tell the class they are going to ask and answer the questions from the exercise. Give them a couple of minutes to prepare. Then ask them to work in pairs. As they do so, go round and listen to their pronunciation, correcting and remodelling things for them if they need it. Also, listen for anything they're trying to say, but don't know how to. Write it on the board.

4 Pronunciation: sentence stress

This activity follows on from **7 Pronunciation** on page 13. Here, capital letters are used to highlight strong stresses in sentences. The sentences here all use language from this unit.

Drill the sentences or play the recording. Make sure students realise the capital letters show the main stress. You could clap your hands, bang your foot or thump a desk to demonstrate stress in these words.

Finally, tell the students to translate 1–10 into their language and to write their translations in the book. If you share the same L1 as the class, check the translations, or with weaker students, simply tell them.

If any of the weaker students have problems translating any of the expressions, it may mean you need to explain them again or ask other students who share the same first language to help them.

Homework
You could tell the class to do **Unit 1** in the **Workbook** for homework, if you haven't done so already.

Alternatively, tell the students to write a short paragraph about their own home town, using as much of the language from this unit as they can.

Collect the writing next lesson and correct any mistakes in language studied in class. Correct any new language the students have produced on the board.

3 What do you do?

Language strip

Ignore the **Language strip** and deal with the language as it comes up in various activities. You could come back to it later as revision. Alternatively, tell students to learn the expressions for homework.

Lead in

Do one of the following:
- Ask students to look at the questions in **3 Using Grammar**, page 15. Give them one minute to study the questions, then ask students to close their books. How many questions can they remember in pairs? As you elicit the questions, write them on the board. Students then ask and answer the questions with a new partner.
- Split the class into two to four groups. Give students two minutes to write down as many jobs in English as they can using dictionaries if they want. The groups then swap papers. Find out which group has thought of the most jobs. Write the jobs on the board as the groups tell you them and drill the words, checking for stress where relevant. Give one point for each job correctly spelt. The winner is the group with the most points.

Conversation

1 Using vocabulary: *What do you do?*

Point to the jobs box and ask students to match each picture with one of the jobs. Give them a couple of minutes and then let them compare in pairs before checking the answers.

Answers

A. a shop assistant   B. a waitress   C. a barman
D. a lawyer   E. a student

Drill the other words as you write them on the board. Ask students if they know what the other jobs are in the box. If they don't know, get them to check in a dictionary.

Go through any new language. For example:
- An *accountant* does the money for a company. Do some big maths equations on the board to show what you mean.
- A *barman* – if it's a woman, she's a *barmaid*.
- A *civil servant* – a government office worker.
- A *waitress* – if it's a man, he's a *waiter*.

Play the recording and drill the words. Tell them to read the two examples given in the book. Ask students if they know anyone who does any of these jobs. Then tell them to tell a partner about any people they know. Elicit answers from the class.

2 Practice

To lead-in, ask some students: *What do you do?* Point to the different pictures in the book. Students answer as best they can using the words they've just learnt. Elicit the question from the students and drill it. Put students in pairs to practise this short conversation.

Ask the question again and elicit some answers, then elicit the next question they would ask by drawing a question mark on the board. For example:

A: *What do you do?*
B: *I'm a doctor.*
A: *Oh right. _____ ?*

Model and drill: *Where do you work?* Ask students to practise the whole conversation in pairs for a minute. Don't worry about mistakes at this stage.

Point to the exercise in the book and tell the students the sentences say where people work. Tell them to use the jobs from **1 Using vocabulary: *What do you do?*** to complete the sentences. You might want to do the first one as a class to model the activity. Then ask students to do the rest individually.

Answers

1. doctor	5. civil servant	9. lawyer
2. barman	6. waitress	10. accountant
3. teacher	7. student	
4. shop assistant	8. businessman	

When most students have finished, get them to compare answers in pairs, then check the answers as a class. Go through any new language and drill pronunciation:
- Clinic – ask another place a doctor works – *hospital*. Say (and gesture) *A hospital is big; a clinic is small.*

- *Pub* – it's like a bar. They sell beer.
- *Primary school* – for young children (5–11). You could also ask: *11–18 – What kind of school?* (Secondary.)
- *Government department* – give examples from the country you are in.
- *Import–export* – draw a rough map of the country you're in. Draw an arrow in and a picture of a car. Say: *import cars.* Draw a picture of clothes and an arrow out of country. Say: *export clothes.* Ask what things their country exports.
- *Law firm* – *firm* means company. We always say *law firm.*
- *Accounting firm* – as with law firm. Sometimes people also say *a firm of accountants.*

You could ask students to test each other. Student A reads the second sentence in **1–10** and Student B closes the book and says the job.

3 Further practice

Tell students to practise the example conversation. Choose one student to demonstrate with. Ask students to practise in pairs. Go round and listen to pronunciation, correcting and remodelling items.

4 Using grammar: more questions

Write up the following on the board:
Where _____ *you from?*
What _____ *you do?*
Whereabouts _____ *you live?*
_____ *it far from here?*
_____ *it a big place?*

Elicit the words in the gaps. Point to the exercise in the book. Tell the students to complete the questions with *is it, are you* or *do you.* You might want to do the first one as a class to model the activity. Give them a few minutes and then let them compare in pairs before eliciting the answers.

As you elicit each answer, ask students if the word after the gap is a verb or not. Establish the rule that *do you* is followed by a verb and *is it / are you*, etc. by words that are not verbs. Tell students to read **Grammar note** G5 on page 137.

Next, give students a piece of paper with a job written on it. Tell everyone to spend 3 or 4 minutes writing answers to questions **1–6** for their job. As they're writing, go round and check that they're writing sensible things. Help them with answers if they need you to. Then tell students to ask and answer the questions in pairs.

As a follow-up, give students another couple of minutes to memorise the questions and answers. Ask them to stand up and find a new partner and repeat the activity, but this time without their books! If students have no room to move, ask them to turn to the student next to them.

Answers
1. do you   2. do you   3. Are you   4. Is it
5. Do you   6. Is it

Round up with corrections or by writing any new language the students have produced on the board.

5 Listening: *What do you do?*

Tell students they are going to listen to four people talking about what they do and where they do it. Tell them to listen and write down the job and where the person works.

Play the conversations once all the way through. Give students a minute or two to compare their answers in pairs. Elicit answers, and if the whole group between them can provide the answers, don't play the conversations again. If they only have some of the answers, play the conversations again, pausing after each conversation.

Answers
1. civil servant in a government department in the capital
2. waiter in a French restaurant
3. shop assistant in a sports shop, lawyer in a big firm
4. doctor in a clinic, teacher in a primary school

6 Listen again

Play Conversation 4 again. Tell students to listen and complete the conversation with the words in the box. Read the words in the box before listening and go through any new language.

Play the conversation and then give the students a minute to compare their ideas with a partner. Play the conversation one more time, stopping after each gap.

Answers
1. doctor   5. helping   9. working
2. clinic   6. primary   10. boring
3. the north   7. enjoy
4. long hours 8. money

Go through any new language in the conversation. For example:
- *Oh right* – drill intonation.
- *And do you enjoy it?* – drill and focus on stress on *enJOY* and link to *it.*
- *Bournemouth* is a town by the sea in the south of England.
- *The money isn't very good* – drill and explain the contraction.
- *I have to* – I don't want to, but I have no choice.
- *Do a lot of paperwork* – explain this. Translate if you can or if you have a register or something similar, show students and mime filling it in and writing notes and filing papers away.
- *That's REALLY boring* (stress).

Ask students to read the conversation in pairs. They can change roles once they finish. As they do so, go round and listen to their pronunciation, correcting and remodelling things for them if they need it.

7 Do you enjoy it?

Point to the book and say that **1–10** are all answers to the question *Do you enjoy it?* Students have to decide if the answer is *Yes* or *No, not really*. Students work individually. Elicit answers from the class.

> **Answers**
> 1. Yes
> 2. No, not really
> 3. Yes
> 4. No, not really
> 5. Yes
> 6. Yes
> 7. No, not really
> 8. Yes
> 9. No, not really
> 10. No, not really

As you elicit the answers, drill the sentences. Go through any new language. For example:
- *The hours* are the time you start and finish. Give an example for yourself.
- *Awful* means very bad (Act out giving the thumbs down).
- *Boring* – yawn and act out another person talking a lot.
- *Great* means very good. (Act looking very pleased.)
- *Work really long hours* – say: *I start at 7 in the morning and finish at 9 in the evening.* Ask if any of the students work *long hours*. What time do they start and finish?

For further practice, ask students which sentences are true for them. Next, give students two minutes to write answers to the three questions in red. Go round and help where necessary. Then get students to ask each other the questions in pairs.

Round up with corrections or by writing any new language the students have produced on the board. Don't forget pronunciation errors. One might be *The hours are awful* – draw attention to the common use of the sound /ə/ in *are* and *hours* to lead into the pronunciation section.

8 Pronunciation: /ə/

Drill the sound /ə/ using the recording. If your students have problems with it, point out the picture on page 144 and focus them on where the tongue is and what the lips do to make this noise.

Read out the eight sentences or use the recording. The first time the students listen, tell them to listen and mark where they think the stressed sounds are in each sentence. Tell students the letters in italics all have the /ə/ sound.

Let students compare their ideas with a partner and then elicit the answers.

> **Answers**
> 1. I'm a <u>law</u>yer.
> 2. I'm an a<u>ccount</u>ant.
> 3. <u>Where</u> are you <u>from</u>?
> 4. Where<u>abouts</u>?
> 5. It's a<u>bout</u> an <u>hour</u> by <u>car</u>.
> 6. It's the <u>second city</u>.
> 7. It's <u>very quiet</u>.
> 8. You <u>pro</u>bably don't <u>know</u> it.

Play the sentences again and drill them.

For homework, ask the students to read **Pronunciation**, page 143 and learn the phonetic symbols. Alternatively, ask students to try to learn the conversation from **6 Listen again** and then test them in the next lesson. You could also get them to write their own conversation with Terry or Lesley, giving responses that are true for them.

Reading

If you are starting a new lesson, begin with a bit of revision. Ask students to try to repeat the conversation in **6 Listen again** from memory. Alternatively, elicit the six questions students studied in **4 Using grammar: more questions** and ask them to interview someone they didn't speak to before. You could also do an activity from the **Teacher's Resource Book**.

1 Before you read

Check students understand the meaning of the words in the box. In pairs or as a class, ask students to decide who said which sentences, (you may want students to cover the text). Go through the **Real English** before students read.

2 While you read

Ask the students to read and find out what each person says about their job, what they do, where they work and if they enjoy it. Do the text as a listening, a reading or both, (see **Introduction** for procedure).

After students finish reading / listening, get them to discuss in pairs what they remember about who said which sentences. Check the answers as a class.

> **Answers**
>
> **Ting Ting:** before she got married, she was an accountant for a big company and now she's a housewife.
>
> **José:** he's a student at Valencia University. He's studying medicine. He also works part-time as a barman in a disco in town.
>
> **Frances:** she's an actor, but when she doesn't have any acting work, she works in an office.
>
> (How much each person enjoys their job is not absolutely clear and students may argue one way or another, but they should refer to words in the text to justify their opinions.)

Don't deal with any unknown vocabulary until after the **Word check**.

3 Speaking

Do this exercise as a class. You could ask the class to vote on each question, then ask some individual students if they can say why – sometimes they might be able to with single words like *busy, difficult,* etc. You could expand these into whole sentences for them and say things like: *Yes. You're usually too busy to work while you're studying. / No, it's quite a difficult job.*

If you can, let students use their own L1 when they justify decisions and translate what they're saying into English for them. Write new things on the board.

4 Word check

Tell the class you're going to look at some of the new language from the text. Point to the exercise and tell students to match the verbs with the words on the right. Tell them to do all the questions and tell them they can look at the text for help if they need to.

Have students compare their ideas in pairs and then check the answers, writing them on the board as you do so. Encourage students to say the words rather than the letter so you can check their pronunciation.

> **Answers**
> 1. c.   2. a.   3. b.   4. d.   5. h.   6. g.   7. f.   8. e.

As you go through the answers, mime, explain or translate some of the meanings and drill pronunciation where relevant. You could also give other collocations and perhaps ask if students know any more, (but don't expect too much at this stage):
- *get divorced*
- *work for a law firm, work for a computer company*
- *take my wife to work (in the car)*
- *do the washing up, do the washing*
- *work in a bank, work in a hospital*
- *study law, study engineering*
- *earn 8 euros an hour, earn 35 thousand a year*

Then ask students to cover **1–8** and complete the seven sentences below by adding one word in each gap. Elicit the answers and write them on the board.

> **Answers**
> 1. earn   2. do   3. work   4. study   5. take   6. for
> 7. married

You could finish by asking a few students if they do the cooking / shopping / washing / cleaning in their house. You could also ask if anyone's married and when they got married.

5 Your future

This activity helps students talk about future hopes and dreams. Point out we use *I want / I don't want* to talk about the future. Highlight that we usually say *don't*

instead of *do not*. Ask students to decide their choices on their own. Answer any questions on vocabulary, but let students use a dictionary as well. Put students in groups of three or four and get them to share their ideas, alternatively discuss the sentences as a class.

Make sure students understand that if you are already doing some of the things in **1–10**, you can't say *I (don't) want to.* For example, some students might try to use this structure, when really they mean to say *I already work with computers* for **8** or *I'm already married* for **9**. Point this out and write these sentences on the board to help them.

You could finish this activity by telling the class a few of your own answers. Simplify your language and try to use some of the language from this unit. Round up with corrections or by correcting any new language the students have produced on the board.

6 Pronunciation: stressed sounds

Put the students in pairs and tell them to practise saying the words and to decide where they think the stresses are. They can then check the answers on page 121. Make sure students understand the capital letters show the main stress, then drill the words using the recording.

Give students five minutes to find sentences in the unit that use these words. Tell them to underline them, then try to memorise as many of the sentences as they can. Ask students to test each other. Student A says the words and Student B closes the book and says as many of the sentences as they can.

Example sentences:
My boss is awful; The money's awful; I earn about £10,000 a year; I earn £25,000 a year; I'm / I was an accountant; I do a lot of paperwork; I work in a government department; I work for the Health department; In the centre of the city; I work in a pub in the centre of town; I work in a big restaurant in the centre of town; I want to / don't want to work in the city centre; I want to / don't want to work for the government; I work for a big computer company; I work for an import–export company; I worked for a big company; I want to / don't want to work for a really big company. — It's quite difficult sometimes; It's really difficult; It's a very difficult job; It's difficult to find work; It's quite difficult sometimes, but I like it; I go to Hull / Valencia University; I study law at Bristol University; I want to / don't want to study at university; I work in a sports shop near the university.

Homework
You could tell the class to do **Unit 2** in the **Workbook** for homework, if you haven't done so already.

Alternatively, tell the students to write a short paragraph about their own job or the jobs that people in their family do using as much of the language from this unit as they can. If none of the class works, ask them to write a short paragraph about the kind of job they want to do in the future.

Collect the writing next lesson and correct any mistakes in language already studied and supply alternatives.

Unit overview

General topic
Talking about your plans for tonight.

Conversation
Five different conversations in which people talk about what they're doing now / tonight / at the weekend.

Reading
Places to visit

Language input
- Free time activities: *going shopping, watching TV,* etc.
- Future time expressions: *tonight, at the weekend,* etc.
- *Going to* + verb: *I'm going (to go) for a meal with friends.*
- Pronunciation: vowel sounds: /iː/ and /uː/
- Describing places: *Everything is included in the price. It's 2000 years old,* etc.
- Pronunciation: vowel sounds: /iː/, /ɪ/, /ʊ/ and /uː/

Language strip
Ignore the **Language strip** and deal with the language as it comes up in various activities. You could come back to it later as revision. Alternatively, tell students to learn the expressions for homework.

Lead in
Do one of the following:
- Elicit the six questions about jobs from **4 Using grammar** on page 17. Put the students into pairs and give them three minutes to note down any questions they remember and then round these up. If students have forgotten any, prompt them. Students then practise the conversations with a different partner. They can give answers that are true for them or invent answers for a different job.
- Do one of the **Unit 3** activities from the **Teacher's Resource Book**.
- Divide the class into two teams. Tell them that when you say a word, they have to call out another word or expression that goes with it. For example:
  Teacher: Live ...
  Student: ... in Madrid.
  Teacher: Work ...
  Student: ... for a computer company.

Give a point to the first correct answer for each verb. The winner is the group with the most points.

Conversation

1 Using vocabulary: activities

Pre-teach the vocabulary by acting out each expression and getting students to copy you and repeat the words. For full instructions on how to do this, see the comments in the **Introduction** about TPR on page 8.

Ask students to match the words with the pictures. Do the first one as a class. Then put students in pairs to do the others so they can help each other. Go round and help where necessary. Give them two or three minutes. Elicit answers and write them on the board. As you do, drill the expressions and if possible, ask students for a translation in their language.

Answers

A. go shopping
B. go for a walk
C. go for a meal
D. go to bed
E. study
F. go to the cinema
G. go back to the hotel
H. go home

If you are happy with how the students have said the expressions, you don't need to do the *Listen and repeat* stage in the book.

Give students one minute to try to remember the vocabulary from the exercise. Get the class to close their books. Put students in pairs to act out some of the verbs. One student can open the book and act them out while the other guesses. After one minute, tell them to change roles.

Tell the students we can also use these verbs with other nouns. Do the first matching with the class. Ask students to try **2–8** individually. Give them two minutes and then let them compare in pairs before asking for their answers.

Elicit the answers from the class and write them on the board. Again, drill the expressions. Ask for translations or ask students to act out the new words to check understanding.

Answers

1. d.   2. c.   3. a.   4. b.   5. h.   6. g.   7. e.   8. f.

2 Using vocabulary: time expressions

You can lead in by presenting the question: *What are you doing tonight?*

Translate the question or write today's date and an evening time with a question mark next to it on the board. Say the question in English and ask students to repeat it. Ask individuals to say the question and as they do so, reply using *I'm going to* + one of the verbal expressions from **1 Using vocabulary**. Next, elicit the question and some possible answers from the students – writing everything on the board. Good classes could practise asking these questions and giving answers using *going to* + verb.

If you don't want to do the presentation above, do the activity with the class instead. Tell the students (in L1 if you prefer) that they are going to hear five conversations where people talk about future plans. Each conversation starts with one of these five questions. Translate the questions for the students and then drill them. It's not necessary at this stage to go through the future tenses.

Answers

1. today   2. after the class   3. now   4. tonight
5. at the weekend

<hr/>

3 | Listening: *What are you doing tonight?*

Look at the activities in **1 Using vocabulary** again. Tell students they are going to listen to five conversations and that in each one they will hear people talk about some of the different activities from **1 Using vocabulary**. Tell them to listen and write down the activities they hear.

Play the conversations once all the way through. Then give students a minute or two to compare their answers in pairs. Elicit answers. If they only have some of the answers, play the conversations again, pausing after each conversation. Write the answers on the board. If possible, write the verbs on the right hand side of the board so you can use them to illustrate how we use *going to* + verb in **5 Using grammar: *going to* + verb**.

Answers

1. play tennis, go for a coffee
2. go home, go to the cinema, go to bed (early)
3. go back to the hotel, go for a drink
4. go shopping, go to a concert
5. go for a meal, read my book

<hr/>

4 | Listen again

Tell the class they are going to hear **Conversation 5** again, between Keith, a man, and Nicola, a woman. This time you want them to listen and complete the conversation with the words in the box. Go through the words before the students listen.

Play the conversation and give the students a minute to compare their ideas with a partner. You may want to elicit the answers immediately or you may want to play the conversation one more time and stop after each gap. Students then call out their answers. Write them on the board.

Answers

1. tonight   2. a meal   3. walk   4. nothing
5. going to   6. want to   7. my own   8. money

<hr/>

Go through any new language. For example:
*   *I'm going to …* describes the future. Not now, tonight. Gesture pointing forward.
*   *I'm going on my own* – say *just me*. Draw two / three people and say: *I'm going with a friend*, then cross them out, so it's *just me – I'm going on my own*.
*   A *hostel* is like a hotel, but really cheap. Give an example from the town you're in if you can.

Next, ask students to read the conversation in pairs. They can change roles once they finish. As they do so, go round and listen to their pronunciation, correcting and remodelling things for them if they need it.

<hr/>

5 | Using grammar: *going to* + verb

Go over some of the activities talked about in the five conversations, if they are not still on the board. Elicit the language the speakers use to talk about the future (*I'm going to*). Write the structure on the board in a table:

I'm going to	stay at home.
	go to the cinema.
	play tennis.

Ask students what you can say if it's more than one person and elicit / give *We're going to* and add this to the table. Ask students to look at the **Tapescript** on page 121 and find some other examples of *going to*. Check with the class. Go through the **Real English** note.

Tell students to close their books and to work in pairs. Tell them to practise the five conversations from memory. Demonstrate the activity with a student. Focus on the basic questions and answers. Give students 3 or 4 minutes. Make sure they change roles. Deal with any problems and corrections on the board as a class.

<hr/>

6 | Who with?

Go through the language in the box. Tell students we often say who we are going with. Give an example such as: *Tonight I'm going to the cinema with my girlfriend*. Translate this if you can. Tell them that in this activity there are more examples of answers like this.

Give them 1 or 2 minutes and then let them compare in pairs before checking the answers.

Answers

1. friends   2. own   3. dad   4. work   5. girlfriend

Now ask individual students questions from **2 Using vocabulary**. Show interest in their answers and ask follow-up questions or make comments such as *That sounds nice* or *Really?*

Next, ask the class to write down the questions and answers that are true for them. Encourage them to add details like who with. Give an example on the board that is true for you. Get students up and moving round the room, having the conversations with different people. Finish with a couple of corrections or by writing on the board any new language students have tried to produce. Go through any pronunciation difficulties, especially with /iː/ or /uː/ to lead into the next activity.

7 Pronunciation: /iː/ and /uː/

Model the sounds yourself or use the recording. Encourage students to use their fingers to feel how the shape of the mouth changes. You could get them to touch the end of their tongues as they say these sounds to feel how the tongue moves back in the mouth, (see the photos on page 144). Also, point to the dots in the phonetic symbols that show it's a long sound and encourage students to extend the sound – exaggerate it a little to help them.

Play the recording of the words for students to repeat. Again, ask students to feel the lip and tongue movement as they say them. As a follow-up, students could mime saying the words in pairs and try to guess each other's words.

Ask students to mark the sounds on the conversation. Check their ideas with the class.

> **Answers**
>
> A: Where are <u>you</u> from? (/juː/)
> B: <u>Greece</u>. (/griːs/)
> A: What do <u>you</u> <u>do</u>? (/ju/, /duː/)
> B: I'm a <u>teacher</u>. (/tiːtʃə/)
> A: Do <u>you</u> enjoy it? (/juː/)
> B: Yes, it's great. What about <u>you</u>? What do <u>you</u> <u>do</u>?
> (/juː/, /juː/, /duː/)

Play the recording. Draw attention to the fact that the first *do* in the questions is weak – it's pronounced with a /ə/ not /uː/.

For homework, get students to learn the conversation from **4 Listen again** and then test them in the next lesson. You could also get them to write their own conversations with a friend about what they're doing tonight, trying to use as much of the language from these two pages as they can.

Reading

If you are starting a new lesson, begin with a bit of revision. Ask students to try to repeat as much of the conversation in **4 Listen again** on page 21 as they can from memory. Alternatively, you could simply ask the students to walk around and ask some different people some of the five questions from **2 Using vocabulary** on page 20, giving answers that are true for them. It's a good idea to repeat this particular activity a few times. The answers will always be slightly different and you'll always be able to round up with a couple of corrections or by correcting any new language the students have produced on the board.

1 While you read

You could lead into this activity by asking if anyone has been to Britain and what they did there. Write any new language on the board.

Tell students they're going to read the text *Places to visit*. Tell them to imagine they are on holiday in Britain and are trying to decide what to do. They should read the text and decide which places they want to go to and which they don't, and why. Tell them they will then use the expressions in **1–6** to tell each other their choices.

You should just check at this stage they understand the vocabulary in **1–6**.

Do the text as a listening, a reading or both, (see **Introduction** for procedure). After students finish reading / listening, get them to read the model conversation and to then briefly discuss their choices in pairs. Their answers will obviously vary.

2 Vocabulary check

Tell the class you're going to look at some of the new language from the text. Ask them to try to complete **1–8** from memory, without looking at the text. There is just one word missing in each gap. After a few minutes, have students compare their ideas in pairs. You could also tell them to go back to the text to check their ideas. Tell them to underline the expressions in the text. Then check the answers as a class, writing them on the board as you do so.

> **Answers**
>
> 1. history   2. centre   3. old   4. train   5. Entrance
> 6. costs   7. walk   8. included

Go through any new language. For example:

- *History* – draw attention to the pattern *The history of …* . Give examples of books and museums the students may know.
- *It's two thousand years old* – give examples of other famous places and how old they are. Ask how old some places in the place the students live in are. You could act 'building something' and give them *It was built in …* .
- *Entrance* – in written English. We usually say *It's free to get in* or *It costs £5 to get in*.
- *It costs about £2* – the price is £1.90, £2, £2.10; I don't know – it costs *about £2*.
- *Walk round* – say other places you *walk round* – the *park, the castle, the old town*, etc. Ask students for other places.
- *Everything is included* – if you pay £20 you get in and then everything is free inside. You don't need to pay again. For example, sometimes you pay to get into a nightclub or disco, but a drink *is included* in that.
- *A castle* – draw a picture. Ask if there are any castles near where you are.
- *You can spend all day looking round* – point out the pattern *spend (time) + -ing*. Give another example: *I spent all day reading my book*. Ask for other possible endings.
- *The Crown Jewels* – point to the picture of the crown and say: *They're the Queen's*.
- *A cathedral* – like a very big, important church. Maybe draw a picture.
- *A shopping centre* – one building, lots of different shops inside. Ask for local examples.
- *Decorated* – draw a picture or use the room you're in to exemplify.
- *Theme park* – like Disneyland. Ask for local examples. Maybe draw some different kinds of rides. Write: *I went on all the rides* on the board.

3 | Role play

Tell students to look at the example conversation at the beginning of the activity. You could then work through the following similar example with the class. Write this on the board:

A: *tomorrow?*
B: *nothing much / stay at home / study / you?*
A: *Legoland*
B: *sounds nice*

Elicit each line from the students and correct / drill where necessary. Tell them to write similar conversations using the other examples. They can do this individually or in pairs.

As students are writing, go round and check and correct any mistakes. Deal with any common problems at the end. Finally, ask students to practise the conversations in pairs.

Alternativiely, do an activities from the **Teacher's Resource Book**.

4 | Pronunciation: /iː/, /ɪ/, /ʊ/ and /uː/

Use a correction from the last activity to lead into this activity if you can. Model the sounds yourself or use the recording. Encourage students to use their fingers to feel how the shape of the mouth changes. You could get them to touch the end of their tongues as they say these sounds to feel how the tongue moves back in the mouth, (see the photos on page 144).

Next, tell students to listen and repeat the ten sentences they hear. Play the recording and drill each sentence. As a follow-up, ask students to cover the sentences and try to say them again – using just the phonetic script as a prompt.

Homework

You could tell the class to do **Unit 3** in the **Workbook** for homework, if you haven't done so already.

Alternatively, tell the students to make a poster of places to visit in the town / city they live or study in. Students each write about one place.

Collect the writing next lesson and correct it. Correct any mistakes with things already studied in class and give students better ways of saying new things that they're trying to say. Make a display using all the pieces of writing.

Unit overview

General topic

Talking about what you did at the weekend.

Conversation

Four different conversations in which people talk about what they did at the weekend.

Reading

My weekend

Language input

- Past simple: *I wrote a latter last night. I bought some new clothes.*
- Pronunciation: vowel sounds: /iː/, /e/ and /æ/
- Useful verb collocations: *He took me to the airport. He took me out for dinner.*
- Pronunciation: vowel sounds: /eɪ/, /aɪ/, /aʊ/ and /əʊ/

Language strip

Ignore the **Language strip** and deal with the language as it comes up in various activities. You could come back to it later as revision. Alternatively, tell students to learn the expressions for homework.

Lead in

Do one of the following:

- Do one of the **Teacher's Resource Book** activities from **Unit 4**.
- Write up the following on the board:

What are you doing tonight? / this weekend? / after the class? / tomorrow?

Ask students to ask and answer the questions in pairs, giving answers that are true for them.

- Start with **6 Pronunciation** on page 25 as this recycles some of the language in **Unit 4** and introduces an example of the past simple as well. See below for procedure.

Conversation

1 Using grammar: past simple forms

To lead in, ask the question: *What did you do last night?* You can show the meaning by writing the time and date of last night on the board with a question mark or by translating it. Drill the question and as students say it individually, answer the question yourself, using a regular *-ed* verb. Write your answer on the board, underlining the verb. Write a selection of other regular *-ed* verbs. Then ask some students the question. Elicit an answer by pointing to the structure on the board and the verbs.

Ask students to ask and answer the question in pairs. Alternatively, you can lead in by simply saying: *In the last lesson we learnt to talk about the future, today we're going to learn how to talk about the past.*

Go through the verbs to make sure students remember all the verbs. Next, tell the class to listen to the recording and repeat the two forms of each verb.

Allow students two or three minutes to try to remember the past forms. Then put them in pairs to test each other. Student A says the basic verb forms and Student B closes the book and says the past simple form. Reverse roles after a couple of minutes.

Ask students to complete the sentences **1–10** with some of the verbs they've just studied in the past tense. Do the first two with the class to model the activity. Then ask students to do the rest individually. Give them a few minutes and then let them compare in pairs before checking the answers. As you elicit the answers, write the verbs in the past simple form on the board.

Answers

1. went	5. wrote
2. played	6. stayed, studied
3. watched	7. read, did
4. went, bought / got	8. went, was
5. wrote	9. read, was
6. stayed, studied	10. went

As you elicit the answer to 7, tell the students to look at the **Real English** note about *newspaper / paper*. You could ask the class if any of them buy a daily paper. Which one?

At this stage, you could also tell students to read the **Grammar note** G7 on page 137 about using the past simple.

2 Practice

Ask students if they did any of the things in **1 Using grammar** last night / yesterday / at the weekend, etc. Give an example yourself. For example: *I stayed at home last night.*

As a follow-up, ask students to move round the room and find someone who did four things this week that they did, too. Demonstrate the activity with one or two students first.

You could also make cards with pictures or with single nouns (shopping / cinema / letter, etc). Give each person one. Students walk round the room and have conversations like this:

A: *What did you do last night?*

B: (sentence based on cue card) *What about you?*

A: (sentence based on cue card)

Students change cards and partners and have the conversation again. Tell them to continue changing cards and partners for four or five minutes.

3 Listening: *Did you have a nice weekend?*

Read out **a–c** and drill them. Ask students to practise saying the questions and answers in pairs.

Next, tell students they are going to listen to four conversations which start with *Did you have a nice weekend?* Tell them to listen and find out which answer each speaker gives.

Play the conversations once all the way through. Give students a minute or two to compare their answers in pairs. Round up what they have and if the whole group between them can provide the answers, don't play the conversations again.

Answers

Conversation 1: It was OK.
Conversation 2: It was OK.
Conversation 3: No, not really.
Conversation 4: Yes, it was great.

Now ask the students to decide in pairs which things were talked about in each conversation. Then go through any new language. For example:

- *The paper* – go through the **Real English** note.
- Act out being *ill*.
- *Went on a trip* – when you visit a place and come back, you *go on a trip*. It's usually for fun. We often *go on a day trip*. Ask for or give examples of places people would go on a trip to. When you come back, people often ask: *How was your trip?*

Tell students to listen and check their answers. Play the recording again. Let students check in pairs again before checking as a class. You can also ask for anything else they heard at this point. Try to reformulate what they say into better English, re-using some of the language heard in the conversations.

Answers

Conversation 1: a and c
Conversation 2: a and c
Conversation 3: b and c
Conversation 4: a and c

4 Listen again

Tell the class they are going to hear Conversation 4 again, between Josh, a man, and Helen, a woman. This time you want them to listen and complete the conversation with the words in the box. Go through the language in the box before listening.

Play the conversation and then give the students a minute to compare their ideas with a partner. You may want to elicit the answers immediately or play the conversation one more time and stop after each gap. Students then call out their answers. Write them on the board.

Answers

1. nice   2. did   3. on   4. with   5. walked   6. saw
7. together   8. sounds

Go through any new language. For example:

- *York* is an old city in the north of England.
- *Together* means with other people.
- It *was beautiful* – very nice. Point to the photo on page 25.

Next, ask students to read out the conversation in pairs. They can change roles once they finish. As they do so, go round and listen to their pronunciation, correcting and remodelling things for them if they need it.

5 Practice

Before doing this exercise replay the four conversations and get students to read the **Tapescript** on page 122 and underline anything they want to ask about. Answer any questions students may have.

Next, write the following on the board:
nice / weekend?
great / went shopping / Saturday / saw a great film / Sunday
A: _____ ?
B: _____ .
A: _____ ?
B: _____ .

Tell the class they're going to write some similar conversations to the ones they just heard. Elicit each line from the students and correct / drill where necessary.
A: *Did you have a nice weekend?*
B: *Yes, it was great.*
A: *Really? What did you do?*
B: *I went shopping on Saturday and then I went to the cinema and saw a great film on Sunday.*

Tell students to write similar conversations using the other examples. They can do this individually or in pairs. If they work in pairs, they can help each other and correct each other's mistakes. As students are writing, go round, check and correct any mistakes. Deal with any common problems at the end.

Tell the students to practise the conversations in pairs. After that, tell the students to stand up and have similar conversations with some different students in the room. This time, encourage them to give answers that are true for them. Help students if they want to say something new. Get them to change partners two or three times.

After 3 or 4 minutes, give some feedback. Say what some of the students did last weekend. You could ask students some follow-up questions. Write up any new language on the board and drill it.

6 Pronunciation: /iː/, /e/ and /æ/

Use a correction from the last activity to lead into this exercise, if you can. Model the sounds yourself or use the recording. Encourage students to use their fingers to feel how the shape of the mouth changes. With these sounds the fingers should be on the top and bottom lip to feel how it opens. You could also get them to touch the end of their tongues to feel how the tongue moves down in the mouth, (see the diagram on p144).

Ask students to listen and repeat the words in the box. Demonstrate the next task by asking: *Which word am I saying now?* whilst saying one of the words in the box silently. Do this two or three times and then ask students to do the same in pairs.

Tell the students to practise the conversations in pairs. After they have finished, play the recording, so students can compare their pronunciation.

Give students a couple of minutes to try to remember the conversations. Play the recording two or three times as they do this. Students close their books and have the conversations again. Correct any pronunciation problems.

For homework, ask students to learn the conversation from **4 Listen again** and then test them next lesson. You could also get them to write their own conversations with a friend about what their weekend was like, trying to use as much of the language from the lesson as they can.

You could also ask them to try to memorise as many of the past simple forms on page 142 as they can. Test them next lesson by reading out the infinitives and eliciting the past simple form. This could be done as a team game, with an extra point if students can then produce a correct sentence using each past simple form.

Reading

If you are starting a new lesson, begin with a bit of revision. Ask students to try to repeat as much of the conversation in **4 Listen again** as they can from memory or do one of the **Teacher's Resource Book** activities for **Unit 5**. If you haven't done it yet, get the class to translate the **Language strip** at the top of page 20 in **Unit 4** and then ask students to test each other in pairs.

1 Using vocabulary: useful verbs

Tell students they're going to read a text about four people's weekends. Pre-teach the verbs using translation, mime, pictures or a mixture. Then do the activity. Explain the task and do the first one with the class. Tell students to do the rest individually or with a partner. As students complete **1–8**, go round and monitor and help out if necessary. Give students 4 or 5 minutes and then let them compare in pairs before checking the answers.

Answers

1. said   2. opened   3. asked   4. gave   5. was
6. took   7. paid   8. hired

Ask for the present form of each verb. Then go through any new language. For example:

* *Marry* – draw a picture of a couple getting married.
* *Ask me to marry him* – mime a man proposing and say: *Will you marry me?*
* A *present* – draw a picture of a present. Ask for examples of good presents.
* A *bunch of flowers* – point to the picture in the book. Point to one flower and say: *a flower*, point to another say: *a flower*. Circle all of them and say: *a bunch of flowers*. You could also show them *a bunch of keys* – if you have one or draw *a bunch of grapes*.
* *Angry* – mime
* *Cold* – mime shivering or draw a symbol with 5°C in it. Ask for / give the opposite *hot*.

* *Took me out for dinner* – ask: *Who pays? Me or someone else? Someone else pays.* Give an example of someone who took you out to dinner.
* *Flight* – point to the photo of the plane and say: *From London to New York, it's a six-hour flight.* Ask the last flight the students went on. How much did they pay?
* If you *hire* something you pay money to take it, but you give it back when you've finished. Usually you hire a car *for a week* or hire a bike *for a day*. Give and ask for other examples of things people hire.

Answers

1. say   2. open   3. ask   4. give   5. am   6. take
7. pay   8. hire

As a follow-up, give students a minute to remember the words, then test them by acting or drawing different expressions. Encourage students to say the whole expression, not just the verb. Then ask them to do the same in pairs.

2 Before you read

Explain the task. You might want to do this with the class, using the expressions from **1 Using vocabulary**. You could then tell students to cover **1 Using vocabulary** and see how many expressions they can now remember in pairs.

3 While you read

Explain the task. Do the text as a listening, a reading or both, (see **Introduction** for procedure). Give students a few minutes to read, then check the answers with the class.

Answers

Emily had a great weekend.
Paulo had a nice / great weekend.
Junko had a bad / awful weekend.
Ron had a great weekend.

Try to elicit some of the things each person did. Students will probably use single words as they do so. Try to rephrase these ideas into whole sentences, so say things like: *Yes, OK. They went to their house in the country.*

4 After you read

Tell students to cover the text. Elicit what happened to Emily, using the words in the exercise. Do this orally or write the expressions on the board like this:
Her boyfriend (came to her house and) took her out for dinner.
She opened the door and he had a big bunch of flowers for her.
He hired a Ferrari just to take her out.

Ask students to re-tell what happened to the next three people in pairs. Then play the recording or let students read the text to check.

Ask the class to cover the text again and re-elicit the expressions from the class. You don't need to write everything on the board this time, just do it orally.

5 Speaking

Tell the students to read the questions and to think about their own answers. If you want to, let students ask YOU some of these questions first. Use some of the words in red in your answers.

Let students ask each other the questions, either in pairs or walking around the class, talking to different people. Round up with a couple of corrections or by writing any new language the students have produced on the board.

6 Role play

Allocate one of the people in the text to each person in the class, or let students choose. Ask them to work in pairs and write a conversation, starting as shown in the book. Give them 5 or 6 minutes. As they are writing, help students with anything new they want to say and correct any mistakes. Give some feedback on any new language or any common mistakes before students practise reading their conversations together.

It's better to do the performances in small groups of fours rather than pair by pair as it is quicker and some students find performing to a class unpleasant. If there is one particularly good pair and they want to, they could do their conversation one last time for the class.

If time is short or if the group is relatively strong, students could role play the conversations without writing them down.

7 Pronunciation:/eɪ/,/aɪ/,/aʊ/and/əʊ/

Use a correction from the last activity to lead into this activity if you can. Explain the activity and see if students can make the single sounds from the phonetic symbols. Correct them yourself or use the recording.

Model the dipthongs yourself or play the recording. Drill the sounds. Ask students to use their fingers to feel the lip movement. The important thing is that the lips move as you say the diphthongs.

Ask the class which sound goes with each group of words and then play the recording.

Answers

1. /aʊ/   2. /eɪ/   3. /əʊ/   4. /aɪ/

Ask students to practise saying the sentences. Model them yourself or use the recording.

Homework

You could tell the class to do **Unit 4** in the **Workbook** for homework, if you haven't done so already.

Alternatively, tell the students to write a short paragraph about their weekend, using as much of the language from this unit as they can.

Collect the writing next lesson and correct it. Correct any mistakes with things already studied in class and give students better ways of saying new things that they're trying to say.

6 What are you studying?

Unit overview

General topic
Talking about your studies.

Conversation
Four different conversations in which people talk about their studies.

Reading
School and university

Language input
- Subjects at university: *history, geography*, etc.
- Conversations in class: *Have you got a rubber?*
- Common classroom expressions: *I'm sorry I'm late. Can I go to the toilet?*
- Pronunciation: the weak form of *are*.
- Pronunciation: regular *-ed* past simple form endings: /d/, /t/ and /ɪd/

Language strip
Ignore the **Language strip** and deal with the language as it comes up in various activities. You could come back to it later as revision. Alternatively, tell students to learn the expressions for homework.

Lead in
Do one of the following:
- Do one of the **Teacher's Resource Book** activities from **Unit 5**.
- If a weekend has passed between this lesson and your last, have students walk around and ask each other: *Did you have a nice weekend?* Round up with a couple of corrections or by correcting and writing any new language the students have produced on the board.
- Put students in pairs. Ask them to compare how much they remember about the text they read on page 27. Round up ideas from the class, then tell students to role-play a conversation between two of the people from the text, starting *Did you have a nice weekend?*

Conversation

1 Using vocabulary: subjects at university

You could lead in to this activity with a brainstorming game. Split the class into 2 to 4 groups, depending on the size of the class. Give them two minutes (no more) to think of as many school / university subjects in English as they can and to write them down. They can use dictionaries if they want, but be strict on the time. The groups then swap papers. Find out which group has the most subjects. Write the subjects on the board as each group tells you them and drill the words, checking

for stress where relevant. Give one point for each subject correctly spelt. The winner is the team with the most points.

With weaker classes, present the vocabulary in the box by translating it for them. You could do this while the class has books closed – as outlined in the section on pre-teaching in the **Introduction** (on page 8).

Alternatively, just tell students that they're going to learn the names of some subjects you study at university. Model the vocabulary yourself or use the recording and ask students to repeat the words. You could also ask what job you would do in each case, (business – businessman, economics – economist / accountant, engineering – engineer, history – teacher, etc.).

Ask individual students which subjects they think are interesting. Ask some different students which they think are boring and other students which ones are difficult. Then put students in pairs to swap ideas for two minutes.

Write the four-line conversation in the book on the board. Explain the next task. You could ask students to try to underline the stressed sounds before they listen. Do the first line together on the board, then get the students to do the rest in pairs. Play the recording and check the answers.

Answers
A: <u>What</u> do you <u>do</u>?
B: I'm a <u>stu</u>dent at uni<u>ver</u>sity.
A: <u>What</u> are you <u>stu</u>dying?
B: Ge<u>o</u>graphy.

Point to the first question and get one student to say it. Continue the conversation, but change the subject. The student will probably not continue the conversation past the four lines given, so add another line to the conversation on the board and try to elicit how the conversation might continue. You might want to prompt the student to say things like: *Do you like it?* and *What year are you in?*, but also be a little flexible and accept other possible questions or comments.

Repeat this process with another student and then ask students to do the same in pairs. You could ask students to move round the room and have several similar conversations with different partners.

2 Listening: *I'm a student*

Tell the students they're going to hear four conversations like the ones they have just practised. Explain the task. You might want to play the first conversation and elicit the information missing from the chart to check they've understood and then play the other three conversations all in one go. Give students a minute or two to compare their answers in pairs. Round up what they have and if the whole group between them can provide the answers, don't play the conversations again.

Answers

1. Business
2. Languages – French and Italian. Likes it a lot. It's really interesting.
3. Second year. Doesn't really like it. It's quite boring.
4. Tourism. In third year. Likes it a lot. It's difficult, but really interesting.

3 Listen again

Tell the class they are going to hear Conversation 4 again, between Carole, a woman, and Mark, a man. This time you want them to listen and complete the conversation with the words in the box. You might want to let them read the words in the box before they listen to see if they understand everything.

Play the conversation and then give the students a minute to compare their ideas with a partner.

You may want to elicit the answers immediately or you may want to play the conversation one more time, stopping after each gap. Students then call out their answers. Write them on the board.

Answers

1. at university   2. in   3. difficult   4. interesting
5. going to   6. want to   7. travel   8. good luck

Go through any new language. For example:

* *What year are you in?* With pronunciation, notice the weak *are* and the link between *you in.* Drill the whole question.
* *What are you going to do after university?* Check pronunciation and point out that *going to* talks about the future. If appropriate, you could ask some of the students the same question.
* *I hope* means you want this to happen in the future. You could accompany this with a gesture like praying or crossing your fingers or whatever may be familiar to students.
* *I hope you get the job you want.* Ask if Mark has a job now to check they understand *hope* again. Give other examples of things we say: *I hope it doesn't rain tomorrow, I hope you have a nice weekend, etc.* Check they understand we're talking about the future here.

Next, ask students to read out the conversation in pairs. They can change roles once they have finished. As they do so, go round and listen to their pronunciation, correcting and remodelling things for them if they need it.

4 Speaking

If students are at college / university, then ask them to write down true answers to these questions. If students aren't at university, get them to choose a subject and invent answers. Give students two minutes to do this. Try to get them to memorise what they have written. They then have conversations with a partner. Again, students could change partners two or three times.

5 Using vocabulary: conversations in class (1)

Tell the students that for the final part of the lesson they're going to learn some language they will need to use in class.

Explain the task. You could do **1–6** with the class or ask students to try it individually with their dictionaries. Go through the answers on the board. As you do so, drill the words individually and then in the question: *Have you got a … ?* As students repeat the questions, answer with one of the two answers given in the example conversations in the book. Then model and drill these answers. Ask students to practise the six conversations in pairs.

A variation would be to get the students to see if they can find someone who has each object – or even all six!

Answers

1. D   2. C   3. A   4. F   5. E   6. B

As a follow-up, get students to ask you other *Have you got … ?* questions that they might want to ask. Give them two minutes to consult their dictionaries. Help them with any new vocabulary. Write their questions on the board. Answer these questions and explain any new vocabulary to the class. Students could again practice these new questions in pairs.

6 Using vocabulary: conversations in class (2)

Explain the task. Do the first two with the class. Ask students to do the rest individually, using dictionaries if they need to. Help out where necessary. Give them a few minutes and then let them compare in pairs before checking the answers. Write the answers on the board.

Go through any new language. For example:

* *Can I go to the toilet?* – elicit / give the answer, *Yes, of course.* Elicit / give other things you might ask with *can: Can I leave early today? Can you close the door? Can you say it again?*, etc. Notice weak form of *can* /kən/.
* *How do you pronounce this word?* Demonstrate by writing a word on board. Say it two or three different ways, then ask and answer the question *How do you pronounce it?* You could then perhaps write the phonetic symbols for the word up and mark the stress as well.
* *Sorry I'm late* – the class starts at 9. It's now ten! Elicit reasons for being late.
* *Underline the words that go together* – demonstrate on the board.
* *Bebek* is Indonesian for *duck.* You could ask the same question using some words from your students' language(s).

Ask students to translate the sentences individually and then compare in pairs. Student A says the sentence in L1 and Student B (with the book closed) says the sentence in English. Monitor and check for any problems. For procedure with multi-lingual groups, see the **Introduction** on page 8.

As a final task, ask students to look at the **Language strip** at the top of page 96. Ask them to underline anything they don't know. Get them to ask their partner *What does … mean?* They can help each other and then ask you anything they're still not sure of!

7 Pronunciation: the weak form of *are*

Start by eliciting the four questions students learnt in **4 Speaking**. Draw attention to the weak form of *are*. Play the recording or model the examples yourself, and ask students to repeat the questions.

Ask students to ask and answer the questions in pairs. Again, monitor and encourage students to use the weak form. However, don't worry if they don't. At this stage, studying weak forms is more important for *receptive* purposes to help students deal with understanding spoken English at natural speed.

Go through new any language or errors when students reply to the questions. Deal with this on the board at the end of the activity.

For homework, ask students to try to learn the conversation from **3 Listen again** and then test them in the next lesson. You could also get them to write their own conversations with a friend about their studies, trying to use as much of the language from these two pages as they can. You could tell them to read the **Tapescript** on page 123 for ideas.

Reading

If you are starting a new lesson, begin with a bit of revision. Ask students to try to repeat as much of the conversation in **3 Listen again** as they can from memory. You could also do one of the **Teacher's Resource Book** activities for **Unit 5**. If you haven't done it yet, get the class to translate the **Language strip** at the top of page 24 in **Unit 5** and then ask students to test each other in pairs, using the L1 translations to elicit the English sentences.

1 Before you read

Tell students they are going to read a text about some different people's time at school and university, but first they're going to look at some of the language from the text to help them understand it.

Explain the task. Give students a couple of minutes to make their decisions individually. Let them compare in pairs. Encourage them to tell each other how they decided before checking the answers.

Answers

1. b and d   2. c and e   3. a

Go through any new language. For example:
- *Do a Master's* – after your first degree, like an MBA or an MSc. Ask how long it takes to do a Master's and if anyone has done one.
- *A primary school* – for children aged 5–11. You could ask where they go after primary school – *secondary school.*

In pairs or with the class, ask students to decide who they think said which sentences, (you may want students to cover the text). This is just to generate some interest in the text, the correct answer is not important.

2 While you read

Ask the students to read and find out what each person actually says about their education. Do the text as a listening, a reading or both, (see **Introduction** for procedure).

After students finish reading / listening, get them to briefly discuss in pairs what they remember about who said which sentences and if they guessed correctly.

Answers

Pardeep said **b**: then he didn't have a job for three years. It was awful!
Charlotte said **e**: she teaches literature to 1st and 2nd year students.
Clare said **a**: she finished her first degree 2 months ago and wants to do a Master's in art history.
Colin said **c**: he loves teaching kids.
Lee said **d**: he really enjoyed it and now he has his own company.

At this stage, don't deal with any unknown vocabulary. Wait until after the **Word check**.

3 Word check

Tell the class you're going to look at some of the new language from the text. Ask them to try to complete **1–10** from memory, without looking at the text. As students try the activity, go round and monitor.

Go through any new language. For example:
- *I was unemployed* – I didn't have a job. Drill it and point out stress.
- *genetics* – translate, or say: *It's why I'm like my mum and dad! I'm clever because my dad's clever and I've got red hair because my mum does too. They gave me my genes. That's what you study if you do genetics.*

After a few minutes, have students compare their ideas in pairs. You could also tell them to go back to the text to check their ideas. Tell them to underline the expressions in the text. Then check the answers from the whole group, writing them on the board as you do so.

Answers

1. didn't   2. make   3. give   4. lucky   5. Master's
6. relax   7. ago   8. grow   9. started   10. doing

As you go through the answers, drill pronunciation where relevant. Go through any new language.
For example:
- *The teacher gives homework; students get / have homework.*
- *Children grow up fast* – maybe they have a boyfriend or girlfriend when they're 12 or 13, they start smoking young, start drinking young, start wearing make-up young, etc.
- If a company is *doing very badly*, it's losing money.

Give students a minute to think about the questions at the end of the activity. Tell them to use their dictionaries if they need to. Do the discussion with the class or put the students into small groups. Round up with a couple of corrections or by writing any new language the students have produced on the board.

4 Role play

Explain the task. Tell students to choose a person from the text to role-play. Give students a few minutes to think about how to answer the three questions. As they are doing so, help students with anything new they want to say. Then tell them to work with a partner who has chosen a different person to them. Before they start, drill the three questions again. Let students have short conversations and then tell them to change and find a new partner. Round up with a couple of corrections or by correcting any new language the students have produced on the board.

As a follow-up, ask students to work in pairs and write one of their conversations. As they are writing, help students with anything new they want to say and correct any mistakes.

5 Pronunciation: -ed endings

Tell the class that the endings of many regular past simple forms are pronounced /d/. Tell them to look at the example for *played* and say it for the class. Drill this. Make sure no-one says *play-ed*! Do the same with *liked* and *wanted*. Put students in pairs and tell them to try saying each of the past simple forms of the verbs in the box by adding /d/. If they think the word then sounds strange, tell them to try with /t/ or /ɪd/. Do one with the class to model the activity. Say: *OK. 'Ask'. The past tense is* (write on board, but DON'T say yet) *'asked'. Does* /ɑːskd/ sound OK? No, it's /ɑːskt/.

Give students 5 or 6 minutes to discuss their ideas then play the recording or model the past forms yourself and tell students to check their ideas. Round up by asking which words use /d/, which use /t/ and which use /ɪd/. Write them in three groups on the board and then drill each group.

Answers

/d/   called, enjoyed, hired, learned (also /t/), listened, lived, loved, moved, opened, paid, played, phoned, rained, stayed.

/t/   asked, learned (also /d/), liked, walked.

/ɪd/   decided, hated, needed, studied, visited, waited, wanted.

Finally, tell students to spend two minutes thinking of five things they did yesterday or that happened yesterday, using the verbs. You could start by modeling this task for them. Tell them, for example: *I just stayed in last night and I phoned my brother. I listened to some music.* Students then compare their ideas in pairs or small groups. Round up with a couple of corrections or by correcting any new language the students have produced on the board.

Homework

You could tell the class to do **Unit 5** in the **Workbook** for homework, if you haven't done so already.

Alternatively, tell the students to write a short paragraph about their education, using as much of the language from this unit as they can.

Collect the writing next lesson and correct it. Correct any mistakes with things already studied in class and give students better ways of saying new language that they're trying to produce.

Review: Units 1–6

Activities **1–6** could be set as homework or done as a short test. If you do them as a test, it's best to give students 20–25 minutes to do them.

You could also do these activities as a slightly more relaxed revision lesson. You can introduce tasks quite simply by saying *Now we're going to revise some questions / vocabulary / grammar we've looked at before* and then explain the tasks. Students can do the tasks in pairs or individually as you wish. When you elicit the answers to each activity, you can ask questions about the language and re-teach any words and expressions students have problems with. After each activity, there is a suggested follow-up that you could do as a way of breaking up the lesson a little. They all provide some opportunities for speaking.

1 Grammar: past, present and future

Answers

2. PA.   3. F.   4. PR.   5. PR.   6. PA.   7. PA.   8. PR.
9. PA.   10. F.

You could follow this up by asking students to translate the sentences and then to test each other. Student A says the translation (or points to the translation, if the pairs don't share the same L1). Student B closes the book and says the sentence in English.

As a follow-up to sentence 5, ask the students if anyone has ever thought THEY were from a different country.

2 Grammar: negatives

Remind students to look back at the examples in **1 Grammar** to help them complete the rules.

Answers

don't,   'm not,   didn't,   wasn't,   'm not

Explain the next task.

Answers

1. don't   2. don't   3. didn't   4. don't, don't
5. didn't   6. don't, didn't

Ask students to write down three things they don't like. As they're writing, go round and check that they've understood and are writing sensible endings down. Help them with any new words. Ask them to compare their answers with other students in the class. Does anyone not like the same things?

You may want to refer students to the **Grammar Organiser** at the back of the **Workbook** for further examples of negatives.

3 Questions and answers

Answers

1. Where are you from?
2. What do you do?
3. What are you doing tonight?
4. Did you have a nice weekend?
5. What did you do?
6. What are you studying?

Ask students to do the first task and check the answers before you get them to match the questions with the answers.

Answers

1. e.   2. a.   3. c.   4. b.   5. d.   6. f.

Get students to ask a partner the questions and find out their answers. Their partner should say answers true for them.

Alternatively, students could write new answers which are not true. Students could then move round the class and try to find the most interesting lies!

4 Adjectives

Answers

1. cold   2. bad   3. easy   4. near   5. interesting
6. great   7. small   8. cheap   9. late   10. empty

You might want to get students to memorise and / or translate the pairs of words first. Students could then test each other. Student A says one expression and Student B, with the book closed, says the opposite.

Before students do the speaking task, you might want to give them 2 or 3 minutes to prepare. Get students to tell each other their ideas. Round up with a couple of corrections or by reformulating into better English interesting things you heard students say. Also, teach on the board any new language the students have produced.

5 Verbs (1)

Answers

1. finish   2. answer   3. learn   4. have dinner
5. play   6. write   7. sell   8. hate   9. see   10. feel

Get students to do the act out or draw to complete the task.

You could read out some sentences and ask students to call out the correct verb when you pause. For example:

*   *I start work at six in the morning and _____ at 8 at night.*

- *They asked me some really difficult questions and I didn't know how to _____ some of them.*
- *He left school when he was sixteen without knowing how to read or _____ .*
- *I love my little brother, but sometimes I really _____ him.*

6 Verbs (2)

Answers

1.	work	7.	live
2.	earn	8.	takes
3.	studying	9.	go
4.	walk	10.	speak
5.	takes	11.	send
6.	do	12.	stay

You might want to give students a couple of minutes to prepare before they discuss the questions. Round up with a couple of corrections or by telling the class some of the interesting things you heard students say.

7 Look back and check

If you have repeated these tasks as a form of revision / warmer in a previous lesson, you may want to skip this activity.

Let students look back at both activities and decide which one they want to do. Take a vote on which one they prefer or do both activities. Give students time to read and ask you questions about the language before they do the speaking task again.

8 What can you remember?

If you have re-elicited these texts as a form of revision / warmer in a previous lesson, you may want to skip this activity.

You could do this activity orally, if you like, instead of getting students to write notes. Students will remember quite a lot about the *content* of a text, but often will not remember the exact expressions or collocations. Try to remind students of these as you go through the answers. For example:
Student: *Junko boyfriend marry, but she say no.*
Teacher: *Yes, OK. Junko's boyfriend asked her to marry him, but she said no.*

An alternative way of doing this is to replay the recording of one or both of the texts. It depends on the time you have available.

9 Vocabulary builder: your house

This page aims to revise and expand on vocabulary, in this case things, activities and rooms in the house. You may want to pre-teach some of this vocabulary by presenting drawings of the furniture and / or by acting out the activities.

Explain the task and ask students to work individually for five minutes. They can use their dictionaries, but also go round and help students with any new language. Answers will vary, but check with students anything that

seems unusual to you, (for example, a sofa in a bedroom, a table in the bathroom, playing video games in the kitchen, etc.). Re-teach the words and ask students if that is what they mean.

Let students compare what they wrote. What things were different? Could anybody find six differences?

For the final task, ask students to spend two minutes memorising the language, close their books and practise the conversations. You could make this into a competition. Each time the students have a new conversation they should change the room or the activity. The first person to repeat a previous example or not be able to think of anything, loses the game.

10 Listening: *I'm quite tired*

Do this listening as you would do a normal listening. Explain the context and the task. Make sure students cover the conversation the first time they hear it. Ask students to compare their ideas in pairs. As they do so, go round and check to see how they've done. Depending on how much they've got, either elicit ideas from the class or play the recording a second time, and then elicit ideas.

Answers

There is no fixed answer, but students should understand the following before moving on to the next task:
Claudio went out with his brother last night. It was his brother's birthday. His brother's 23. He's studying law. Claudio's going to see a film later.

Tell the class they are going to hear the conversation again and that this time you want them to listen and complete the conversation by writing the word they hear in each gap. There is only ONE word missing each time. You could get them to try and complete the conversation first *before* they listen. Play the conversation and then give the students a minute to compare their ideas with a partner. Elicit the answers immediately or play the conversation one more time and stop after each gap. Students then call out their answers. Write them on the board. As you do so, deal with any new language.

Answers

1. tired 2. How 3. studying 4. year 5. did
6. surprised 7. going 8. doing

Ask students to discuss the questions in small groups or as a class. Round up as above.

11 Pronunciation: the letter 'a'

This activity looks at the relationship between spelling and sound. Use the recording or model the sounds and words yourself and ask students to repeat them. Explain the task. As this is the first time students have done this activity, it's probably best to explain things in the students' L1, if you can. You may also want to do the first few examples with the class. Read out all the words that are possible moves to show students how they should move through the board. For example, after *made* it is either *past* or *paid*. After *paid* it is either *paper* or *relax*, etc.

Ask students to do the rest of the route as a race in pairs. See which pair finishes first. Stop the task when the first pair finishes. Let the students read out their route. If they give a wrong answer, stop them and let another pair try to finish the route. The pair with the correct route wins.

Answers

made, paid, paper, Monday, take, game, say, wait, played, e-mail, great, late, April, came

12 Collocations

The collocation exercise also uses the grid of words from **11 Pronunciation**. The idea is to find a different route by completing each group of expressions with one word from the grid. Again, explain this quite thoroughly as this is the first time students have done this kind of activity. You could do this as a race with students working in pairs or threes in the same way as **11 Pronunciation**.

Answers

1. made	6. all	11. great
2. paid	7. last	12. late
3. relax	8. wait	13. April
4. answer	9. played	14. came
5. ask	10. August	

As this is revision, there's no need to ask questions about the language here. You could re-use the grid now or at another time. Read out some sentences, but say *blank* (or whistle or hum) instead of saying the word in the grid. Students listen and try to follow the route by deciding the missing word.
For example:

1. I _____ some pasta for dinner.
2. It's twenty _____ six.
3. Have you got any _____ I can write on.
4. It's a very _____ train.
5. It _____ me about 20 minutes to get home.
6. Did you see the _____ last night?
7. What did you _____ ? I didn't hear.
8. _____ here. I'll be back in five minutes.
10. I'm really tired. I _____ tennis for about three hours this morning.
11. I'm going to visit some friends in Berlin in _____ .
12. I like your _____ . It's really nice.
13. My dad _____ home really late last night.

7 What did you do last night?

Unit overview

General topic
Talking about what you did last night, your likes and interests.

Conversation
Three different conversations in which people talk about what they did last night.

Reading
Pen Pal Friends International

Language input
- Free time activities: *play golf, go to my aerobics class, go sightseeing*, etc.
- Questions: *How often do you do that? How long've you been doing that?*
- Past simple forms: *I went, I played*, etc.
- Questions with *Who* and *What: Who's your favourite singer?*
- Pronunciation: consonant sounds: /f/ and /v/

Language strip
Ignore the **Language strip** to begin with and deal with the language as it comes up in various activities. Come back to it later as revision. Alternatively, tell students to learn the expressions for homework.

Lead in
Do one of the following:
- Put students in pairs and give them two minutes to think of as many school / university subjects as they can. Elicit answers and write them on to the board, marking the stress and drilling the words. Then ask the students to find a new partner and tell each other which subjects they think are interesting / boring / difficult.
- Do one of the **Unit 6** activities from the **Teacher's Resource Book**.
- Play the seven sentences from **7 Pronunciation** on page 29 again, but this time, do them as a dictation. Ask students to close their books and try to write down what they hear. Stop briefly after each question and give students a minute or two to compare ideas before eliciting the answers. Drill the questions and then get students to ask and answer them with a partner.
- Tell students to look at the verbs in the box on page 31 and to work with a partner, saying the past simple forms. Tell them to make sure they agree on how the endings of the verbs are pronounced – /d/, /t/ or /ɪd/.

Conversation

1 Using vocabulary: free time activities

To lead in, ask students to go round the room and ask and answer the question: *What did you do last night?* Demonstrate with one or two students. Ask follow-up questions like *Did you enjoy it?* and write them on the board. Go round, helping students with any new vocabulary.

Alternatively, split the class into two to four groups, depending on the size of the class. Give them two minutes (no more) to think of as many free-time hobbies in English as they can and to write them down. They can use dictionaries if they want to, but be strict on the time. The groups then swap papers. Find out which group has the most hobbies. Write the hobbies on the board as each group tells you them and drill the words, checking for stress where relevant. Give one point for each hobby correctly spelt. The winners are the team with the most points.

Students could then tell each other which hobbies they do.

Tell the students they're going to learn some new vocabulary for activities they do in their free time. You could pre-teach this vocabulary using drawings or through TPR, (see the **Introduction** on page 8). Alternatively, simply ask the students to look at the words in the box and to look up the words they don't know in a dictionary. Then ask them to match the activities with the pictures. Elicit the answers from the class.

Answers		
A. aerobics class	B. driving lesson	C. go jogging

Deal with pronunciation as you go through the answers or play the recording afterwards and get students to repeat the expressions.

Next, put students in pairs. Student A closes their book while Student B tests them by acting or drawing the activities. Do one or two as an example with the class first.

As a follow-up, ask if anyone does any of these activities. You could do this with the class and ask follow-up questions where relevant. Ask: *How often do you do that?* and: *How long have you been doing that?* Don't spend more than a few minutes on this; don't ask everyone in the class.

2 Listening: *So what did you do last night?*

Tell students they are going to listen to three conversations and that in each one they will hear people talk about what they did last night. Tell them to listen and take notes about the things they hear.

Play the conversations once all the way through. Give students a minute or two to compare their answers in pairs. Round up what they have and if the whole group between them can provide the answers, don't play the conversations again, unless the class really wants you to. If they only have some of the answers play the conversations again, pausing after each conversation. Elicit the answers and write them on the board.

Answers

1. had a driving lesson; have them twice a week; has got a test next month.
2. went running, has been doing that for six weeks, goes 2 or 3 times a week, went to bed early.
3. One speaker played golf with a friend (for a couple of hours), plays once or twice a month; the other speaker had a piano lesson – second lesson.

3 | Listen again

Tell the class they are going to hear Conversation 3 again, between Dean, a man, and Jan, a woman. This time you want them to listen and complete the conversation by writing the words they hear in the gaps. Tell them they might need to write one word, two words or sometimes even three words in the gaps.

Play the conversation and then give the students a minute to compare their ideas with a partner.

You may want to elicit the answers immediately or you may want to play the conversation one more time and stop after each gap. Students then call out their answers. Write them on the board.

Answers

1. not too bad   2. How often   3. twice   4. learning the piano   5. How long   6. Not very long

Go through any new language. For example:
- *A couple* means two. Give other examples – *a couple of* days, *a couple of* years, *a couple of* friends.
- *How often do you do that?* – draw or use a calendar and point to different days when you *play golf*. Give some possible answers.
- *Once or twice* – once is one time; twice is two times. We say *once or twice a week*, but *2 or 3 times a week, 3 or 4 times a week*, etc. Note pronunciation of *once*.
- *I beat her* means I won the game. Write the score on the board (6–4, 6–3) and *I beat her. You win something* (a match, a game, a competition), but *you beat someone* or *you beat another team*. Elicit opposites (*I lost* the game and *I lost to her*).
- *How long have you been doing that?* – stretch out your arms to illustrate length of time and say *one week? two weeks?* or draw a timeline on the board. Mark *now* and then draw a line backwards to illustrate *how long*. Again, give possible answers. You could also ask some students *How long have you been studying English?*
- *Good luck with it* means *I hope you enjoy it* or *I hope it goes well*. Give a thumbs-up or similar gesture students might know.

Next, ask students to read out the conversation in pairs. They can change roles once they finish. As they do so, go round and listen to their pronunciation, correcting and remodelling things for them if they need it.

4 | Using grammar: *How often / How long ...?*

Tell students they're going to learn some more ways of answering these questions. You could ask them to translate the questions before you begin. You don't need to treat these questions as aspects of the different tenses at this stage. Treat them as whole expressions and simply deal with their meaning. If you need to, use a calendar or time lines to illustrate *How long* and *How often*.

Explain the task and ask students to try it individually and to then check their answers in pairs. Elicit the answers and write them on the board.

Answers

1. b, c, g, h   2. a, d, e, f

As you go through the answers, drill the language and draw attention to how the words link together as you say them. For example: *nine or ten, once or twice, once a month, about a month*, etc. Students could practise asking and answering the questions in pairs.

After completing this part of the activity, ask students to cover the answers **a–h** and to try to complete the six sentences underneath with one word in each space. Again, do the first one with the class.

Answers

a. very, or   b. very, maybe   c. every   d. very, about
e. very, only   f. time, nine

You could ask students to read **Grammar note** G8 on page 137 before moving on. Check to see if they have any questions.

5 | Practice

Ask students to choose one or two of the expressions in 1 **Using vocabulary** or simply allocate one to each person by giving each person a piece of paper with one of the words on it. Ask students to write answers to the two questions they have just learnt. Tell them to memorise them.

Now ask them to have conversations with different people in the room. Demonstrate with one person. If they have pieces of paper, they could swap them each time they change partner.

6 | Further practice

Explain the task. Give a couple of examples yourself, ideally ones that are true. Ask students to complete the sentences individually. As they're writing, go round and check that they've understood. Help with any new vocabulary.

Return to your examples and get students to ask you the two follow-up questions they've learnt. You might need to write an example A: / B: dialogue (where you are A) on the board to elicit this.

Ask students to have similar conversations in pairs. Monitor and listen for any mistakes, particularly in the use of the two questions and answers. Deal with these on the board after students have finished and also tell the class about any interesting things you heard students say.

7 Using vocabulary: free time

Tell the students they're going to learn some more useful vocabulary to talk about what they do in their free time. Most of the words in this activity appear in the text students will read in the second part of the unit.

Explain the task and let students work individually or in pairs, using dictionaries if they need to. Elicit the answers from the class and write them on the board.

> **Answers**
> 1. films   2. travelling   3. music   4. art   5. religion

As you elicit the answers, go through the new language and drill some of it where appropriate:

- *Laugh* – act this out.
- *Cry* – act this out.
- *Go sightseeing* means to go and see famous places. Elicit examples of places you go to see if you go sightseeing in the country you are in.
- *Get a visa* – give examples of places you need to get a visa to visit. Ask if anyone has ever got a visa. You could add *go to the embassy* to get a visa.
- When you *go to a concert* you go and see someone play live music / sing. Ask where, (*concert hall, nightclub, stadium*). Has anyone been to a concert? Who did they see? Where?
- *Be a big fan* – you really like someone famous. You have all their CDs. You go to their concerts a lot. It's also used for football. Go through the **Real English** note.
- *Download* – get things from the Internet. Elicit / give other things you can download (*pictures, music, articles, films*).
- *Paint* – draw a paintbrush and mime it.
- *Draw* – draw a pencil and mime it.
- *Temple* – a church for Hindus or Buddhists or Sikhs.
- *Pray* – mime.

Next, put students in pairs. Student A closes their book while Student B tests them by acting out or drawing the activities. Do one or two as an example with the class first.

For homework, ask students to try to learn the conversation from **3 Listen again** and then test them in the next lesson. You could also get them to write their own conversations with a friend about what they did last night, trying to use as much of the language from these two pages as they can.

Reading

If you are starting a new lesson, begin with a bit of revision. Ask students to try to repeat as much of the conversation in **3 Listen again** on page 36 as they can from memory.

Alternatively, give students two minutes to write down as much of the vocabulary from **7 Using vocabulary** on page 37 as they can remember. You could help them by giving them the five topics: art, films, music, religion, travelling. After two or three minutes, ask students to compare in pairs and to explain any words their partner has forgotten. You could extend this by asking the class to think of one or two more words / expressions for each topic. You could also do an activity from **Unit 7** of the **Teacher's Resource Book**.

1 Speaking

Tell the students to read the questions and the model conversation. Ask if there is anything they don't understand. Tell the students to choose three questions to ask you. Give true answers to demonstrate the activity, making sure you use some of the language highlighted in red. Ask students to practise the conversations in pairs. Monitor and encourage students to extend their answers by saying how often they do these things. Round up with a couple of corrections or by writing any new language the students have produced on the board.

2 While you read (1)

Explain what a pen pal is (someone you write letters to, but don't usually meet) and explain the reading task. Tell students they should read the text and decide if they would answer any of the adverts or not. Do the text as a listening, a reading or both, (see Introduction for procedure).

Go through any new language. For example:

- *Religion* – give examples such as Muslim, Catholic, Hindu, etc.
- *Share my interests* means to be interested in the same things.
- *Bad experiences* – bad things that have happened.
- *An invitation letter* – a letter asking someone to come to a party / wedding or to stay / visit.
- *Catholic* – translate or say *the main religion in Italy, Spain, Latin America*. Drill and point out the silent 'o'.
- *Classical music* – act violins, cellos, etc. Say *Like Beethoven, Bach*, etc. Notice it's *classical* and NOT *classic*.
- *I race cars* – act it out, (like Formula One).

When students have finished reading, give them a few minutes to read the five sentence prompts at the bottom of the activity and to write appropriate names in the gaps. If anyone asks about the use of *would* here, either translate it or explain *it's imaginary, not real. Would* means you're not really going to write to them, it's just thinking, imagining. You may also need to explain *I don't think he / she only wants to write*.

Next, put students in pairs to discuss their ideas. Give an example yourself, using one or two of the sentence frames.

3 While you read (2)

Explain the task. Note here that the recording includes the names of the people they are writing to, so DON'T play the recording at this stage. Give students five minutes to read the texts. Then put them in pairs to compare what they think before rounding up ideas from the class. Don't give any definitive answers at this stage, but encourage students to give examples from the texts to justify their ideas.

Play the recording and tell students to check if they were right. As they listen, you could also ask students to underline anything they don't understand or want to ask you about.

Answers

Sam is writing to Justine.
Gustav is writing to Sara.
Izzy is writing to Antonio.

Go through any new language. For example:
- *I've been to see him* – this means *before now*. We often use it to say how many times before now.
- *Ballet* – act it out. Drill it, pointing out the silent /t/.
- *Theatre* – like the cinema, but for live acting; for plays like *Hamlet*.
- *Latin dance clubs* play music from Latin America.
- *Salsa* – act it out or just say: *it's a kind of Latin dance and dance music*.
- *For short* – give examples: *My name's Andrew, but people call me 'Andy' for short*. Write this on the board. Ask if the students have any short names.
- *Graphic design* – translate or say: *designing books or magazines*. You work on a computer to make the pages look good.
- *Goya* is a famous Spanish artist.

Afterwards, answer any questions students have and then go through the **Real English** note.

If you want to, you can skip the last speaking task here. Alternatively, perhaps just ask the class if they think anyone will write to Isaac, Baz or Jurgen. Ask them to explain their ideas. Reformulate things the students try to say into better English.

4 Using grammar: *who* and *what*

Introduce the task by referring to the two questions from the e-mail. Tell students we use *who* to ask about people and *what* to ask about things. Explain the task and do the first two with the class. Ask students to do the rest individually. Monitor and help with any unknown language. When most students have finished, get them to compare in pairs. Then check the answers.

Answers

1. Who's	2. What's	3. What's	4. What's
5. Who's	6. Who's	7. Who's	8. What's
9. Who's	10. What's		

Elicit the answers, drill the questions and go through any new vocabulary:
- A *writer* is someone who writes books. Elicit examples.
- *Director* – elicit examples.

Get students to choose three questions they want to ask you. Reply with answers that are true for you.

Write any new language on the board and translate if you can, so students can also try to use it. Next, ask students to ask and answer the questions in pairs. Round up with a couple of corrections or by correcting any new language the students have produced on the board.

A variation is to get students to find people who like the same things as they do. When students have changed partners once or twice, finish the activity.

Get students to write an e-mail to a partner. You could set this for homework. A project you could do is to get students to actually find an English-speaking pen pal through websites on the Internet.

5 Pronunciation /f/ and /v/

Model the sounds or use the recording and ask students to repeat the sounds. The difference between the two sounds comes from using your voice for /v/. You can feel this by touching your throat. You also expel more air with /f/. If you put your hand in front of your face, you should be able to feel the air when you say /f/, but not when you say /v/. You can show these techniques to students as well as using the photos and diagrams on page 145.

If students don't have a big problem with these sounds, don't spend a lot of time on them, but move on to the dictation. Play the recording. Pause at the end of each sentence to give students time to write. Get students to compare their answers and then play the ten sentences once more. Let students then compare what they have written again, before you go through the answers on the board, playing each sentence once more and pausing after each one as you do so. Alternatively, students can just compare with the **Tapescript** on page 124.

Students then practise reading out the sentences either individually or as a class. Help with any problems. If students say /b/ instead of /v/ or /p/ instead of /f/, point out that the teeth should show on the lips for /v/ and /f/. Contrast this with /b/ and /p/.

Homework

You could tell the class to do **Unit 6** in the **Workbook** for homework, if you haven't done so already.

You could also ask them to write an advert about themselves, like those on page 38. Alternatively, use the pen pal ideas already given.

Collect the writing next lesson and correct it. Correct any mistakes with things already studied in class and give students better ways of saying new things that they're trying to say.

8 Do you like ... ?

Unit overview

General topic
Talking about what things you like and don't like.

Conversation
Three different conversations in which people talk about what they like doing in their free time.

Reading
Living abroad

Language input
- Questions: *What kind of ... , do you ... ? Do you like ... ?*
- Expressions for (not) liking something: *I quite like it, I really like them.*
- Agreeing: *Me too, Me neither.*
- Describing things and people: *He's very friendly, It's not very good for you.*
- Comparatives: *The weather here is better than in England.*
- Pronunciation: weak forms: *of, to, than*

Language strip
Ignore the **Language strip** to begin with and deal with the language as it comes up in various activities. Come back to it later as revision. Alternatively, ask students to learn the expressions for homework.

Lead in
Do one of the following:
- Ask students to work in pairs and repeat **6 Further practice** on page 37.
- Ask students to look at the **Expressions Organiser** for the first four units on pages 146–7. Ask students to translate the expressions in pairs then check their ideas. Students can then test each other by saying a translation, acting it out or drawing a picture, while their partner guesses. To make this easier, let both students look at pages 146–7.
- Test the students on the expressions in the **Language strip** in **Unit 7**. Give students two minutes to look at the **Language strip** and remember as much as they can. They can ask you questions during this time. Ask students to close their books, then put them into two teams. If you can, use L1 to test them on different expressions, draw them on the board or act them out. The first person to call out the correct expression wins a point for their team.

Conversation

1 What kind of...? / Do you like...?

Ask students to work in groups of three to find eight things they all like. Let them decide how to do the task and what language to use. Monitor and help with any problems. Once one group has finished, stop the task. Find out the eight things the first group all liked and also some things other groups all liked. Don't spend more than two minutes on this.

Tell the students they're going to learn some questions we ask to find out what people like. Explain the task. Translate the two kinds of question, if you can. Ask students to do the activity individually, then check their answers in pairs. Go through the answers on the board, eliciting from the class.

> **Answers**
> 1. d.   2. a.   3. b.   4. e.   5. c.

As you go through the answers, drill the questions. Point out the linking and weak forms of *kind of* and *do you*. Go through any new language. For example:
- *Dance* – act it out.
- A *band* is music group. Elicit examples.
- *Spicy* means hot, usually when we're talking about food – act it out.

You could also ask one or two students some of these questions and help them answer.

2 Practice

Ask students to cover **1 What kind of ... ? / Do you like ... ?** and complete the two conversations by adding one word in each space. Do the first one with the class, then ask students to do the rest individually. When they've finished, go through the answers with the class. As you do so, deal with new vocabulary and highlight how we answer the questions.

> **Answers**
> 1. kind, read / like, Do, favourite
> 2. music, to, like, my, band

Explain *detective novels*.

Now ask students to work in pairs and write three similar conversations using the other questions from **1 What kind of ... ? / Do you like ... ?** and the different kinds of answers given. You might want to work through one example with the class on the board. Tell students to give answers that are true for them.

As a follow-up, students could read out their conversations to another pair.

3 Listening: free time

Tell students they are going to listen to three conversations and they will hear people talk about what they like doing in their free time. Tell them to listen and to tick the things in the box they hear. Before they listen, students could discuss in pairs which words they think go together, for example *dancing* and *salsa*.

Play the conversations once all the way through. Give students a minute or two to compare their answers in pairs. Round up what they have and if the whole group between them can provide the answers, don't play the conversations again, unless the class really wants you to. If they only have some of the answers, play the conversations again, pausing after each conversation.

Answers

Conversation 1: Wimbledon, tennis and running
Conversation 2: reading, *About a Boy* and Paulo
               Coelho
Conversation 3: salsa, dancing, shopping, cinema,
               action movies, Harry Robbins

Before students listen again, ask if they remember who or what was described using the adjectives. You may have to explain *embarrassing* by acting out and saying: *your face goes red*.

Play the recording again. Students compare their answers in pairs. Go round and check how they've done and based on what you see, decide whether to play the recording one more time or go through the answers with the class. If students listen again, you could let them also read the **Tapescript** on page 124.

Answers

great: Harry Robbins (and going to the cinema together!)
not very good: at playing tennis, (and at dancing)
a bit boring: running
quite funny: *About a Boy*
sad and funny: Dan Jackson's books
embarrassing: dancing

---

4 Listen again

Tell the class they are going to hear Conversation 3 again, between Penny, a woman, and Dennis, a man. This time you want them to listen and complete the conversation with the words in the box.

Play the conversation and then give the students a minute to compare their ideas with a partner.

You may want to elicit the answers immediately or play the conversation one more time and stop after each gap. Students then call out their answers. Write them on the board.

Answers

1. class	6. love
2. been	7. kind
3. dancing	8. too
4. very	9. should
5. embarrassing	10. great

Go through any new language. For example:

- *I'm not very good at it* – draw attention to the pattern *I'm (quite) good at …* and *I'm not very good at … .* Give examples: *I'm not very good at tennis, I'm quite good at cooking.* Mime the examples if you can. Ask some students to tell you what they are good / not very good at.
- *Step on people's feet* – act it out with a student.
- *Embarrassing* – drill it. Ask if students find dancing or anything else embarrassing.
- *Action movies* usually contain lots of guns and explosions and are very fast.
- *Comedies* are films that make you laugh.
- If an actor or director *has got a film out* it means it's at the cinema now. Give / elicit examples from the country you are in.

5 Using grammar: *me too / me neither*

Next, ask students to read out the conversation in pairs. They can change roles once they have finished. As they do so, go round and listen to their pronunciation, correcting and remodelling things for them if they need it.

Write the following sentences on the board:
A: *I love basketball.*
B: *I love basketball.*

A: *I don't go out much.*
B: *I don't go out much.*

Ask the students: *What can B say to agree with A instead of repeating the sentence? What does Dennis say in the conversation in 4 Listen again?* Elicit *Me too* and write it on the board. Then ask: *So in the second example, what do you say to agree?* Students will probably say: *Me too.* Draw their attention to the negative *don't* and write *Me neither* on the board.

Ask students to read the grammar explanation. Answer any questions. If they ask about how to show you DON'T agree, add: *Really? I hate it* and *Really? I go out a lot* to the conversations on the board.

Explain the task. All the responses are grammatically correct. Give an example of how you could use both answers by adding an extra comment to each. For example:
1.a: *Yes, me too. I go dancing every week.*
1.b: *Really? I don't like it. I find it very embarrassing.*

Ask students to make their choices individually for two minutes. Give students a couple minutes to try to remember what they have written. Demonstrate the task. Students close their books. You say some of the statements to 2 or 3 students. Then put students in pairs to do the task. Student A can keep the book open.

6 Practice

Explain the task. Ask students to do this individually. As they're writing, go round and check that they've understood. You could deal with any common problems before you start the speaking part of the activity. For example, students might not follow **1–4** with an *-ing* form or might try to use an *-ing* form for **5** and **6**.

Get one or two students to read out their sentences to you. Respond using *Me too* or *Me neither*. Continue the conversation with one of the follow-up questions in red.

Ask students to have similar conversations in pairs. Monitor and check for mistakes. Correct any new language you heard students produce on the board.

For homework, ask students to try to learn the conversation from **4 Listen again** and then test them in the next lesson. You could also get them to write their own similar conversations with a friend about what they are doing tonight, trying to use as much of the language from these two pages as they can.

Reading

If you are starting a new lesson, begin with a bit of revision. Do one of the following:

*   Ask students to try to repeat as much of the conversation in **4 Listen again** on page 40 as they can from memory.
*   Do an activity from **Unit 8** of the **Teacher's Resource Book**.
*   Ask students to walk around and ask some other students the five questions from **I What kind of … ? / Do you like … ?** on page 40. Tell them to give true answers and to continue the conversations by asking *Do you like … ?* questions.

1 Using Vocabulary: describing

Tell students they're going to learn some new vocabulary to describe aspects of the country you live in. Check they understand the words in the box. You may have to explain *prime minister*. Give an example of current famous prime ministers. Explain the task – each group of three sentences describe one of the words in the box. Ask students to do the task in pairs. Elicit the answers from the class and write them on the board. As you do so, deal with any new language.

Answers
I. people   2. weather   3. prime minister 4. TV   5. food

Go through any new language. For example:

*   Act out *friendly* by smiling, shaking hands, etc. Elicit the opposite *unfriendly* or *not very friendly*.
*   *Warm* – show difference with hot and cold by writing different temperatures, (0°C, 20°C, 35°C).
*   In this context *weak* means you can't decide. Opposite – *strong*.
*   *There's lots of choice* – lots of different things, you can choose what you want. Give the example of TV or restaurant menus where there is *lots of choice* or *not much choice*.
*   *Stupid* means the opposite of intelligent.
*   *Delicious* is an adjective for food: it tastes very nice. Mime!
*   Foods that are *good for you* are fruit, vegetables, etc. They make you healthy. Contrast with *bad for you*. Give and elicit examples of each.

Ask students to decide which expression they would use to talk about their own country. Let them do this individually and then get them to compare in small groups and see if they agree.

2 While you read

Explain the task. Note here that the recording includes the complete questions, so DON'T play the recording at this stage. Give students about five minutes to complete the text. Then put them in pairs to compare answers before rounding up ideas from the class. Don't give any definitive answers at this stage, but encourage students to give examples from the text to justify their ideas.

Play the recording and tell students to check if they were right.

Answers
I. food   2. weather   3. people   4. prime minister 5. TV

Write the answers on the board and ask students which country you think Robert is living in. There is no fixed answer to this question, but ask students to justify their ideas as best they can.

At this stage, don't deal with any unknown vocabulary. Wait until after the **Word check**.

3 Word check

Tell the class you're going to look at some of the new language from the text. Ask them to try to complete **1–6** from memory, without looking at the text. After a few minutes, get students to compare their ideas in pairs. You could also tell them to go back to the text to check their ideas. Tell them to underline the expressions in the text. Then check the answers from the whole group, writing them on the board as you do so.

Answers
I. healthy   2. way (*food* is also possible)   3. with 4. difficult (or *easy*)   5. how   6. owns

As you go through the answers, drill pronunciation where relevant. Go through any new language. For example:

*   Ask for examples of *healthy* food. Give examples of how you can be healthy, (eat vegetables, do lots of exercise). Elicit the opposite – *unhealthy*.
*   *To begin with* means *at first*. Note that this shows a change and usually goes with *but* by giving other examples. *I didn't like him to begin with, but now we're good friends. To begin with, I found English difficult, but now it's easy!*
*   *Owns* – they're his. He bought them. If you *own* a business, you get all the money!
*   Give examples of *TV channels* from the country you are in.

Give students a minute to think about the questions in red at the end of the activity. Tell them to use their dictionaries if they need to. Do the discussion with the class or put the students into small groups. Let them use L1 if they need to, and then translate for them into English. Round up with a couple of corrections or by orally reformulating into better English interesting things you heard students say. Correct anything new language the students have produced on the board.

You could get students to ask you the questions if you are living in a foreign country! Also, ask if students have any other questions they want to ask about the text.

4 Using grammar: comparatives

If you can, use some corrections from the last activity to lead into this one. Students may say things like: *My country is more good here.* Write this on the board and see if any students can correct it.

Write up *better than* and *worse than* on the board. Ask students to read the short explanation in the book and translate the words. Check they understand by referring to the text. Ask: *In the text, what things does Robert think are better than in Britain?* (The food, the weather.) What does he think is worse? (TV).

Explain the task and do the first one with the class. Get students to do the rest individually. Monitor and help with any problems. Elicit the answers from the class and write them on the board.

> **Answers**
> 1. better   2. better   3. better   4. worse
> 5. better   6. better   7. worse   8. better

Next, draw attention to the first sentence and write up *She's stronger (than our leader)*. Say: *Our leader is quite strong, but yours is stronger* and underline -er. Tell students that with long adjectives, we don't add -er, we use *more*. Write up *interesting – more interesting* on the board. Now ask students to underline the other comparatives in the activity.

Check with the class and drill the whole expressions.

Tell students to read the **Grammar note** G9 on page 138 and let them ask any questions, if you have time.

5 Practice

Explain the task and demonstrate by giving examples yourself first. Write three places you know well on the board. Try to make them a mixture of places that are better and worse than the place you are in. Tell the students how they are different using *better than* and *worse than* and some comparative adjectives to explain why.

Ask students to write their own examples before they tell a partner. When they compare their ideas, put these short conversations on the board and tell students to begin like this:
A: Do you know X?
B: No, what's it like?
A: It's better / worse than here …

OR
A: Do you know X?
B: Yes. What do you think of it?
A: It's better / worse than here …

Round up with a couple of corrections or by orally reformulating into better English interesting things you heard students say. Also correct on the board any new language the students have produced.

6 Pronunciation: weak forms – *of, to, than*

Model and drill the expressions yourself or use the recording. Play the recording. Pause at the end of each sentence to give students time to write. Get students to compare their answers and then play the ten sentences once more. Let students then compare what they have written again, before you go through the answers on the board. Play each sentence once more and pausing after each one as you do so. Then drill the sentences individually or as a class. Help with any problems.

For alternative ways to do this section see the **Introduction** on page 10–11 of this **Teacher's Book**.

Homework
You could tell the class to do **Unit 7** in the **Workbook** for homework, if you haven't done so already.

You could also ask them to write an imaginary interview with a famous foreigner living in their country. To set this up, you could spend three minutes in class brainstorming any famous foreigners know; footballers, pop stars, TV personalities, etc. Students then use the questions from the interview with Robert on page 42 and as much of the language from this unit as they can.

Collect the writing next lesson and correct it. Correct any mistakes with things already studied in class and give students better ways of saying new things that they're trying to say.

Unit overview

General topic
Talking about things to do in the future.

Conversation
Three different conversations in which people talk about what they are doing now.

Reading
Things I'd like to do

Language input
- Shops and places: *supermarket, internet café, etc.*
- *Need to: I need to phone a friend.*
- Pronunciation: vowel sounds: /iː/, /uː/, / ɔː – as in or/ and /aː/
- *I'd like to: I'd like to buy a new car.*
- Time expressions: *sometime in the next 3 or 4 months*
- Using the present simple to describe someone: *She sounds really nice.*
- Pronunciation: consonant sounds: /s/ and /z/

Language strip

Ignore the **Language strip** to begin with and deal with the language as it comes up in various activities. Come back to it later as revision. Alternatively, ask students to learn the expressions for homework.

Lead in

Do one of the following:
- Ask students to work in pairs and repeat **5 Practice** on page 43. This time they should use different places or talk to a different partner.
- Ask students to look at the **Expressions Organiser** for **Units 5** and **6** on page 148. Ask students to translate the expressions in pairs then check their ideas. Students can then test each other by saying a translation, acting it out or drawing a picture, while their partner guesses. To make this easier, let both students look at page 148.

Conversation

1 Using vocabulary: shops and places

A good way to lead in to the lesson is to ask students to discuss what they're doing after class or at the weekend, whichever is more appropriate. Ask students to move round the class and have several short conversations. Round up with a couple of corrections or by orally reformulating into better English interesting things you heard students say. Correct any new language the students have produced on the board.

Tell students that in this lesson they're going to get better at having conversations like this.

Ask students to look at the photos and to translate the names of the kinds of shops. You could ask students to close their books and test each other using their translations, (for ways of doing this with multilingual groups, see the **Introduction** on page 8). As they do so, go round and listen to their pronunciation, correcting and remodelling things for them if they need it.

Put students into pairs to tell each other the names of the most famous examples of these kinds of shops in their country. If it is a monolingual group, round up by seeing if the class agrees.

You could do the next part of the activity with the class. At this stage students only really need to say the names of streets or that it is near here. However, you could help students with other language they might want to use such as *opposite, next to*, etc. (This language is formally introduced in **Unit 11**.) To follow-up students tell each other about the shops near their house. Let the class decide whose house is best for the shops.

Put students in pairs to do the next task. The point here is not to give personal examples, though students can if they want to, but to elicit the NAMES of the kinds of places where you do these things.

As students discuss their ideas, go round and help out, but let them also use their dictionaries. Elicit the answers from the class and write them on the board. Drill and explain language where appropriate.

Answers
1. an internet café
2. a bank
3. a bookshop
4. a supermarket
5. a photo place
6. a newsagent's (or supermarket)
7. a restaurant (or café)
8. a chemist's
9. a café

Go through any new language. For example:
- *Send a few e-mails* – ask for the opposite *check my e-mail.*
- If you *change* some money you change dollars or pounds into euros, for example. You could elicit the currency of students' countries and the exchange rate, (for example 1.8 dollars *to the* pound).
- *Get your film developed* – draw a film, draw an arrow to a picture of photo(s). Ask *and if they're digital photos?* (*You print them out* or *put them on a disk.*)
- Check students understand *paper* means *newspaper* as opposed to *some paper*. Underline *the* and find out which papers the students read.
- *Get something to eat* – drill it. Point out the weak form of *to* and the linking in *to eat.*
- *Go for a coffee* – point out the weak form of *for a* and linking.

2 Listening

Tell students they are going to listen to three conversations and that in each one they will hear people talking after class. Tell them to listen and answer the questions about each one.

Play the conversations once all the way through. Give students a minute to compare their answers in pairs. Round up the answers. If the class missed anything from **1 Using vocabulary**, play the recording once more before doing the true or false questions.

Answers

Conversation 1: get something to eat (and *get* some money). They're going to do this together.

Conversation 2: go for a coffee. They're maybe going to go together *tomorrow*. (They also talk about going home, finishing homework).

Conversation 3: send a few e-mails. They decide to do these things on their own and meet up later.

Ask students to do the true or false questions in pairs before they listen to the conversations again. Then play the recording so that they can check their ideas. Elicit answers from the class and write them on the board.

Answers

1.a. F   1.b. T   2.a. T   2.b. F   3.a. T   3.b. F

3 Listen again

Tell the class they are going to hear Conversation 3 again, between Rod and Michael. This time you want them to listen and complete the conversation with the words in the box.

Play the conversation and then give the students a minute to compare their ideas with a partner.

You may want to elicit the answers immediately or you may want to play the conversation one more time and stop after each gap. Students then call out their answers. Write them on the board.

Answers

1. need to   2. about   3. some presents   4. left
5. better   6. somewhere   7. two hours   8. see you

Go through any new language. For example:

*   *I need to* – translate or act a stomach pain or a broken leg and say *I need to go to the doctor.* Or act having no money and say *I need to go to the bank.*
*   *I've only got three pictures left* – say: *On my film, there were 24 pictures. I took 21 pictures. I've only got three left.* OR say: *This morning, I had £10. I spent £7. Now I've only got £3 left.*
*   *You should* – translate or pretend a student has stomach-ache and say: *You should go to the doctor. I think this is a good idea.*
*   *Shall we* – Do you want to? Give other examples: *Shall we take a break? Shall we stop there?*
*   *I'll* – it's a promise. *I'll = I will.* Rod's deciding / promising at the time of speaking.

*   *A couple of hours* is two hours. Tell students to read the **Real English** note.

Next, ask students to read out the conversation in pairs. They can change roles once they finish. As they do so, go round and listen to their pronunciation, correcting and remodelling things for them if they need it.

4 Using grammar: *need to*

In Conversation 3, Michael says *he needs to send a few e-mails.* Ask the students if they can remember why. (The last time he wrote to his family was about 2 weeks ago.) Tell them we often say *why* we need to do things. Write on the board: *I need to go to the bank … .* Elicit reasons. Try to organise these reasons into two groups. For example:

… *to open an account.*

… *to get some money.*

… *to change some money.*

… *(because) I haven't got any money.*

… *(because) I've got a problem.*

… *(because) the cash machine ate my card.*

Explain the task. Do the first two with the class to model the task. Ask students to do the rest individually. Monitor and help with any unknown language. Let students compare in pairs, and then elicit the answers from the class. Write them on the board. Drill and explain language where appropriate.

Answers

1. e.   2. d.   3. c.   4. b.   5. a.   6. h.   7. i.   8. j.
9. g.   10. f.

Go through any new language. For example:

*   In **1–5**, highlight the weak forms of *to* and drill the sentences.
*   Act out *photocopying* using a book. Drill it and mark the stress on the board – photocopying.
*   A *parcel* – draw a picture of one on the board and act wrapping it, tying it, writing the address on and sending it.
*   *Sun cream* – draw a picture of someone sunbathing and act out putting on sun cream.

Explain the next task. Tell students it's fine if they have different reasons than those written here. Give some examples yourself. For example:
I need to go to the post office to send an airmail letter.
I need to call my mum. I haven't spoken to her for weeks.

Ask students to tell each other their ideas for two or three minutes. Round up with a couple of corrections or by orally reformulating into better English interesting things you heard students say. Correct any new language the students have produced on the board.

5 Practice

The first part of this activity is a way of using the class to generate new language. Explain the task. As the students are writing, go round and check that they've understood and are writing sensible endings down. Give them a few minutes and then let them compare in pairs before rounding up their ideas. Reformulate some of their ideas into better English as you're doing this. For example:

Student: I need to go to the doctor tomorrow because my back pain.

Teacher: OK, yes. Because my back really hurts.

Next, tell the students to think of two more things they need to do today / this week. Give them two minutes to write down their ideas. Go round and help out as they do so, then ask students to talk to each other to see if they can find someone else who needs to do the same thing. Deal with any common mistakes or new vocabulary.

6 Role play

Tell the class they're going to practise having similar conversations to the ones they heard on the recording. Give them two minutes to read the prompts. You could drill some of the language here: *What about you? What're you doing? / Do you want to meet later after you've finished?* You could also model the task with a good student.

Let students have the same conversation two or three times, with different partners. Round up with a couple of corrections or by orally reformulating into better English interesting things you heard students say. Correct on the board any new language the students have produced.

7 Pronunciation /iː/, /uː/, /ɔː/ and /aː/

Model the sounds yourself and demonstrate the position of the tongue and lips or use the recording and the photos on page 144. Ask students to repeat the sounds, both chorally and individually. Draw attention to the two dots /ː/ that follow each letter. These show that the sounds are longer. Encourage students to lengthen the sounds, exaggerating them slightly to begin with.

Answers

/uː/ *couple* is wrong: /kʌpl/
/ɔː/ *foreign* is wrong: /fɒrən/
/aː/ *camera* is wrong: /kæmərə/
/iː/ *present* is wrong: /preznt/

To follow up, students could test each other. Student A says some words silently. Student B reads their lips and guesses the words. They can both have their books open while they do this.

For homework, ask students to try to learn the conversation from **3 Listen again** and then test them in the next lesson. You could also get them to write their own similar conversations with a friend about what they are doing now, trying to use as much of the language from these two pages as they can.

Reading

If you are starting a new lesson, begin with a bit of revision. Do one of the following:

• Ask students to try to repeat as much of the conversation in **3 Listen again** on page 44 as they can from memory.

• Do an activity from **Unit 9** of the **Teacher's Resource Book**.

• Do a quick class test. Divide the students into two groups. Tell them you're going to say the thing you do and the students have to call out the place you do it. For example:

I need to get some money out. (cash point / bank)

I want to get the paper. (newsagent's / supermarket)

Give a point to the team that calls out the answer first. The winning team is the one with the most points.

1 Using grammar: *I'd like to ...*

Tell the students some things about your life that you don't like at the moment. Then elicit / give some changes. For example: *I'd like to have a holiday. I'd like to have children.*

Write these on the board and drill them. Translate them if you can. Leave these examples on the board, if possible, so you can use them to introduce the next activity.

Ask students to read the brief note on page 46, then give them a couple of minutes to do the matching task. Elicit the answers from the class and write them on the board.

Answers

1. c and f   2. d and g   3. b and e   4. a and h

2 Using grammar: time expressions

Go back to the examples about your life on the board. Ask students when you want these things to happen. The main point here is that students should recognise these are all talking about the future, but you could also feed in some new expressions such as *sometime soon* or *sometime in the next year or so* if students try to say them. Write them on the board, adding them to the ends of the sentences from the previous activity.

Ask students to read the examples in the book and then explain the task. Ask students to do this individually or in pairs. Elicit the answers from the class and write them on the board.

Answers

1. sometime in the future
2. sometime in the next year
3. sometime in the next few years
4. sometime in the next few weeks
5. sometime in the next three or four months

As a follow-up, ask students to put the phrases in order starting with the soonest to the last one, (4, 5, 2, 3 and then 1).

Next, ask students to tell each other what they'd like to do using similar examples to those you gave. You might need to give the class a couple of minutes to prepare. Round up with a couple of corrections or by orally reformulating into better English interesting things you heard students say. Correct on the board any new language the students have produced.

Tell the students to read **Grammar note** G11 on page 138.

The aim here is to predict and to generate a bit of interest in the text, so don't tell the students if they are right or wrong, but correct any errors in the use of grammar and vocabulary.

3 Before you read

Ask the students to read and find out what each person would like to do in the future. Do the text as a listening, a reading or both, (see **Introduction** for procedure).

4 While you read

When students have finished reading, ask them to cover the text and tell each other what each person would like to do. Go round and check they have understood.

> **Answers**
>
> Karen would like to go to Japan sometime in the next 2 or 3 years.
> Alan would like to buy a big red sports car and learn how to play the guitar.
> Rick would like to spend less time with his wife and kids, and see his old friends more.
> Charlotte would like to lose weight, go dancing more often, go swimming more often and join a singing group.

Go through any new language. For example:

- *I've always wanted to go there* – from a long time ago to now – draw a timeline.
- *One day* – some time in the future, not *for* one day. Give some more examples, *I'd like to go to Morocco one day*, etc.
- A *rock star* – act out *rock music* and then name a very famous rock musician. Give / ask for examples from the country you're in.
- *Make my dreams come true* – make the things I've always wanted to do happen.
- *Haven't had* – from the past to now, 'for one and a half years'.
- A *good night's sleep* – act it out and act out the opposite – tossing and turning and waking up a lot.
- *Put on a lot of weight* – got fat. Act it out if you want to. Say you can *put on 5 kilos* or *10 kilos*. Ask for / give the opposite – *lose weight*.
- *Get thinner* means to lose weight.

5 Comprehension

Ask students to keep the text covered to begin with and to discuss in pairs what they can remember about each question for 2 or 3 minutes. You could also tell them to go back to the text to check their ideas. Tell them to underline the expressions in the text. Then check the answers from the whole group, writing them on the board as you do so. Ask the class how they made their decisions.

> **Answers**
>
> 1. Alan (I've got quite a lot of money.)
> 2. Rick (My son was born a year ago.)
> 3. Charlotte (I was very ill a year ago.)
> 4. Karen (I'm learning Japanese.)
> 5. Alan (I started working for a big company.)
> 6. Charlotte (I'd like to lose weight and go swimming more often.)
> 7. Rick (I haven't had a good night's sleep for a year and a half.)
> 8. Karen (I'd like to go to Japan.)

6 Speaking

Give students a minute to read the questions and expressions first. Then ask them to discuss what they think of the four people in pairs. You could ask them to change partners before they talk about whether or not they'd like to do any of the things mentioned in the text.

Round up with a couple of corrections or by orally reformulating into better English interesting things you heard students say. Correct on the board any new language the students have produced.

7 Pronunciation: /s/ and /z/

Model the sounds yourself and demonstrate the position of the tongue and lips or use the recording and the photos on page 144. Ask students to repeat the sounds, both chorally and individually.

Now put the students in pairs and get them to say the sentences to each other and to decide which sounds are /s/ and which are /z/. Play the tape to check and go through the answers with the class.

> **Answers**
>
> | | |
> |---|---|
> | 1. /s/, /s/ | 5. /s/, /s/ |
> | 2. /s/, /z/, /z/ | 6. /z/, /s/, /s/ |
> | 3. /s/, /z/, /s/ | 7. /s/, /s/, /z/ |
> | 4. /s/, /s/, /z/, /z/ | 8. /z/, /z/, /s/ |

Finally, give students a few minutes to read 1–8 again and decide if the statements are true for them. Ask them to read the three examples and to then discuss their feelings in pairs or as a class.

Homework

You could tell the class to do **Unit 8** in the **Workbook** for homework, if you haven't done so already.

You could also ask them to write a paragraph about things they'd like to do in the future, using as much language from this lesson as they can.

Collect the writing next lesson and correct it. Correct any mistakes with things already studied in class and give students better ways of saying new things that they're trying to say.

10 Have you been to ... ?

Unit overview

General topic
Talking about places you go to on holiday.

Conversation
A conversation about places people have been to and places they're going to.

Reading
You should go to ...

Language input
- Past time phrases: *last week, the day before yesterday*, etc.
- Present perfect: *Have you been to Morocco?*
- Describing places: *It's got great nightlife*, etc.
- Should: *You should go to Milan.*
- Pronunciation: contractions: *I haven't, I've been there.*

Language strip
Ignore the **Language strip** to begin with and deal with the language as it comes up in various activities. Come back to it later as revision. Alternatively, ask students to learn the expressions for homework.

Lead in
Do one of the following:
- Ask students to work in pairs and repeat **6 Role play** on page 45. This time the students should have different plans or talk to a different partner.
- Ask students to look at the **Expressions Organiser** for **Units 7** and **8** on page 149. Ask students to translate the expressions in pairs then check their ideas. Students can then test each other by saying a translation, acting it out or drawing a picture, while their partner guesses. To make this easier, let both students look at page 149.
- Test the students on the expressions in the **Language strip** in **Unit 9**. Give students two minutes to look at the **Language strip** and remember as much as they can. They can ask you questions during this time. Then ask students to close their books and put them into two teams. If you can, use L1 to test them on different expressions, draw them on the board or act them out. The first person to call out the correct expression wins a point for their team.
- Students test each other in pairs using the language in **4 Using grammar** on page 45. Give the class one minute to memorise the language. Student A then reads out **1–5**, while Student B closes the book and tries to repeat **a–e**. They then swap roles for **6–10** and **f–k**.
- Do one of the **Teacher's Resource Book** activities for **Unit 9**.

Conversation

1 Using vocabulary: past time phrases

A good way to lead in to the lesson is to write up the sentence starters *I've been to ...* and *I'd like to go to ... sometime* on the board. Give / ask for the translations and then complete the sentences in ways that are true for you by adding the names of some cities / countries.

Students then write down endings that are true for them. Get one or two students to tell you their sentences. Respond with questions like: *What's it like? Is it nice? When did you go there? Why?* etc. If students struggle to answer, let them use L1 and translate for them or reformulate their ideas into better English. Don't expect too much at this stage.

Next, get students to tell each other their sentences and have short conversations.

Round up with a couple of corrections or by reformulating into better English interesting things you heard students say. Correct on the board any new language the students have produced. Tell students they are going to learn how to have more conversations like this in this unit.

Explain the matching task. Point out that the date today is 12th August. Do the first one with the class and then let students try the rest individually.

Give them a couple of minutes and then let them compare in pairs before checking the answers. Write the answers on the board. Go through any new language, drilling where necessary. For example:
last weekend; yesterday morning; a couple of weeks ago; a few days ago

Answers							
1. d.	2. e.	3. f.	4. a.	5. b.	6. g.	7. c.	8. h.

- *Last weekend* – you could also elicit / give other last phrases like *last year*.
- *Yesterday morning* – elicit other times with yesterday – *yesterday afternoon / evening*. Note last night.
- *A couple of weeks ago* – note the weak forms and linking when you drill and ask: *How many weeks?* (Two.)
- *A few days ago* – ask: *How many days?* (More than two.)

Give the students a minute to remember the expressions then get them to test each other as suggested in the **Coursebook**.

2 Practice

Explain the task or model it. Try to give examples that are true for you or just point out the two examples. You might need to give the class a couple of minutes to prepare. Then get them to tell a partner their ideas.

51

Round up with a couple of corrections or by reformulating into better English interesting things you heard students say. Correct on the board any new language the students have produced.

3 Before you listen

Tell the students they're going to listen to a conversation between some people travelling around Europe by Inter Rail, like those in the photo. Read the short paragraph as a class, then discuss the questions quickly. Teach *hostel*.

As a homework activity or as a class project, students could look up Inter Rail on the Internet and plan where they would like to visit. This could be combined with descriptions of places to visit (like those in the reading on page 51) and made into a class poster.

4 Listening: *Have you been there?*

Tell students they are going to listen to three people talking in a hostel in Florence, Italy. All three are travelling by Inter Rail. Before students listen, go through any new language in the box. For example:
* *Hill* – draw a picture of a hill and a mountain to compare.
* *Istanbul* is a famous city in Turkey.
* *Vienna* is the capital of Austria.

Tell students not to read the **Tapescript** on the next page, but simply to listen and tick the places in the box the three people talk about.

Play the conversation once all the way through. Give students a minute or two to compare their answers in pairs. Round up the answers. If the class missed anything, simply tell them or play the recording once more before doing **4 Listening**.

Answers
* **The cathedral:** two of them are going to go there today. One of them went there a few days ago and says it's lovely.
* **The tower:** Stefan didn't go up the cathedral tower because he didn't want to pay.
* **The hill outside the city:** Stefan walked to the hill outside the city a few days ago. You get a really good view from there. Edward and Kirsty went there yesterday, but the weather was awful. It rained really badly. They got wet.
* **Vienna:** Stefan is thinking of going there this afternoon. Edward and Kirsty went there a couple of weeks ago. It's nice, but quite expensive.
* **Istanbul:** Stefan might go there after Vienna. Edward went there a few years ago with his ex-girlfriend. It's amazing – and cheaper than Florence!

5 Listen again

Tell the class they are going to hear the conversation again and that this time you want them to listen and complete the conversation with the words in the box. Play the recording and then give the students a minute to compare their ideas with a partner. Elicit the answers immediately or play the conversation one final time and stop after each gap. Students then call out their answers. Write them on the board.

Answers
1. cathedral
2. went
3. view
4. weather
5. yesterday
6. leave
7. couple
8. few
9. pack
10. enjoy

Go through any new language. For example:
* *A good view* – what you can see when you look down from somewhere. Ask where you can get a good view of the place you're in.
* *It rained really badly* means it rained a lot.
* *Ex-girlfriend* – she was a girlfriend before, but now she's not! Give other examples: *my ex-husband, our ex-president*.
* *Istanbul IS amazing* – we stress *is* to emphasis / make our point stronger.
* *You should go there* – I think it's a good place for you to go. I recommend it.
* *Pack my bag* – put all my clothes, shoes, etc. in my bag to take with me. Act it out.
* *It was nice meeting you* – we usually say this at the end of the first meeting with someone, as we're saying goodbye.
* *Your trip* – your Inter Rail holiday – you start from home, travel round Europe, then go home again. Give other examples: *I'm going on a day trip, I went on a business trip, We're going on a fishing trip*.

Next, ask students to read out the conversation in pairs. They can change roles once they finish. As they do so, go round and listen to their pronunciation, correcting and remodelling things for them if they need it.

6 Using grammar: *Have you been to … ?*

Ask students to find the three examples of *Have you been … ?* in the conversation and explain the meaning as written at the beginning of the activity. Now ask them to find the replies.

Elicit the full questions from the students and write them on the board. Elicit the answers and underline the common feature which is: *Yes, I went there …* + a past time phrase. Point out that we DON'T use the present perfect with past time phrases.

The three examples in the conversation are:
A: *Have you been there?*
B: *Yes, I went there a few days ago.*

A: *Have you been there?*
B: *Yes, we went there yesterday.*

A: *Have you been to Vienna?*
B: *Yes, we went there a couple of weeks ago.*

Ask the students to look at the five example conversations in the book. Read them out if you like. Point out the negative responses as you do so. Elicit the adverbs and translate them, if you can.

> **Answers**
>
> *Ever* and *never* mean any time in your life.
> *Recently* means some time near to now.

Next, get students to read out the conversations and continue them, if they can. Demonstrate this with one student. For example:
A: *Have you ever been to Glasgow?*
B: *No, I haven't. Is it nice?*
A: *I don't know. I'd like to go there this summer.*
B: *Oh, OK.*

As students are doing this, write the following on the board:
A: *Japan?*
B: *never / you?*

A: *the theatre recently?*
B: *a few weeks ago*

Give some feedback on the students' conversations or just move on and work through the two examples on the board, eliciting the full questions and answers from the class.
A: *Have you ever been to Japan?*
B: *No, never. Have you?*

A: *Have you been to the theatre recently?*
B: *Yes, I went a few weeks ago.*

Next, get students to write the conversations for **1–5** individually or in pairs. As they're writing, go round and check that they've understood and are writing sensible endings down. Correct where necessary. You might want to deal with common problems on the board when the students have finished.

Elicit the answers from different students. It may take too long to write everything on the board, but make sure you drill the correct answers with the class.

> **Answers**
>
> 1. A: *Have you been to the castle?*
>   B: *Yes, I / we went there yesterday afternoon.*
> 2. A: *Have you been to the restaurant across the road?*
>   B: *Yes, I / we went there last Friday with some friends.*
> 3. A: *Have you been to the new sports centre in town?*
>   B: *No, I / we haven't. Is it nice?*
> 4. A: *Have you been to the cinema recently?*
>   B: *Yes, I / we went (there) a few days ago.*
> 5. A: *Have you ever been to the States?*
>   B: *No, never. Have you? / What about you?*

As a follow-up, students could read the conversations in pairs and try to continue them. Alternatively, get students to write four or five *Have you been to … ?* questions that they want to ask other people in the class. Check the questions and then ask students to walk around asking and answering each other's questions.

Round up with a couple of corrections or by reformulating into better English interesting things you heard students say. Correct any new language the students have produced on the board.

For homework ideas, see the suggestions at the end of the notes for **3 Before you listen**.

Reading

If you are starting a new lesson, begin with a bit of revision. Do one of the suggested follow-up activities for **6 Using grammar** on page 49 that you haven't done already. Alternatively, do an activity from **Unit 10** of the **Teacher's Resource Book**.

Refer back to the listening. In the conversation, Edward says: *You should go to Istanbul.* He means it's a good place to go. Ask students if they remember why. (It's great there and it's cheaper than Florence.) Here there are seven more sentences that recommend places and say why they are good.

1 Using vocabulary: describing places

Ask students to read **1–7** and to see if there are any words they don't understand. Go through any new language. For example:

- *Incredible* means really good, amazing.
- The *nightlife* is the places to go at night to enjoy yourself. Elicit examples: pub, bar, club, restaurant, cinemas, theatres etc. Point to the photo of people clubbing on the left.
- *Sandy beaches* – point to the photo on the left.
- *Buildings* – point to some different buildings in the photos in this and the previous unit. Say: *A shop is a building, a cathedral is a building*, etc.
- The *scenery* is the countryside outside the city. Point to the photos of the beach and the tropical scenery on the left. They're both examples of scenery.

Ask students to complete the sentences by adding the names of places they know. Elicit a couple of examples from the students for **1** to give them the idea and to check they understand. As they're writing, go round and check that they've understood.

Get a couple ideas from the students and reply with one of the following:
Really? That sounds nice.
Really? Where is that?
Yes, I've been there. It's great.
No. X is much better!

You could write these responses on the board, if you want to and / or drill them. Now ask students to compare their ideas in pairs or groups of three and if they can, to use some of the responses above.

2 While you read

Explain the task. Ask students to read and think if they've been to any of the places and if not, whether they would like to go sometime in the future. Do the text as a listening, a reading or both, (see **Introduction** for procedure).

When the students have finished reading, ask them to discuss the questions in pairs for three or four minutes. Next, discuss the questions with the class. Ask if anyone has been to any of the places and find out if they agree with what was said. If they don't agree, ask them why not. Then ask a few students if they would like to go to any of the places and why. Don't spend more than a few minutes on this. You probably won't be able to speak to everyone in the class.

As a follow-up, write the following on the board:
the Alhambra
the Lake District
biscuits
the Scottish islands

Ask students to close their books and to compare what they remember about these places in pairs. After a couple of minutes, elicit ideas from the class and re-tell some of what was written in the text. For example:

Teacher: So, what can you can remember about the Alhambra?
Student: Very old.
Teacher: Yes. It's over 500 years old. Anything else?

Go through any new language. For example:
- *Tourists* are people on holiday.
- *Sunbathe* – act this out. Lying on the beach in the sun. Ask why. So you *get brown / get a suntan*.
- *First of all* is the first thing. There are more things coming.
- *Museums* – give / ask for local examples.
- *Of course* means *I'm sure you know this already, I don't need to tell you this*. Give other examples: *Can I sit here? / Yes, of course.*
- A *wild area* is a place with no houses or roads, a long way from the town, not many people live there.
- *Quiet and peaceful* mean the same thing. They're often used together.
- *Lakes* – draw one.
- *Very green* means lots of trees and plants.
- *Biscuit* – draw one.
- *It depends what you like* – translate or say *I'm not sure. It depends what you like. If you like swimming, go here, but if you like nightlife, go there.*
- *Bars* are like pubs – they sell beer and other kinds of alcohol.
- The *wildlife* is birds and animals.

3 Role play

Explain the task. Demonstrate the conversation with a strong student. Start as in the example given in the Coursebook. Put the students in pairs. You might want students to write the conversation first and then read it out, particularly with weaker classes. Otherwise, let students do the whole thing orally. Ask students to change roles once they have finished.

Monitor and check for mistakes in the language you've just taught. Round up with a couple of corrections or by reformulating into better English interesting things you heard students say. Correct on the board any new language the students have produced.

4 Using grammar: the present perfect

Write: *Have you been to Spain?* on the board. Explain this is an example of the present perfect, which we make

with *have* + past participle. This is often a third form of the verb. In this case, *be* (am / are / is) – present, *was / were* – past simple, and *been* – the past participle. With regular verbs, the past participle is the past *-ed* form. Ask students to read the explanation in the book.

Now explain the task. Do the first one with the class, then get students to do the rest individually. When most students have finished, get them to compare in pairs. Then check the answers.

> **Answers**
> 1. eaten   2. decided   3. travelled   4. known
> 5. met   6. seen   7. heard   8. gone

As you go through the answers, write them on the board and drill the questions. As students say them individually, you could model some answers to the questions.

Next, elicit some of the typical answers to: *Have you been to Spain?* Draw attention to the fact that we usually use the past simple in positive replies. Ask a few of the students the questions and elicit replies. Correct where necessary and perhaps ask the occasional follow-up question. Then put the students in twos or threes to ask and answer the questions. Monitor and check for mistakes, particularly any errors in the language you've just taught. Round up with a couple of corrections or by reformulating into better English interesting things you heard students say. Correct on the board any new language the students have produced.

Tell students to read **Grammar note** G12 on page 138.

5 Pronunciation: contractions

If you can, lead in to this activity using a correction from the role-play. Model the expressions yourself, or use the recording, and ask students to repeat them.

Before you do the dictation of the ten sentences, ask students to read the conversation in **5 Listen again** or the text on this page and to find examples of contractions. Ask them what the full forms are.

Play the recording. Pause at the end of each sentence to give students time to write. Get students to compare their answers and then play the sentences once more. Let students then compare what they have written again, before you go through the answers on the board, playing each sentence once more and pausing after each one as you do so. Alternatively, students can just compare with the **Tapescript** on page 126. Then drill the sentences either individually or as a class. Help with any problems.

Homework

You could tell the class to do **Unit 9** in the **Workbook** for homework, if you haven't done so already.

You could also ask students to write a paragraph telling tourists where they should go in their country and why. Tell them to use the four paragraphs on page 51 as models and to use as much language from this unit as they can.

Collect the writing next lesson and correct it. Correct any mistakes with things already studied in class and give students better ways of saying new things that they're trying to say.

Unit overview

General topics

Asking for and giving directions.
Basic travel experiences and getting lost.

Conversation

Three different conversations in which people ask for and give directions.

Reading

I got lost

Language input

- Prepositions of place: *opposite the station, next to the bank*, etc.
- Useful expressions for giving directions: *It's the second on the right.*
- Making requests: *Could you post this for me, please?*
- Pronunciation: consonant sounds: /θ/ and /ð/
- Travel language: *What time does it leave?*

Language strip

Ignore the **Language strip** to begin with and deal with the language as it comes up in various activities. Come back to it later as revision. Alternatively, ask students to learn the expressions for homework.

Lead in

Do one of the following:

- To revise language from **Units 9** and **10**, ask students to discuss which shops they've been to this week and why.
- Do one of the **Teacher's Resource Book** activities from **Unit 10**.
- Test the students on the expressions in the **Language strip** in **Unit 10**. Give students two minutes to look at the **Language strip** and remember as much as they can. They can ask you questions during this time. Ask students to close their books then put them into two teams. If you can, use L1 to test them on different expressions, draw them on the board or act them out. The first person to call out the correct expression wins a point for their team.

Conversation

1 Using vocabulary: prepositions of place

You could pre-teach this language by drawing larger versions of the maps and then using them to teach the six expressions to the class. Ask the question: *Is there a bank near here?* and drill it. Then elicit / give one of the expressions using a picture as a prompt. Drill this new expression and ask students to practise this 2-line

conversation in pairs. Repeat this process for all six expressions, going back over ones you have taught already from time to time. You could also teach: *Sorry, I'm not sure. I don't know this area.*

Ask students to do the exercise in pairs. After a few minutes, elicit the answers from the class and write them on the board. If you have not pre-taught the language, drill each answer. Point out the weak form of *there's* and the words which are stressed in the sentence. Explain that *up the road* just means it's near here, on this road. People also often say *down the road.* It means the same thing.

You could ask students to memorise the answers for one minute and to then test each other. The class covers the writing. Student A then points to a picture and says: *Is there a bank near here?* Student B then says the appropriate sentence.

Demonstrate the next task. Ask some students: *Is there a newsagent's / bank near here?* Encourage them to use the prepositional expressions as they answer and help them with anything new they might want to say. Next, get students to ask and answer similar questions in pairs.

For more controlled practice, give each student a piece of paper with a different shop / place written on it. Students then move round the room, asking: *Is there a X near here?* Students swap cards each time they change partners. Round up with a couple of corrections or by reformulating into better English interesting things you heard students say. Correct any new language the students have produced on the board.

2 Understanding directions

Explain the task. Ask students to work in pairs. After a few minutes, elicit the answers from the class and write them on the board.

Answers
1. d.   2. c.   3. b.   4. e.   5. a

As you go through the answers, drill the language and explain it using diagrams and gestures.

3 Listening: *Is there one near here?*

Tell students they are going to listen to three conversations and that in each one they will hear people ask for directions. Tell them to listen and to draw on the map where each person is going. The places are not marked. You could tell students the places to help them, (an internet café, a bookshop and a good restaurant). To help them further, drill the names of the streets / roads on the map.

Play the conversations once all the way through. Give students a minute or two to compare where they think the places are. Round up what they have and if the whole group between them can provide the answers, don't play the conversations again, unless the class really wants you to. To check the answers, point to the map in your book. As you elicit the answers, explain again how to get to the places. Ask the class where they think each place is, point to the places on the map and then give the directions yourself.

Answers
- The internet café is on James Street, opposite the supermarket.
- The bookshop is on Cloone Street, near the end of the road, next to the church.
- The restaurant is on Lincoln Street: turn left at the traffic lights and it's on the right.

4 Listen again

Tell the class they are going to hear Conversation 3 again, between Lenny, a man, and Kim, a woman. This time you want them to listen and complete the conversation by writing the words they hear in the gaps. Tell them they might need to write one word, two words or sometimes even three words in the gaps.

Play the conversation and then give the students a minute to compare their ideas with a partner. You may want to elicit the answers immediately or you may want to play the conversation one more time and stop after each gap. Students then call out their answers. Write them on the board.

Answers
1. I'd like to   2. on   3. Could you   4. come to
5. turn left   6. on the right

Go through any new language. For example:
- *Get some lunch* means buy / have some lunch. Give other examples: *I need to get a coffee. Do you want to get something to eat?*
- *How to get there* means the way / route.
- *I think I know where you mean* means I think I know the restaurant you're talking about.

Next, ask students to read out the conversation in pairs. They can change roles once they finish. As they do so, go round and listen to their pronunciation, correcting and remodelling things for them if they need it.

5 Practice

Divide the students into pairs. With weaker classes, put students in groups of 4 with 2 As and 2 Bs in each group, so they can help each other. Model the task with one of the better students. Then ask students to work together to complete the task.

Monitor for errors and help students with new language. At the end of the task, students should compare their maps to see if they were right. Round up with a couple of corrections or by reformulating into better English things you heard students say. Correct on the board any new language the students have produced.

6 Using grammar: making requests

Translate and / or explain *Could you ... , please?* Say it means *I want you to do this for me.* Ask students to look through the **Tapescript** of the conversations on page 126 and find examples of *Could you ... ?* questions and how people reply to them. Elicit these from the students and drill them.

Explain the task and do the first one with the class. Ask students to do the rest individually. Monitor and help with any unknown language. After two minutes, let students compare in pairs before eliciting the answers from the class and writing them on the board.

Answers
1. write down   2. draw   3. show   4. open
5. post   6. help

Go through any new language. For example:
- *Show me how to get there* means *you go with them.* You could also give other examples of *show*, e.g. *Show me the way. Show me where to go. Show me how to do it.*
- *Open the window* – act it out and then elicit the opposite *close.*
- *Post this letter* – act it out. Ask where you do it – *post office* or *post box.*
- *Move the table* – act it out. Elicit / give other examples of *move.*

Ask students to look at the 3-line example conversation and then get them to ask and answer the questions in pairs. As they do so, go round and listen to their pronunciation, correcting and remodelling things for them if they need it.

Finally, ask students to write two extra *Could you ... ?* questions they'd like to ask other students. Give them a couple minutes to write. As they do so, go round and check they're writing realistic questions. They then practise asking and answering in pairs again.

7 Pronunciation: /θ/ and /ð/

Tell the students they're going to do some work on pronunciation and their listening skills. Model the sounds yourself and demonstrate the position of the tongue between the teeth or use the recording and the photos on page 145. Ask students to repeat the sounds, both chorally and individually.

Now put the students in pairs and get them to say the sentences to each other and to decide which underlined sounds are /θ/ (as in *thin*) and /ð/ (as in *mother*). Play the tape to check and go through the answers with the class.

Answers
1. /ð/, /ð/
2. /ð/
3. /ð/
4. /θ/, /ð/, /ð/
5. /θ/, /θ/

Explain the next task. Play the recording. Pause at the end of each date to give students time to write. Ask students to compare their answers in pairs. Play each date again and pause again as you do. Elicit the answers from the class and write them on the board.

Alternatively, students can just compare their ideas with the **Tapescript** on page 126. Drill the sentences, either individually or as a class. Help with any problems.

For homework, ask students to try to learn the conversation from **4 Listen again** and then test them in the next lesson. You could also get them to write their own similar conversations with a friend about what they are doing now and how to get to somewhere in their town, trying to use as much of the language from these two pages as they can.

Reading

If you are starting a new lesson, begin with a bit of revision. Ask students to try to repeat as much of the conversation in **4 Listen Again** on page 53 as they can from memory. Alternatively, do an activity from **Unit 11** of the **Teacher's Resource Book**.

1 Using vocabulary

Tell students they're going to learn some useful vocabulary for having conversations when taking trains or buses. Explain the task. You could do the first conversation with the class, if you like, and then ask students to work individually. Monitor and help out with any new vocabulary. Give them a few minutes and then let them compare in pairs before checking the answers. Explain and drill any new vocabulary / expressions.

> **Answers**
> 1. go, take, get off
> 2. take, station, line
> 3. taxi, cost, driver
> 4. change, leave, The next one, 25 past
> 5. explain, problem, change, take

Go through any new language. For example:
- *Take an 87 bus* – we often add the number. For example, *take the number 3 bus. You need to take a number 19.*
- *Get off at* – act this out. Ask for the opposite (*get on*). Give examples: *Get off at the stop outside the supermarket. Get off when you get to the park. Get off at Heaton station.* (Here it's best to use shop names and station names which students would be familiar with.)
- *The underground* – the underground train is what students might call *the metro*. In London, it is called the *tube*.
- *Line* – draw a map to illustrate or give an example if your city has an underground.
- Taxis are also often called *cabs*.
- *25 past every hour* – write down 10.25, 11.25, 12.25 etc. to illustrate. You could also give other examples: *10 past every hour*. Also give *They run every half hour / every 20 minutes.* Ask: *So how many in one hour?* If students have already told you they take the bus or train to work or school, you could ask: *How often do the buses run?*

Ask students to practise the conversations in pairs, but to change the names of the places. Encourage them to use places they know. As they do so, go round and listen to their pronunciation, correcting and remodelling things for them if they need it.

2 Speaking

Ask students to read the sentences and examples individually and to choose which words and sentences they want to use. Then put students into groups of three and ask them to tell their partners about their city. If you are in a monolingual group from the same city, students can see if they agree with each other or not. They can also talk about their habits – the transport they usually use.

Round up with a couple of corrections or by reformulating into better English interesting things you heard students say. Correct on the board any new language the students have produced.

3 Before you read

Tell the class that all these verbs are from the text the students are going to read. Explain the task. Ask students to do it in pairs, using dictionaries if they want. Point out that the verbs are in the past, so they may need to look up the present forms. Elicit answers from the class and write them on the board. Ask for translations or act them out. You could also check the present forms as you go through the answers.

> **Answers**
> 1. d.   2. c.   3. a.   4. e.   5. b.

Go through any new language. For example:
- *Missed the train* – you could also elicit / give other things we miss: *my bus, my class, my flight, the meeting, the beginning of the film,* etc. Students might confuse this with *lose*. Give examples of things you *lose* (*some money, my keys, my wallet*).
- *Got lost* – we often say *I got lost on the way here / to somewhere.*
- *Fell asleep* – not usually when we go to bed, but instead *I fell asleep in the class / in front of the TV / on the train.* You could ask why, e.g. *It was very boring* or *I was very tired.*
- *Woke up* – for example, *I woke up at 6 this morning. I woke up late this morning and I was late for work.* Act it out to show the difference between waking up and getting up.

Ask students to test each other in pairs by acting out or drawing the verbs.

4 While you read

Explain the task. Note here that the recording includes the complete questions, so DON'T play the recording at this stage. Give students about five minutes to read the text. Then put them in pairs to compare what they think before rounding up ideas from the class. Don't give any definitive answers at this stage, but encourage students to give examples from the texts to justify their ideas.

Play the recording and tell students to check if they were right or not. Ask students to underline anything they don't understand or want to ask you about as they listen.

> **Answers**
> 1. c.   2. d.   3. a.   4. b.

After you have checked the answers and written them on the board, answer any questions students have. Then go through any new language. For example:

- *All the way to Scotland* – it was a long journey. Use your arms to show long. Use local examples to say, for instance: *I once drove all the way to X* or *I ran all the way to Y.*
- *Exactly at the moment* – at the same time.
- *Didn't recognise* – she saw the place, but she didn't know it. Ask why you sometimes don't recognise people – they've got fatter / thinner, they've had their hair cut, etc.
- *Unfortunately* – it was bad luck. Give other examples: *I took my driving test last week, but unfortunately I failed.*
- *Couple* – boyfriend and girlfriend or husband and wife.
- *Had an interview* – act it out and ask when else you have interviews.
- *Walked round in circles* – act it out. It means I was lost and walked a lot, trying to find the right place.

5 | Comprehension

In pairs, ask students to cover the text and use the notes and pictures to re-tell as much of the stories as they can. Go round and monitor for any errors. You could go through these on the board after they have finished. Alternatively, just elicit what the class can remember and reformulate this into better English, using as much of the actual language from the texts as you can. For example:

Teacher: OK, so what can you remember about the first story?
Student: Woman have accident.
Teacher: Yes, OK. She HAD an accident. And then?

You can decide if you want the students to try to remember and re-tell the last story without any prompts or not. If you are short of time, leave out this part of the activity.

6 | Speaking: *Have you ever got lost?*

Ask students to read the sentences first and check they understand them. Explain the task. You could model it by telling a story yourself, using some of the expressions. You might also need to give the class a couple of minutes to prepare or ask students to write their stories first. If they do write them, encourage students to try to memorise what they have written *before* they tell their partners.

Students tell their stories in pairs or groups. Monitor and help out with any new vocabulary. Round up with a couple of corrections or by reformulating into better English interesting things you heard students say. Correct any new language the students have produced on the board.

Homework
You could tell the class to do **Unit 10** in the **Workbook** for homework, if you haven't done so already.

You could also ask students to write a paragraph about a time they got lost. Tell them to use as much language from this unit as they can.

Collect the writing next lesson and correct it. Correct any mistakes with things already studied in class and give students better ways of saying new things that they're trying to say.

Unit overview

General topics
Meeting people while you're abroad.
Places to stay and booking rooms.

Conversation
Two conversations that happen while people are abroad.
A telephone call in which a woman books a room in a bed and breakfast.

Reading
Places to stay

Language input
- Useful expressions for meeting people: *Where are you staying? How long've you been here?*
- Present continuous: *I'm travelling all round Europe.*
- Holiday activities: *going sightseeing, going camping,* etc.
- *Not very* + positive adjective: *It wasn't very clean.*
- Pronunciation: consonant sounds: /b/ and /p/

Language strip
Ignore the **Language strip** to begin with and deal with the language as it comes up in various activities. Come back to it later as revision. Alternatively, ask students to learn the expressions for homework.

Do one of the following:
- Ask students to test each other on the expressions from **Activities 1** and **2** on page 52. Let them look at the page for one minute and then ask them to close their books. In pairs, ask students to write down as many of the expressions as they can remember in two or three minutes, then check by looking back at the book again. Finally, students role-play the three conversations from the listening, using the map as a prompt.
- Ask students to work in pairs and repeat **5 Comprehension** on page 55. Round up ideas from the class and retell the four stories in the text.
- Ask students to look at the **Expressions Organiser** for **Units 9** and **10** on page 150. Ask students to translate the expressions in pairs then check their ideas. Students can then test each other by saying a translation, acting it out or drawing a picture, while their partner guesses. To make this easier, let both students look at page 150.
- Do one of the **Teacher's Resource Book** activities from **Unit 11**.

Conversation

1 Meeting people for the first time

A good way to lead in to the lesson is to ask students to brainstorm questions they might ask when they meet someone when they are on holiday in another country. You could ask them to do this in teams or do it as a class. If students work in pairs, give them three or four minutes to prepare and then elicit ideas from the class. You might need to reformulate the students' ideas into better English. Write up the questions on the board and drill them.

Ask students to role-play a conversation between a tourist and a local in pairs. Tell students they are going to learn how to have more conversations like this in this unit.

Explain the matching task and do the first one with the class. Ask students to do the rest individually. Monitor and help with any unknown language. After a few minutes, elicit the answers from the class and write them on the board. Drill the questions as you go through.

Answers							
1. e.	2. c.	3. f.	4. b.	5. d.	6. a.	7. h.	8. g.

Go through any new language. For example:
- *Is it business or pleasure? Business* means anything to do with work. *Pleasure* – just to enjoy yourself. Elicit / give examples of each.
- *Where are you staying?* – check students understand this applies to the present. You could draw the timeline from page 57. Elicit other examples of places you stay.
- *How long've you been here?* – this is looking back from now to the past. Elicit other replies: *since Wednesday, since March, quite a long time, we arrived here last night,* etc.
- *When are you leaving?* – ask if this is talking about the present or the future? (The future.) Elicit other replies: *next week, we're going on Friday, in two weeks time,* etc.
- *Are you doing anything later?* – again, point out it's talking about the future. There's no need to explain WHY yet.

Ask students to say the questions in pairs and to guess where the stress in each is. Go through the questions with the class and drill them. Ask students to mark the stressed sounds. You can say the stressed words first and then repeat the whole question.

Answers
1. ENGlish
2. DOing HERE?, BUSiness, PLEAsure
3. WHERE, STAYing
4. LONG, HERE
5. BEEN, beFORE
6. WHEN, LEAVing
7. WHAT, THINK, HERE?
8. DOing, LAter

2 Listening: *What are you doing here?*

Tell students they are going to listen to two conversations. In the first, a German man is talking to a British woman on a train from London to Scotland. In the second, a Colombian woman is talking to a French man in Paris. Explain the task and play the recording once all the way through. You might want to stop the tape after each conversation so that students can compare notes, but don't go through the answers at this stage.

After students have listened to both conversations once and compared their answers, check which questions the speakers used and write the answers on the board.

Answers

Conversation 1: Questions 4, 2 (and 5 is acceptable *Have you been to Glasgow before?*)
Conversation 2: Questions 1, 2, 5, 7, 3 and 8.

Now ask students to discuss what they remember about the answers to these questions. Elicit ideas from the class to get a feel for how much students understood and then play the recording once more. Let students compare their answers in pairs again and then elicit the answers from the class.

Answers

Don't expect students to get all of the following, but mention it as you round up what they did hear.

Conversation 1:
4. Not very long. He arrived in London last Thursday.
2. It's business. He works for an export company.
5. Yes, a few times.

Conversation 2:
1. *Yes, sure.*
2. She's on holiday. She's travelling all round Europe.
5. No, it's her first time.
7. She thinks it's great. It's very romantic.
3. In a hotel near Monmartre.
8. She'll probably just get something to eat and go to bed early!

---

3 Listen again

Tell the class they are going to hear the conversations again and that this time you want them to listen and complete the sentences from each one by adding one word in each gap. You could see if students can fill in the gaps BEFORE they listen to the recording again.

Play the recording and then give the students a minute to compare their ideas with a partner. You may want to elicit the answers immediately or you may want to play the conversation one final time and stop after each gap. Students then call out their answers. Write them on the board.

Answers

1. a. free   b. Glasgow   c. Thursday   d. good
e. company
2. a. find   b. direction, like   c. holiday, Europe
d. romantic   e. nightlife   f. early

Go through any new language. For example:

- *Is this seat taken?* means the same as *Is this seat free?* – act it out. The answers differ, though: *No, go ahead, Help yourself* or *Yes, sorry. I'm saving it for someone.*
- The *Louvre* is a famous art gallery in Paris.
- *I'm going in that direction* means *You're going that way? Oh, me too. I can show you where it is, if you want.*
- *Travelling round* means to spend quite a long time going from one place to another to another. For example, *I spent three months travelling round China. It was amazing!*
- *Romantic* – draw a love heart on the board! It's a good place to fall in love, to go with your boyfriend, etc. Give other examples: *a romantic dinner, a very romantic film*, etc.
- A *guide* is someone to show you the good places to go and tell you about them. Ask for / give any local sights where tourists can get guides.
- *I think I'll probably* – I'm not 100% sure, but this is my idea for what to do in the future. Refer students to the **Real English** note. Drill both of B's responses.

You could follow up the listening by having a short discussion about whether the students have ever made friends with people on holiday or had any bad experiences with the people they have met.

Round up with a couple of corrections or by reformulating into better English interesting things you heard students say. Correct on the board any new language the students have produced.

4 Speaking

Ask students to role-play the conversations in pairs. You might want to let them read the Tapescript on page 126–7 first or give them two or three minutes to prepare. As students try the role-play, monitor for problems of pronunciation or usage and correct where necessary. Ask students to change roles. Finish by dealing with any common problems and any new language that came up.

5 Using grammar: present continuous

Elicit examples of the present continuous that students have seen in this lesson. Highlight the use of the verb *be* + *-ing* in these examples. Point out that the present continuous is used to talk about both unfinished temporary activities around now and the near future. Students learn more about this second usage in **Unit 24.** This activity looks at unfinished activities.

Ask students to read the short explanation and then explain the task. Students should do the task individually or in pairs. Go through the answers on the board. The task is essentially a vocabulary test, but as you go through the answers, draw attention to the grammar.

Answers

1. doing   2. visiting   3. feeling   4. studying
5. trying   6. getting   7. talking   8. opening

Go through any new language. For example:

- *In the shower* – act it out. Tell students we also say *in the bath*.
- *Getting ready to go out* – ask what you do when you get ready to go out: have a shower, get changed, do your hair, put your make-up on, etc.

Next, ask students to memorise the eight sentence pairs in **1–8**. Demonstrate the task. Student A can have their book either open or closed.

Finally, ask students to cover the sentences in **1–8** and to complete **a–g** with the correct form of the verb *be*. Let students refer back to **1–8** before eliciting the answers and writing them on the board.

Answers

a. 'm   b. Are   c. 's   d. 's   e. 's   f. 're   g. 're

At this point, ask the class to read **Grammar note** G14 on page 139.

6 Practice

Write the following on the board:
A: Where / you? / We / wait / for you?
B: Sorry. / the bus. / It / come along Tyne Street now.
A: OK. / We / wait / outside the cinema.

Elicit the sentences from the class and write them on the board. Ask students to write the other three conversations in pairs. As they're writing, go round and check that they've understood and are writing sensible endings down. Note any common mistakes on the board and correct them with the class after students have finished writing. You don't have to write all the conversations on the board, especially if you have monitored and help students closely.

Possible answers:

1. A: *Where are you? We're waiting for you?*
   B: *Sorry. I'm on the bus. It's just coming along Tyne Street now.*
   A: *OK. We're waiting for you outside the cinema.*

2. A: *Hi. Are you on your own? Where's Carlos?*
   B: *He's at home in bed. He's not feeling very well.*
   A: *Oh, I'm sorry.*

3. A: *Hi. Where's Dave?*
   B: *He's just having a shower.*
   A: *Oh, OK.*

4. A: *What're you doing here in Brighton?*
   B: *I'm on holiday. I'm just staying for a week.*
   A: *Where are you staying?*
   B: *In a youth hostel near the park.*
   A: *Is it nice?*
   B: *Well, it's not very clean, but (at least) it's cheap.*

Next, ask students to read their conversations in pairs. Monitor and correct any problems with pronunciation or any other language mistakes you missed first time round. With quick finishers, get them to change roles or to memorise the conversations.

To finish, ask students to read **Grammar note** G14 on page 139, if they haven't done so already.

For homework, ask students to write their own mobile phone conversations with friends, using the present continuous where relevant.

Collect the conversations next lesson and read them. Correct any mistakes with things already studied in class and give students better ways of saying new things that they're trying to say.

Reading

If you are starting a new lesson, begin with a bit of revision. Test the students on the expressions in the **Language strip** on page 56. Give students two minutes to look at the **Language strip** and remember as much as they can. They can ask you any questions during this time. Tell students to close their books and put them into two teams. If you can, use L1 to test them on different expressions, draw on the board or act them out. The first person to call out the correct expression wins a point for their team.

Alternatively, ask students to practise the four conversations in **6 Practice** on page 57 again, using the notes as a prompt. You could also do an activity from **Unit 12** of the **Teacher's Resource Book**.

1 Speaking

It's probably best to do both parts of this activity in one go. Ask students to read **a–d** first and to check they understand them, before then reading the second part of the activity. Go through any new language.
For example:
• *Relatives* are cousins or aunts or uncles, etc.
• A *5-star hotel* is a very expensive, top quality hotel. Give / ask for local examples.
• A *bed and breakfast* is a small family-run / owned private house. The family live there and maybe have three or four rooms for guests. You get breakfast.
• A *self-catering apartment* is a flat / apartment you rent for a week or two when you go on holiday and where you can cook. Teach *a self-catering holiday*, too. Drill the expression.

Explain the task. Model it by telling students where you usually stay when you go to other places and if you've ever stayed in any of the five places. Remind students that we use the past simple to talk about <u>when</u> we stayed in a place.

Ask students to discuss the questions in pairs. Monitor and help out with any new vocabulary. Round up with a couple of corrections or by reformulating into better English interesting things you heard students say. Correct any new language the students have produced on the board.

2 While you read

Explain the task. Note here that the recording includes the complete descriptions, so DON'T play the recording at this stage. Give students about five minutes to read the text. Then put them in pairs to compare what they think before rounding up ideas from the class. Don't give any definitive answers at this stage, but encourage students to give examples from the texts to justify their ideas.

Play the recording and tell students to check if they were right or not. Write up the answers on the board.

As you do so, check that students understand why the answers are as they are. For example:

Teacher: OK. So Western House is a bed and breakfast. How do you know? What else tells you in the text?
Student: Family.
Teacher: OK. It's run by a very friendly family and a full English breakfast is included.

At this stage, don't deal with any unknown vocabulary. Wait until after **3 Comprehension.**

3 Comprehension

Ask students to cover the text to begin with and discuss the questions in pairs. Next, ask students to check their ideas by looking back at the text and underlining the words that helped them decide. Elicit answers from the class and write them on the board. As you go through the answers, ask how the class made their decisions.

Answers

a. Hill farm – you can put your tent up there.
b. The Go-Go – it's very close to all the pubs and clubs.
c. The Clifford – there's a swimming pool there or Western House – it's 10 minutes by car from the sea.
d. The Clifford – it's close to all the famous sights like Big Ben and Buckingham Palace.
e. The Clifford – there's a gym and a swimming pool there.
f. The Home from Home – you can use the computer there.
g. The Home from Home – it's self-catering, so you do your own cooking there or The Go-Go – you can cook for yourself there.

Discuss which places students would like to go to with the class. Ask students why and help them with any new vocabulary they need. It's not worth spending more than about five minutes on this, so you may not have time to ask everyone.

Go through any new language. For example:
- *A two-hundred-year-old house* – when we put an article at the front of this, we don't say *years*. Give other examples: *a 5-minute walk, a two-hour exam, a three-hundred dollar suit*, etc.
- *Historic* means very old and important, with lots of old buildings. Ask for / give local examples.
- *Per person per night* – for each person for each night.
- *In the middle of* – draw a picture to illustrate this.
- *Hills and mountains* – draw pictures to show the difference.

4 Conversation: booking a room

Explain the context and the task. Ask students to try to complete the conversation in pairs before they listen. You may need to explain *book* first. (You phone some time before you go to the hotel and ask for a room. You can *book a room / a table / your flight*). Play the recording so students can check their ideas. Elicit answers from the class after each gap or at the end of the conversation and write them on the board. Deal with new and interesting language as you do so.

Answers

1. book   2. arriving   3. leaving   4. checking
5. pay   6. take

Go through any new language. For example:
- *A single room* – ask for how many people and then elicit *a double room*.
- *Madam* – a polite, formal thing to call to a woman in a shop / restaurant, etc. This is what staff say to customers. Customers don't say it to staff. Ask what you say to a man in this situation. (*Sir.*)
- *How are you going to pay?* – elicit the different answers – *by credit card, by cheque, in cash*.
- *The full cost* – the cost of everything: It's £50 a night, so for two nights the full cost is £100.
- *The expiry date* – show students on any card you have. Tell them you can't use it after this date – it expires. Elicit other things that have an expiry date or expire: passport, visa, driving licence, etc.
- *Your name as it appears on the card* – again, show a card and contrast this with the name people usually call you, if it's different.
- *Look forward to seeing you* is a common way to end these kinds of conversations. It means we're happy that we're going to see you.

If you like, ask students to read the conversations in pairs. As they do so, go round and listen to their pronunciation, correcting and remodelling things for them if they need it. However, you may want to miss these stages and move straight on to the practice where the students slightly adapt the conversation.

5 Practice

Put the students in pairs. Student A is the receptionist at The Clifford Hotel from the text. Ask the students to re-read the conversation in **4 Conversation** and decide what information they will need to change, (e.g. the price) and which questions and expressions they can use again.

Student B is going to book a room. Again, ask them to re-read the conversation and decide which information they will need to change. For example, the dates of the visit and the credit card details.

Then ask students to practise the conversations in pairs. They can read out relevant sections from the conversation.

A follow-up would be to get students to change roles and to spend a few minutes trying to remember the relevant language. They then repeat the role-play with their books closed. Make it clear that if they forget exactly how it was said, they should just keep going and not look at the book.

6 | Using vocabulary: *How was your holiday?*

You could introduce this activity by telling a short personal story about somewhere you've been to recently where things weren't very good. Write up a couple of examples of *not very* + positive adjective on the board as you do so. Explain / check students understand them and then explain the task. Do the first one with the class and then ask them to do the rest individually. After a couple of minutes, let students compare in pairs. Then elicit the answers from the class and write them on the board. Drill each sentence as you do so.

Answers

1. The weather wasn't very good.
2. The hotel wasn't very clean.
3. The English breakfasts weren't very nice.
4. The owners of the bed and breakfast weren't very friendly.
5. The town wasn't very interesting.
6. Our hotel room wasn't very warm.

Now ask students to tell each other about their own experiences. You might need to give the class a few minutes to prepare. You could also tell them one or two personal examples following the model in the book or simply ask them to read the examples given.

When students tell each other their stories, get them standing up and mingling so they change partners several times. You could ask them to decide who had the worst experience.

Monitor and check for mistakes, particularly any errors in the language you've just taught. Round up with a couple of corrections or by reformulating into better English interesting things you heard students say. Correct any new language the students have produced on the board.

7 | Pronunciation: /b/ and /p/

Tell the students they're going to do some work on pronunciation and their listening skills. Model the expressions yourself and demonstrate the position of the lips or use the recording and the photos on page 144. Ask students to repeat the sounds chorally and individually. Point out that the difference between the two sounds comes from using your voice for /b/. You can feel this by touching your throat. You also blow out more air with /p/. If you put your hand in front of your lips, you should be able to feel the air coming out when you say /p/ but not /b/. Show this technique to the students.

Now ask students to practise saying the sentences to each other in pairs. Play the recording so students can check their pronunciation or simply go round and listen to their pronunciation, correcting and remodelling things for them if they need it.

Homework

You could tell the class to do **Unit 11** in the **Workbook** for homework, if you haven't done so already.

You could also ask students to write either a paragraph describing somewhere they have stayed on holiday or a paragraph about some problems they've had while on holiday. Tell them to use as much language from this unit as they can.

Collect the writing next lesson and correct it. Correct any mistakes with things already studied in class and give students better ways of saying new things that they're trying to say.

Review: Units 7–12

Activities **1–5** could be set as homework or done as a short test. If you do them as a test, give students 10–15 minutes.

You could also do these activities as a slightly more relaxed revision lesson. You can introduce tasks quite simply by saying: *Now we're going to revise some questions / vocabulary / grammar we've looked at before*, and then explain the tasks. Students can do the tasks in pairs or individually. When you elicit the answers to each activity, you can ask questions about the language and re-teach any words and expressions students have problems with. After each activity, there is a suggested follow-up that you could do as a way of breaking up the lesson a little. They all provide some opportunities for speaking.

1 Questions

Answers

1. c. 2. a. 3. d. 4. e. 5. b. 6. i. 7. h. 8. j.
9. f. 10. g.

You could follow this up by asking students to memorise the answers and to then test each other. Student A says the question. Student B closes the book and says the answer.

Alternatively, get Student A to ask Student B the same questions, but Student B should give a different answer. You may need to model this with a student. Get the student to ask you 2 or 3 questions and give new replies. You could round up by writing on the board some of the new answers you heard students say.

2 Grammar: tense and questions

Answers

1. the present tense: 2, 3, 7
2. the past tense: 1, 5, 6, 9
3. the present perfect tense: 4, 8, 10

3 Grammar: questions

Do the grammar rules either as a class or in pairs.

Answers

The present: a. do you b. is it
Specific times in the past: a. did you b. was it
General experiences before now: have you

If you wish or more particularly if students ask, you can give third person forms. However, there is no particular need to do so at this stage or for this activity.
Ask students to do the gap fill task.

Answers

1. did you   2. do you   3. Was it   4. Have you
5. did you   6. did you   7. Do you   8. Have you

Ask students to write their questions for you in pairs. They can copy ones they've seen already or make new ones. Go round and correct their questions if necessary. If you have a big class, put students into groups of 4 or 6 to compare and then choose just 2 or 3 questions from the ones they have written. Get them to ask you their questions and answer them.

Refer students to the **Grammar Organiser** at the back of the **Workbook** for further examples of questions.

4 Verbs

Answers

1. send   2. get   3. change   4. get off   5. need
6. spend

Ask students to discuss the questions in pairs or small groups. You might want to add some more questions of your own such as:
How many e-mails do you send a day?
When was the last time you got lost?
Which bust stop do I need to get off at to go to your house?

Round up with a couple of corrections and correct on the board any new language the students have produced.

5 What's the forecast for tomorrow?

Explain what *forecast* means and / or translate it.

Answers

1. d.   2. e.   3. f.   4. a.   5. c.   6. b.

You could follow this up by asking students to memorise the expressions. Cover the expressions. Student A says: *What's the forecast for tomorrow?* and points to a symbol. Student B says the expression.

You could get students to ask about the forecast for this afternoon / tomorrow / the weekend / next week, etc. Their partner replies truthfully, with one of the expressions.

6 Look back and check

If you have repeated these tasks as a form of revision / warmer in a previous lesson, you may want to skip this activity.

Let students look back at both activities and decide which one they want to do. Take a vote on which one they prefer or do both. Give students time to read and ask you questions about the language before they do the speaking task again. Round up as above.

7 What can you remember?

If you have re-elicited these texts as a form of revision / warmer in a previous lesson, you may want to skip this activity.

Students will remember quite a lot about the content of a text, but often will not remember the exact expressions or collocations. Try to remind students of these as you go through the answers. For example:

Student: In England you should go to lake place. Very nice.

Teacher: Yes, OK. It's called The Lake District and it's very beautiful.

An alternative way of doing this is to replay the recording of one or both of the texts, depending on the time you have available. Get students to discuss the questions with a new partner.

8 Vocabulary builder: People and clothes

This page aims to revise and expand on vocabulary, in this case ways of describing people and words for clothes.

Get students to discuss the questions and help with any new language they might want to use. Explain the task and ask students to work in pairs. After a few minutes, elicit the answers from the class and drill the words where appropriate, (blonde, leather, skirt, suit). You could also ask who in the class is wearing these things. Ask students to study the names of the people and what they look like for a minute. They should cover the pictures and in pairs try to answer the questions.

Answers

Paul: gray hair, suit, leather shoes
Sally: T-shirt
Patrick: jacket, jeans
Lita: black hair, skirt
Sharon: blonde hair, glasses

1. Patrick
2. Sharon
3 Patrick
4. Paul
5. Lita
6. Sally
7. Sharon

Now get students to ask similar questions about other people in the room. Model this by asking about two or three people yourself.

Ask students to read the short dialogue. Ask them to think about where they got some of the things they are wearing. Then do one or two similar conversations with a student. Get the class to move round the room complimenting each other on different clothes. Monitor and check for mistakes or help out with any new language students want to use. Round up with a couple of corrections or interesting things students said. Also, teach anything new you heard students trying to say.

9 Listening: *My brother's there now*

Do this listening as you would do a normal listening. Explain the context and the task. Make sure students cover the conversation the first time they hear it. Ask students to compare their ideas in pairs. As they do so, go round and check to see how they've done. Depending on how much they've got, either elicit their ideas from the class or play the recording a second time and then do so.

Answers

There is no fixed answer to the first task. It's up to you how much you want students to get. However, as a guide, it's best for students to have understood the following before moving on to the next task:

He's living in Uzbekistan. His wife is from there. He's an engineer. He's teaching English.

Tell the class they are going to hear the conversation again and that this time you want them to listen and complete the conversation by writing the word they hear in each gap. There is only ONE word missing each time. You could get them to try and complete the conversation first *before* they listen. Play the conversation and then give the students a minute to compare their ideas with a partner. You may want to elicit the answers immediately or you can play the conversation one more time and stop after each gap. Students then call out their answers. Write them on the board. As you do so, deal with any new / interesting language.

Answers

1. awful   2. read   3. doing   4. do   5. moment
6. wife   7. did   8. been   9. think   10. speak

Ask students to discuss the questions in small groups or as a class. Round up as above.

10 Pronunciation: the letter 'o'

This activity looks at the relationship between spelling and sound. Use the recording or just model the sounds and words yourself and ask students to repeat them. Explain the task. Do this as a race – ask students to do this in pairs and see which pair finishes first. Stop the task when the first pair finishes. Let the students read out their route. If they give a wrong answer, stop them and let another pair try to finish the route. The pair with the correct route are the winners!

Answers

hot, cost, sorry, lost, job, on, wrong, stop, a lot, top, long, golf, problems

11 Collocation

The collocation exercise also uses the grid of words from **10 Pronunciation**. The idea is to find a different route by completing each pair of expressions with one word from the grid. You could do this as a race with students working in pairs or threes in the same way as the activity above. You might need to do the first two as a class.

Answers

1. hot
2. open
3. Sorry
4. lost
5. job
6. Could
7. once
8. road
9. wrong
10. window
11. long
12. corner
13. problems

As this is revision, there's no real need to ask questions about the language here. However, after students have got the answers, ask if anyone has any questions about the language.

You could re-use the grid now or at another time. Read out some sentences in **1–10**, but say *blank* (or whistle or hum), instead of saying the word in the grid. Students listen and try to follow the route by deciding the missing word. For example:

It's really _____ here in the summer.

How much did your new computer _____ ?

We've known each other _____ years.

Can you help me _____ this table please?

I hate playing games. I always _____ ?

I'm trying to _____ smoking, but it's really difficult.

You look sad. What's _____ ?

I live on a big _____ . It's very noisy.

I'd like to work for a computer _____ .

I hate watching any sport, but especially _____ . It's so boring.

I've had a lot of _____ with my computer.

Homework

You could tell the class to do **Unit 11** in the **Workbook** for homework, if you haven't done so already.

13 What time is it?

Unit overview

General topic
Talking about time and the first time you did things.

Conversation
Four different conversations about time.

Reading
Do you remember the first time?

Language input
- Telling the time: *It's half past six, It's quarter to ten.*
- Common questions using the word *time*: *What time's your flight?*
- Making suggestions using *Let's*: *Let's go and see a film.*
- Past simple interrogative: *When was the first time you went on a plane?*
- Pronunciation: /ʃ/

Language strip
Ignore the **Language strip** to begin with and deal with the language as it comes up in various activities or come back to it later as revision. Alternatively, ask students to learn the expressions for homework.

Lead in
Do one of the following:
- Ask the class to work in pairs and see how many of the eight questions from **1 Conversation** on page 56 they can remember. Then give them one minute to look back at the questions and have them role-play two or three conversations using these eight questions. Split the group into two halves, tourists and locals, and have the locals ask these questions to some different tourists. Round up with a couple of corrections or by correcting and writing any new language the students have produced on the board.
- Give students two minutes to try to remember **1–8** from **5 Using Grammar** on page 57. They then work in pairs. Student A closes their book. Student B reads out the first sentences in **1–8**. Student A tries to remember all the present continuous sentences. Alternatively, do the activity as a class.
- Do one of the **Teacher's Resource Book** activities from **Unit 12**.

Conversation

1 | Using vocabulary: telling the time

Ask the group what the time is, what time they got up, what time they went to bed last night, etc. See how well they answer and then tell them they're going to look at ways of talking about time.

Ask students to match the times in **1–8** with the clocks in **a–h**. Go round and help out as they do so. You might need to explain that *past* means *after* and *to* means *before*. You could draw a circle on the board and divide it in half to clarify this. Elicit the answers from the class and write them on the board. Drill each expression as you do so.

Answers
1. f.   2. b.   3. e.   4. g.   5. c.   6. h.   7. d.   8. a.

Ask students to read the **Real English** note. Then round-up by asking some different students again what time it is, what time they got up, what time they went to bed last night, and so on.

2 | Listening: *What time?*

Tell the class you're going to play them four different conversations and in each one they will hear people mention different times. Tell them to listen and to try to write down the times they hear in the gaps.

Play the conversations once all the way through. Give students a minute or two to compare their answers in pairs. Then round up what they have. If the whole group between them can provide the answers, don't play the conversations again, unless the class really wants you to. If they only have some of the answers, play the conversations again, pausing after each conversation.

If you do play the conversations again, you might want to ask the class if they heard anything else and rephrase their ideas using the language heard in the recording.

Answers
1. 8 o'clock
2. a. 2.30   b. 7
3. a. 9.45   b. 1
4. a. 8   b. 7

3 | Listen again

Tell the class they are going to hear Conversation 4 again, between Roger, a man, and Jane, a woman, but before they hear it you want them to try to complete the conversation on their own.

Give them two minutes to do this and then let them compare their ideas in pairs. Tell the class to listen and check if they were right or not. After playing the conversation, give them one more minute to compare their ideas with a partner. Elicit the answers immediately or play the conversation one more time and stop after each gap. Students then call out their answers. Write them on the board.

Answers

1. do   2. sure   3. does   4. need   5. change
6. take   7. let's   8. cinema

You might want to mark the stress on _cinema_ and drill it.

Go through any new language. For example:
- _Have a shower_ – act it out.
- _Change my clothes_ means take off these clothes and put some different clothes on. Act it out.
- _Take me an hour_ means I will need an hour to do it.
- _Let's meet at seven_ means I want to meet at seven; this is my suggestion.
- We often finish conversations by saying: _See you later_ and _Bye_.

Ask students to read out the conversation in pairs. As they do so, go round and listen to their pronunciation, correcting and remodelling things for them if they need it. Do this with each pair rather than the whole group, unless you hear something everybody has trouble with, then deal with it at the end of the activity as a class, remodelling and drilling.

Tell the students to translate **1–6** into their language and write their translations in the book. If you share the same L1 as the class, check the translations with weaker students or simply tell them.

Point out the use of _take_ again in **4**. The question means _How much time do I need for my journey there?_

In **6**, the word _just_ adds the meaning of _nowhere special_ or _nowhere very interesting_.

4   Common questions

Tell the class they are going to look at some very common questions people ask about time. Ask them to match **1–4** to **a–d** and then match **5–8** to **e–h**. Have them compare their ideas in pairs and then check the answers from the whole group, writing them on the board as you do so.

Answers

1. b.   2. c   3. a.   4. d.   5. f.   6. e.   7. h.   8. g.

As you go through the answers, check the understanding of some of the words. The most efficient way is to translate if you can.

Go through any new language. For example:
- A _match_ – is a game between two teams.
- A _stadium_ is a big place where people go to watch matches. You could draw one on the board or ask the name of any big local stadiums.
- _What time are you going to get to the party tonight?_ means _What time are you going to arrive at the party tonight?_
- _Midnight_ is twelve o'clock at night. Twelve o'clock in the morning is _midday / noon_.

Put the students in pairs to ask and answer the questions. Go round and listen to their pronunciation, correcting and remodelling things for them if they need it. Ask the students to change partners and to ask the

same questions, but to think of new answers for each one. Refer them to the example given. Walk round and check their answers.

5   Using grammar: _Let's_

Tell the class they're going learn how to make suggestions. If you share the same L1, translate _Let's meet outside my office at half past five_ and see if they tell you in English.

Read the conversation. If anyone asks what the _'s_ in _Let's_ mean, say it means _Let us_, but that it's almost always said as just one word – we use it to suggest things to do together.

Ask students to try to complete the five conversations using the five pairs of words in the box. You might want to do the first one as a class to model the activity. Give them a few minutes and then let them compare in pairs before checking the answers.

Answers

1. do + go   2. see + try   3. go + try   4. get + take
5. meet + say

Go through any new language. For example:
- We often say _go and + verb_. You could give a few more examples: _Let's go and have a coffee, Let's go and talk to him_, etc. In American English, it's _Let's go see a film_.
- _Miss Snowblood_ is a movie.
- _It looks good_ means I've seen / heard information about something and like what I've seen.
- _It's quicker_ means the train is quicker than any other way of travelling, like the bus or walking.

6   Practice

Tell the class that now they're going to have conversations like the ones they've heard.

Before you start this, ask the students to read the **Grammar note** G15 on _Let's_ on page 139.

If you want to give students some preparation time, let them write the short conversations first and then have them practise them without looking at the writing. You could ask them to repeat the conversations with a different partner.

Round up with a couple of corrections or by reformulating into better English interesting things you heard students say. Correct any new language the students have produced on the board.

For homework, ask students to try to learn the conversation from **3 Listen again** and then test them in the next lesson. You could also get them to write their own similar conversations with a friend about what time and where to meet tonight, trying to use as much of the language from the lesson as they can.

Reading

If you are starting a new class, begin with a bit of revision. Put the students in pairs and ask them to look at the clocks on page 64. Tell them to cover **1–8** and check they can remember the times shown. Alternatively, ask them to repeat **6 Practice** on page 65 with a new partner.

1 Using grammar: making questions with the past simple

Tell the group that in this part of the unit they're going to look at ways of talking about the first time they did things.

Ask them to complete questions **1–8** by adding the past simple forms of the verbs in brackets. You might want to do the first one as a class to model the activity. Let them compare their ideas in pairs and then elicit the answers from the whole group, writing them on the board as you do so.

Answers

1. travelled   2. went   3. kissed   4. met   5. stayed
6. bought   7. saw   8. had

As you go through the answers, drill the whole questions.

Go through any new language. For example:
- *Abroad* means go to a different country.
- A *record* is an old way of listening to music. DJs often still use records. They're big, round and black. You could draw one on the board.

Go over the expressions *when I was at school / university*, and say we use *at* not *in*. You could also explain that if an experience was bad or very personal and you don't want to tell people about it, you can say *I don't want to talk about it* and add *if you don't mind* to sound polite.

If you want to, let students ask you some of these questions first. Try to use the expressions in your answers.

Now let students ask each other the questions in pairs or walking around the class, talking to some different people. Round up with a couple of corrections or by reformulating into better English interesting things you heard students say. Correct any new language the students have produced on the board.

2 Before you read

Check students understand the meaning of the words in the box.

Go through any new language. For example:
- Your *grades* are the marks you get for work or for exams or school. Write B+ or 65% on the board.
- *Nervous* is a feeling you get before flying or something your afraid of doing. Act this out.
- *I felt really grown-up* – I was only young, but I did something adult. I felt older, like I was now a man / woman, not a child.

- *I got paid* – I did some work and my boss gave me some money.
- *I wrote to a pen pal* – a friend in a different place. I write him / her letters, but maybe I've never met him / her.
- You do the *washing-up* after dinner, to clean the dirty plates and cups. Act it out.

In pairs or as a class, ask students to decide which words go with which pictures, (you may want students to cover the text). This is just to generate some interest in the text; the correct answer is not important.

3 While you read

Ask the students to read the text on page 67 and find out which words from **2 Before you read** go with each person. Do the text as a listening, a reading or both, (see **Introduction** for procedure).

When students have finished reading / listening, ask them to discuss in pairs what they remember about which words went where. Round up with the class and try to retell some of the text while you do so.

Answers

Awful: Jeremie thought his trip to England was going to be great, but really it was awful: it rained all the time and he didn't like his pen pal.
Grades: Ruth's teacher gave everyone grades for their presentations from A+ to E.
I felt really grown-up: Hugh felt like this the first time he got paid. He was only 15, but was already earning his own money!
I got paid: Hugh gets paid £15 a night and he can still remember the first time he got paid. It was brilliant!
I wrote to a pen pal: Jeremie wrote to a pen pal in England. Everybody in his English class at school did the same.
It went really well: Ruth spent weeks planning her presentation and it went really well. She got a good grade for it.
Nervous: Ruth was really nervous before speaking in public for the first time. She couldn't sleep!
Not very friendly: when Jeremie stayed with his pen pal's family in England, they weren't very friendly.
Washing up: Hugh has a job in a restaurant and he does the washing up, (as well as chopping vegetables).

At this stage, don't deal with any unknown vocabulary. Wait until after the **Word check**.

4 After you read

Let students discuss these two questions in pairs. For **1**, they may well simply say things like *Hugh ... enjoy ... brilliant*. You can respond by saying: *Yes, OK. Hugh really enjoyed it. He said it was brilliant!* You can do this with each pair as you go round.

For **2**, let students try to tell their stories, using L1 if they have to. Round up with a couple of corrections or by reformulating into better English interesting things you heard students say. Correct any new language the students have produced on the board.

As students use the words in the box and the pictures to re-tell the text help them to say things in a better way.

5 Speaking

This is a chance for students to ask about things they'd like to know. Give them two or three minutes to write their questions. Go round and help out as they're doing so. You might need to point out possible questions for **2**, e.g. *What was the first film you saw?*

Round up with a couple of corrections or by correcting any new language the students have produced on the board. Alternatively, round up by retelling two or three of the more interesting stories you heard students trying to tell.

6 Word check

Tell the class you're going to look at some of the new language from the text. Ask them to try to complete **1–8** using the words in the box, all of which are from the text. Let them compare their ideas in pairs and then check the answers as a class, writing them on the board as you do so.

Answers

1. exciting   2. divorced   3. proud   4. all   5. afraid
6. frightening   7. give   8. spent

As you go through the answers, mime some of the meanings and drill pronunciation where relevant.
You could also give other collocations and perhaps ask if students know any more, (but don't expect too much at this stage). Some things you might need to explain are:

* Point out it's *GOT divorced* and maybe add you *get married* and *get re-married*.
* We use *I'm afraid* to introduce bad news. Give more examples: *I'm afraid I can't come to class tomorrow, I'm afraid I didn't do my homework*, etc.
* You can act out *It was really frightening*. You might want to add *so I was really frightened*; *-ing* endings describes the thing, *-ed* ending describes my feelings.
* Point out you *GIVE a presentation* and add: *I don't want to, but I HAVE TO*.
* Point out you *spend time doING things*.

7 Pronunciation: /ʃ/

Drill the sound /ʃ/ yourself or use the recording.
If your students have problems with making the sound, point out the picture on page 145 and focus them on where the tongue is and what the lips do to make this noise. One good way to practise is to put a finger up to your lips as if you're telling small kids to *shh*.

Drill the words in the box and then play the eight sentences for students write down.

Play them once, give students a chance to compare their ideas and then play them again, stopping after each one to round up the students' ideas. Finally, look at the answers on page 128. If you want to, drill these sentences too or get students to repeat them in pairs.

To round up, tell students you want them to talk about one of the following three topics:
the first time they spoke in public / went abroad / got paid.

Give them a few minutes to plan what they want to say. Help out with any language they're looking for. Then tell a partner about their experiences. You could begin by telling them your own memories about one of these things.

Round up with a couple of corrections or by correcting any new language the students have produced on the board.

Homework

You could tell the class to do **Unit 12** in the **Workbook** for homework, if you haven't done so already.

You could also ask students to write a paragraph about the first time they did one of the things discussed in this unit. Tell them to use as much new language as they can.

Collect the writing next lesson and correct it. Correct any mistakes with things already studied in class and give students better ways of saying new things that they're trying to say.

Unit overview

General topic
Taking about things you can't do; asking for and offering help.

Conversation
Eight different conversations asking for and offering help.

Reading
The kindness of strangers

Language input
*   *Can't: I can't read without my glasses.*
*   Adjectives and adverbs: *He's a good cook. She does it well.*
*   Expressions for helping people: *Can you show me where to go?*
*   Offering with *I'll: I'll take you there, if you want.*
*   Pronunciation: /k/ and /g/

Language strip
Ignore the **Language strip** to begin with and deal with the language as it comes up in various activities. Come back to it later as revision. Alternatively, ask students to learn the expressions for homework.

Lead in
Do one of the following:
*   Put the students into pairs and ask them to look at the clocks on page 64. Ask them to cover 1–8 and check they can remember the times shown.
*   Ask students to repeat **6 Practice** on page 65 with a new partner.
*   Put the students into pairs and ask them to write down as much as they can remember about the text on page 67. Round up the students' ideas and reformulate things into better English, using as much of the language from the actual text as you can.

Conversation

1 Using grammar: *I can't*

A good way to lead in to the lesson is to ask the group to write down three things they can't do, but would like to. Ask them to share their experiences in pairs or small groups – maybe give an example yourself first. Then tell them they're going to look at ways of talking about things they can't do better.

Ask students to match the sentences in 1–8 with the pictures in **a–h**. Go round and help out as they do so. You might need to explain what *I can't get the top off* means: act out trying to get the top off a jam. Elicit the answers from the class and write them on the board. Drill each expression as you do so – the stress is usually

on the verb and also the object noun, if there is one – *top, exercise, board, map, etc.*

Answers
1. C   2. E   3. A   4. F   5. B   6. G   7. D   8. H

Tell the students to translate 1–8 into their language and to write their translations in the book. If you share the same L1 as the class, check the translations or with weaker students, simply tell them.

Give students one minute to try to remember the eight sentences. Put them in pairs. Tell student B to close their book. Student A points to the pictures **a–h** and B tries to repeat the whole sentences. If B gets stuck, A can help them.

Tell the class to read **Grammar note** G16 on using *can* and *can't* on page 139.

2 Practice

Tell the class they're going to tell each other about things they can't do. Read through the phrases together and check for understanding. You might need to give examples of musical instruments: the piano, the guitar, the drums, the violin, etc.

Put the students in pairs and tell them to compare the things they can't do, responding as in the two example conversations. You could either start or finish by telling which of these things you can't do yourself.

3 Listening: *Sorry, could you help me, please?*

Tell students they are going to listen to eight different conversations and that in each one they will hear people asking for help. Tell them the situations in the conversations are the same as in the eight pictures on page 68.

You could let them read 1–8 first to check they understand all the vocabulary. You might need to explain *curtains* – point to the ones in the room or draw some. Tell them to listen and complete the questions they hear, using one or two words in each gap.

Play the conversations once all the way through. Give students a minute or two to compare their answers in pairs. Round up what they have and if the whole group between them can provide the answers don't play the conversations again. If they only have some of the answers, play the conversations again, pausing after each one. Then elicit the answers from the class and write them on the board.

Answers
1. help me   2. open this   3. top shelf   4. this exercise
5. speak up   6. down   7. close   8. show me

Put the students into pairs to go over the words in the box and try to remember who or what was described by each word in the conversation. Elicit answers from the class and then decide whether you think the students need to hear the conversations again to check their answers.

> **Answers**
>
> The suitcase is heavy.
> The top of the jar is very tight.
> The music's loud.
> The student is very quiet when she speaks.
> The sun's bright.

Play the eight *can / could* questions and drill them, both chorally and individually. Point out we usually say /kən/ instead of /kæn/.

Tell the students to read the **Real English** note about *Could you ... ?* and see if they have any questions about this.

4 Speaking

If you want to, give students five minutes to plan what they are going to say. Put students in pairs and tell them to role-play the conversations they heard. Tell them to use the pictures, the eight sentences in **1 Using Grammar** as well as the eight questions in **3 Listening** to help them.

After they have finished, you might want to tell them to read the **Tapescript** on page 128. They could then practise reading the conversations in pairs.
As they do so, go round and listen to their pronunciation, correcting and remodelling things for them if they need it.

If students asks about the stressed *is* in Conversation 4 and 7, explain that it's for emphasis, to make the sentence stronger.

5 Further practice

Tell the class they are going to work in pairs and write four conversations like those they heard in the recording. Tell them to look at the Tapescript on page 128 and to use this as a model for the four conversations they are going to write.

With weaker classes, let students keep page 128 open while they write, though stronger students should try to write without referring to it directly. As students write, go round, monitor and help out where necessary. Make sure students add *please* at the end of questions.

After a few minutes, get pairs to swap what they've written and check each other's writing for mistakes. Alternatively simply check the answers by eliciting from the class orally.

> **Answers**
>
> 1. A: *Excuse me, could / can you move (a bit), please? I can't see the (white / black) board.*
>   B: *Yes, sorry. Can you see now?*
>   A: *Yes, thanks.*
> 2. A: *Sorry, could / can you turn the stereo up (a bit), please? I can't hear it.*
>   B: *Yes, sure. It IS a bit quiet.*
>   A: *Thanks.*
> 3. A: *Sorry, could / can you turn the light on. I can't see the writing (on the board) very well.*
>   B: *Yes, sure. It IS a bit dark. Is that better?*
>   A: *Yes, thanks.*
> 4. A: *Sorry, could / can you help us? We're looking for a restaurant called La Mancha.*
>   B: *Yes, it's in Thames Road.*
>   A: *Could / can you show us on the map?*
>   B: *(Yes.) Of course.*

Students then role-play the conversations. As they do so, go round and listen to their pronunciation, correcting and remodelling things for them if they need it.

6 Using grammar: *well* and *good*

To lead in to this exercise, try to elicit an example of *well* and *good* from the class by saying: *Student X said that he / she can't cook very ... ?* You can then write on the board: *I can't cook very well.* Then write up the opposite: *I'm a really ... cook,* and see if you can elicit *good.* You could tell the class *well* is an adverb and describes the verb. Draw an arrow from *well* to *cook.* Tell them *good* is an adjective and describes the noun. Draw an arrow from *good* to *cook.*

Ask the class if they know the opposites of *good* and *well* (*bad; badly*). You could maybe ask a couple of students if they're a good cook or a bad one. Ask them what they can cook.

Ask students to choose the correct word in 1–8. Tell them to think about the position of the words in the sentence and what the words describe – verb or noun. You might want to do the first one as a class to model the activity.

Let students compare their ideas in pairs, then elicit the answers from the class, writing them on the board as you do so.

> **Answers**
>
> 1. well   2. good   3. bad   4. well   5. badly   6. well
> 7. bad   8. well

As you are eliciting the answers, ask students how they know. Focus on the position of words and what the words describe. This helps to reinforce the concept for the students.

As you go through the answers, you might need to act out being a bad driver. You could also ask: *If you can't see very well, you need to wear ... ?* You could then write on the board: *I usually wear glasses / contact lenses.* In **8**, check students remember that *gran* means *grandmother.* Ask if they remember the shorter way of saying *grandfather – grandad.* You could also write on the board: *She has to wear a hearing aid* and explain this.

Next, ask students to tick the sentences that are true for them and try to change the others so that they become true. Go through the two examples and model one or two in ways that are true for you.

Put the students in pairs and ask them to tell each other their sentences. Round up with a couple of corrections or by reformulating into better English interesting things you heard students say. Correct any new language the students have produced on the board.

Finally, ask the students to read **Grammar note** G17 on *adverbs* and *adjectives* on page 140.

Consolidate what students have done so far in this unit by asking them to repeat the eight conversations they heard in new pairs, but this time ONLY using the pictures in **1 Using Grammar** to help them.

For homework, ask students to try to learn the four conversations from **5 Further practice** and then test them in the next lesson. You could also get them to write three other similar conversations, using some of the other questions they have seen in this lesson.

Reading

If you are starting a new lesson, begin with a bit of revision. If you haven't yet asked the class to repeat the eight conversations they heard using only the pictures on page 68, you could do this now. Alternatively, have them read out the four conversations they wrote for **5 Further practice** on page 69, using only the ideas given in the Coursebook. You could also do an activity from **Unit 14** of the **Teacher's Resource Book**.

1 Before you read

Tell the class they are going to read two stories about people who were helped by strangers, but that first you're going to look at some of the difficult language from the text. In pairs or with the class, ask students to divide the ten sentences into two groups. They can then compare their ideas in pairs. This is just to generate interest in the text, the correct answer is not important.

You might need to explain:
- *The night before* – yesterday was (for example) Tuesday, so Monday night was *the night before*.
- A *nurse* can be a man or a woman. A *nurse* helps the doctor in hospitals.
- *Ambulance* – point out the stress and drill it. Point to the picture.
- *The date was wrong* – ask the class what the date today is. Check they understand it means January the 10th, May the 16th, etc.
- *Several* means quite a few, maybe four or five or six. We don't pronounce the second 'e'.

2 While you read

Ask the students to read the text and find out if they were right about the two groups of sentences. Do the text as a listening, as reading or both, (see **Introduction** for procedure). When the students have finished reading / listening, let them check their answers in pairs and then elicit the answers from the class. Try to retell some of the text as you do so.

Answers

Terry's story: he went to the airport to fly home. He didn't have enough money for a hotel and he had an early flight, so *he got to the airport the night before. He slept there.* In the morning, he couldn't see his flight on the screens. *They checked the time on the computer, but the date was wrong.* He had to wait two days for the flight! *He was really hungry!*

Li Ying's story: she was in London. *She got hit by a bus* in the street because she didn't look when she crossed the road. *She was hurt quite badly.* Some people got off the bus and helped her. There was *a tall black man who was a nurse.* A woman with a mobile *called an ambulance.* They took her to hospital. She'd *broken several bones* and had to stay in hospital for a week.

3 Comprehension

Put the students in pairs. Ask them to discuss the answers to the eight questions without looking at the text. As they do so, go round, listen and help out. Ask them if they can remember what the text said about each question.

When they've finished, ask them to check their ideas against the text. They might want to underline the parts of the text that refer to the answer. Then elicit the answers from the class. You don't need to write the answers on the board.

Answers

1. January 23rd
2. He didn't have enough money to stay in a hotel and /or his flight was very early.
3. He had to wait another two days and he didn't have any money
4. £50 in shekels (Israeli currency)
5. He paid for somewhere to stay and bought some food.
6. She was knocked over by a bus because she wasn't looking when she crossed the road.
7. She didn't think they were very nice.
8. She'd broken several bones.

Go through any new language. For example:
- *The Middle East* – an area east of the Mediterranean Sea; countries like Egypt, Jordan, Syria, Iran and Iraq.
- *I'd spent it all* – if anyone asks about the use of the past perfect here, just say: Yes, I **had** spent it all – it means *before then*.
- We ask: *What's the matter?* if we think someone is hurt or sad or angry.
- *I've got some money left* – I had a thousand pounds. I spent 900. I've got 100 left.
- *The Old Bailey* is a famous building (a court) in London.
- *Came round the corner* – draw a picture to illustrate it.
- *Rude* is the opposite of polite – translate it or act out somebody being rude – putting feet on the table, shutting the door in your face, etc.
- *Though* means *but*.

4 Speaking

This is a chance for students to talk about any experiences they've had that are similar to those described in the text. Tell them to read the questions and the examples and to make sure they understand everything. You might want to give them a few minutes planning time. Tell them to ask you if they're not sure of how to say something in English.

Ask students talk to each other. They can do this in pairs or walking around, talking to different people.

Round up with a couple of corrections or by reformulating into better English interesting things you heard students say. Correct any new language the students have produced on the board.

5 Using vocabulary: helping people

Ask students to complete 1–8 by adding the words in the box. The verbs in the box can be used with both endings in each number. You might want to do the first one as a class to model the activity.

As students are doing the exercise, go round and help out with anything they don't understand. Let them compare their ideas in pairs, then elicit the answers from the class, writing them on the board as you do so.

> **Answers**
>
> 1. take me 2. show me 3. lend me 4. stay
> 5. carry 6. give me 7. push 8. help me

Go through any new language. For example:
1. *Take me* – in your car.
2. *Show me how to do it* – act this out: show them how to use a machine in the class.
3. *Lend me* – you can also say: *Can I borrow?* You could add that if someone lends you money, you have to *pay them back*.
4. *Stay with you* – in your house / flat.
5. *The buggy* – a thing you put babies in and push them along in. Draw or act it out. Act out carrying bags as well.
6. *Help me move house* – carry boxes, drive the van, etc.
7. *Help me look for my keys* – because *I've lost them. I can't find them anywhere.*

Ask the class as a whole what the past forms of the verbs are and maybe drill any they have problems with. Write the answers on the board to show spelling, if you want to.

> **Answers**
>
> 1. took 2. showed 3. lent 4. stayed 5. carried
> 6. gave 7. pushed 8. helped

Tell the class they're going to talk about a time someone helped them or they've helped someone. Give the class a few minutes to prepare. Tell them to ask you if they're not sure of how to say something in English.

Before students talk to each other, tell them a story from your own experience. Then get students to talk to each other in pairs or walking around talking to different people.

Round up with a couple of corrections or by reformulating into better English interesting things you heard students say. Correct any new language the students have produced on the board.

6 Using grammar: *I'll do it*

Tell the class you're going to look at ways of offering to help people.

To lead in to this activity, try to elicit what the students would say if they wanted to offer to help you. Tell them you're at home. Your kitchen is a mess. You're upset about it. Say: *Look at this mess! It's so dirty.* Tell them to offer to help you. See what kind of language they use to do so and then tell them this exercise will help them get better at making offers like this.

Alternatively, just tell the class you're going to do some grammar and ask them to look at the presentation.

Students can work individually or in pairs. Let them check their ideas with another student once they've finished and then elicit the answers from the class. Write the best answers on the board and drill them.

> **Possible answers**
>
> 1. It's OK. I'll lend you some, if you like.
> 2. It's OK. I'll help you look for them, if you like.
> 3. It's OK. I'll take you to the station, if you like.
> 4. It's OK. I'll lend you an umbrella, if you like.
> 5. It's OK. I'll show you (where to go / on the map), if you like.

Ask the students to read out their conversations in pairs. Walk round and listen as they do so, correcting any pronunciation problems you hear.

Tell the class to read **Grammar note** G18 on page 140.

7 Pronunciation: /k/ and /g/

Drill the sounds with /k/ and /g/ yourself or use the recording. If your students have problems with it, point out the picture on page 145 and focus them on where the tongue is and what the lips do to make this noise.

Drill the words in the box and then play the eight sentences, which students write down.

Play them once, give students a chance to compare their ideas and then play them again, perhaps stopping after each one to round up the group's ideas. Finally, look at the answers on page 128. If you want to, drill these sentences too or get students to repeat them in pairs.

Homework

You could tell the class to do **Unit 13** in the **Workbook** for homework, if you haven't done so already.

You could also ask students to write either a paragraph about a time when someone helped them or when they helped someone. Tell them to use as much language from this unit as they can.

Collect the writing next lesson and correct it. Correct any mistakes with things already studied in class and give students better ways of saying new things that they're trying to say.

15 What're you doing this weekend?

Unit overview

General topics
Your plans for the future.

Conversation
Three conversations in which people talk about what they're doing this weekend.

Reading
The meeting

Language input
- Weekend activities: *play computer games, tidy up the flat,* etc.
- Talking about the future using *will* and *going to: I think I'll probably just stay at home. I'm going to study for my exam.*
- Expressions for not being sure: *It depends how I feel.*
- Saying sorry for being late: *Sorry I'm late. I overslept.*
- Pronunciation: consonant sound: /l/

Language strip
Ignore the **Language strip** to begin with and deal with the language as it comes up in various activities. Come back to it later as revision. Alternatively, ask students to learn the expressions for homework.

Do one of the following:
- Put students in pairs. Give them two minutes to try to remember the eight pairs of collocations in **5 Using vocabulary**, page 71. Student A closes their books. Student B reads out the eight verbs, and Student A tries to remember the two collocations for each verb.
- Ask students to look at the **Expressions Organiser** for **Units 11** and **12** on page 151. Ask students to translate the expressions in pairs then check their ideas. Students can then test each other by saying a translation, acting it out or drawing a picture, while their partner guesses. To make this easier, let both students look at page 151.
- Ask students to repeat **5 Further Practice**, page 69 with a new partner, using only the prompts given in the book for support.
- Test the students on the expressions in the **Language strip** on page 68. Give students two minutes to look at the **Language strip** and remember as much as they can. They can ask you questions during this time. Ask students to close their books then put them into two teams. If you can, use L1 to test them on different expressions, draw them on the board or act them out. The first person to call out the correct expression wins a point for their team.
- Do one of the **Teacher's Resource Book** activities from **Unit 14**.

Conversation

1 Using vocabulary: weekend activities

Explain the task. Do the first one with the class. Ask students to do the rest individually. It's best to ask them to do both parts **1–5** and **6–10** in one go. After three or four minutes, ask students to compare answers in pairs. Elicit the answers from the class and write them on the board. Drill the collocations and ask for other nouns that can be used with each verb.

> **Answers**
> 1. cook 2. see 3. go 4. stay 5. play 6. take
> 7. go 8. tidy up 9. study 10. meet

Go through any new language. For example:
- *See a play at the theatre* – give examples of a play that may be familiar to students. Ask what other things you might see at the theatre, (a musical, a concert, etc.).
- *Take it easy* means *relax*. Ask what you do when you *take it easy, sit around, watch TV, go to bed early).* Point out that lots of younger people say: *Bye / See you. Take it easy!* when they say *goodbye* to friends.
- *Tidy up* – act this out. Ask why you need to tidy up. (*It's in a mess.*) Point out that it isn't the same as *clean:* you *clean the flat / the car* when it's dirty.

Ask students to read the questions and the sentence starters. Draw attention to the two different structures they will need to use: the present simple for habits and things they generally do and *be going* to + verb for this weekend (future). Put students into pairs to discuss the questions. Monitor and check for any mistakes, particularly with the language just taught.

Round up with a couple of corrections or by reformulating into better English interesting things you heard students say.

2 Listening: *So what're you doing this weekend*

Tell students they are going to listen to three conversations and that in each one they will hear people talk about what are doing this weekend. Tell them to listen and to note which things in **1 Using vocabulary** they hear.

Play the conversations once all the way through. Give students a minute or two to compare their answers in pairs. Round up what they have and if the whole group between them can provide the answers, don't play the conversations again, unless the class really wants you to. If they only have some of the answers, play the conversations again, pausing after each conversation. Elicit the answers from the class and write them on the board.

Answers
1. meet some friends, see a play, cook dinner for some friends
2. stay at home, take it easy, tidy up the flat, study English
3. stay at home, study English, go shopping for some new clothes

3 Listen again

Tell the class they are going to hear Conversation 3 again, between two women, Shona and Mel. This time you want them to listen and complete the conversation by writing the words they hear in the gaps. Tell them they might need to write 2 or 3 words in the gaps. Play the conversation and then give the students a minute to compare their ideas with a partner. You may want to elicit the answers immediately or you may want to play the conversation one more time and stop after each gap. Students then call out their answers. Write them on the board. Go through any new language. For example:
- *I might study some English – might* here means *maybe* and is followed by a verb in the infinitive. You could refer students to the **Real English** note on page 73.
- *It depends how I feel – if I feel lazy, I'll just watch TV. If I have lots of energy, I'll study.* You could give other examples of *depends: It depends on the weather. It depends what time you're going. It depends what time I finish work.* In each case, tell students the variety of options and possible results.
- *I'll probably* – ask students if Shona has already decided? (No – it depends.) Which is more sure – studying or watching TV? (Watching TV.)
- *Why don't you … ?* – this is a suggestion. Give / elicit other examples.

Next, ask students to role-play the conversation in pairs. They can change roles when they have finished. As they role-play, go round and listen to their pronunciation, correcting and remodelling things for them if they need it.

Answers
1. any plans
2. how I feel
3. watch TV
4. That sounds
5. come with me
6. do you want
7. Is eleven OK
8. No problem

4 Using grammar: *going to / will*

Refer back to the conversation in **3 Listen again** and the examples of *I'll probably* and *I'm going to + verb*. You could ask students to underline them. Ask again which one shows you are 100% sure. (*I'm going to* – it means you've already decided.)

Ask them to read the presentation and examples. Then explain the task. Do the first one with the students, then ask them to do the rest individually. Give them a few minutes and then let them compare in pairs, before eliciting the answers from the class. As you go through the answers, ask if the person is 100% sure. Ask what

words tell us this and draw attention to the use of *probably*, but also to the other language such as *I think, I'm not really sure yet, It depends on my husband*, etc.

Answers
1. I'll
2. I'm going to
3. I'm going to
4. I'll
5. I'm going to
6. I'll
7. I'll
8. I'm going to
9. I'll
10. I'm going to

Drill the *going to / 'll probably* expressions as you elicit the answers or play the recording and ask students to repeat them.

You could finish by asking students to read **Grammar note** G19 on page 140.

5 Using vocabulary: *I'm not sure*

Tell students that they're going to learn some expressions for saying they're not sure. If you haven't done so already, begin by asking them to read the **Real English** note on *I might. I might* is one way we can show we're not sure yet.

Explain the task. Do the first one with the class and then ask students to do the rest individually. Encourage students to write out the whole expression. Give students a minute or two and then elicit the answers from the class. Write them on the board and drill the expressions.

Answers
1. I don't know.
2. I'm not really sure yet.
3. I don't have any plans.
4. I haven't really decided.
5. It depends how I feel.
6. It depends on the weather.

6 Practice

Explain the task. Model by asking a couple of students the questions. Ask some follow-up questions and tell students they should try to continue the conversations if they can. Ask students to move round the class and have similar conversations with different people.

Monitor and check for mistakes, particularly any errors in the language you've just taught. Help students with new vocabulary. Round up with a couple of corrections or by reformulating into better English interesting things you heard students say. Correct any new language the students have produced on the board.

For homework, ask students to try to learn the conversation from **3 Listen again** and then test them in the next lesson. You could also get them to write their own similar conversations about what they are doing this weekend, using as much of the language from these two pages as they can.

Reading

If you are starting a new lesson, begin with a bit of revision. Ask students to try to repeat as much of the conversation in **3 Listen again** on page 72 as they can from memory. Alternatively, do an activity from **Unit 15** of the **Teacher's Resource Book**. You could also give students one minute to remember the ten collocations from **1 Using vocabulary on** page 72. Students then test each other in pairs. Student A closes the book. Student B says the verbs and Student A says the collocations.

1 Using vocabulary

Tell the students they're going to read a short story, but first they're going to learn some vocabulary that appears in the story.

You could lead in by acting out and presenting each verb with one collocation, instead of finishing with students acting out the collocations in pairs. For example, you could act out the following: *look out of the window, pour some wine, taste horrible, look embarrassed*. Say each verb collocation as you act it out. Next, ask students to act out each word before testing each other and then finally doing the collocation exercise. For more detail on this procedure, see the notes on TPR in **Introduction** on page 8.

Alternatively, just explain the task. Do the first one with the class and then ask students to do the rest individually. It's best to ask them to do both parts **1–5** and **6–10** in one go. After a few minutes, ask students to compare in pairs. Elicit the answers from the class and write them on the board. As you go through the answers you could act out some of the verbs or ask for a translation. You could also check the past form of the verbs at this stage. Make sure you also drill the collocations as a whole.

Answers				
1. look	2. wear	3. feel	4. order	5. take
6. serve	7. pour	8. forget	9. sit	10. taste

Go through any new language. For example:
*   *Feel uncomfortable* – this could be a physical feeling (act out sitting in an uncomfortable chair) or an emotional one. You feel nervous and bad. For example, you go out for dinner with two friends and they have a big argument. Ask for other situations.
*   *Feel embarrassed* – elicit situation when you might feel like this.
*   *Take a seat* – often said at the start of an interview. It means sit down, not to literally take the seat somewhere.
*   *Pour* – perhaps also teach *spill*. Show the difference in meaning by acting them out.

If you didn't start the activity by pre-teaching the verbs and collocations, demonstrate the task and then put students in pairs to test each other by acting out the expressions.

You could follow this up by asking students to use their dictionaries to find one more collocation to go with each verb.

2 While you read (1)

Explain the task. You could ask students to also think about *why* Rick is going to meet this person as well as *who* he is going to meet. Do the text as a listening, a reading or both, (see **Introduction** for procedure).

After students finish reading / listening, ask them to discuss the two questions in pairs for a couple of minutes. Ask the class to share ideas.

The answers will vary, but students should recognise that he's meeting a woman called Debbie. It's probably their first date. Accept other comments if they can be justified. In terms of what happens next, students can answer more or less however they want. The idea here is more to generate interest in the next part of the text rather than give a definitive correct answer at this stage.

Go through any new language. For example:
*   *Seeds* – draw a picture or explain they're things you put in the ground if you want to grow plants. Birds like to eat them.
*   *Chasing birds* – point to the picture.
*   *Is this seat taken?* – you can also say *Is anyone sitting here?* and *Is this seat free?* They all basically mean the same thing.

3 While you read (2)

Do this text as a listening, a reading or both, (see **Introduction** for procedure). Ask students to read / listen to the rest of the text and see if their predictions were correct.

Go through any new language. For example:
*   *Getting dark* – in the evening, when the sun goes down. You could also teach *It's getting late / cold / warmer*.
*   *Olives* – translate or draw them.
*   *Pick it up* – act it out.
*   *Steak* is a big piece of meat from a cow. You could also teach *rare / medium / well-done steak*. Ask some students how they like their steak.
*   *The Champions League* – a European football competition. It happens every year. It used to be called the European Cup.

4 Comprehension

None of these questions have a definitive answer. You could ask students to discuss them as a class or in pairs. Students should try to justify their comments by referring to the story. Let students use L1 and translate their ideas if you can.

When you have finished this discussion, you might want to let students go back through the text and check if there is anything they want to ask about.

5 Listening

Tell the students they're going to hear the six messages that were left on Rick's phone. Students can check if their ideas in **4 Comprehension** were correct. Explain the task and play the recording through once. Ask students to compare what they wrote. Then play the recording again and stop it after each message. Elicit the answers from the class and write them on the board.

Answers

1. late, problem   2. traffic, message   3. paper
4. fault   5. checking, Love   6. number

Ask students to discuss the three questions. Again, you may choose to do this with the class rather than in pairs. In the fifth message, Lucy is calling Rick. She's presumably his girlfriend. You could teach the expressions: *He's cheating on his girlfriend / He's a liar.*

As a follow-up, ask students to write a conversation between Debbie and Rick.

6 Saying sorry for being late

Introduce the activity by recapping why Debbie was late – she had a problem at work, then the traffic was awful, then she lost the piece of paper with the name of the place on. Next, tell the students they're going to learn some more language to explain why you are late. After a couple of minutes, let students compare in pairs. Then elicit the answers from the class and write them on the board.

Answers

1. lost   2. missed   3. problem   4. awful   5. work
6. forgot   7. left   8. overslept

Go through any new language. For example:
- *Missed the bus* – elicit other things you can miss – *my flight, the train, the start of the movie*, etc.
- *The traffic was awful* – very bad. There was *a traffic jam.* Draw a picture to explain and elicit possible reasons, *There was an accident*, etc.
- *I had a problem at work* – point out the preposition *at* and give other examples (*at home, at school*), but also *have a problem with my computer / my bike / the car.*
- *I was talking to a friend and …* – act out the situation of talking and suddenly realising the time. You could give / elicit other examples to show the pattern, *I was reading the paper* and … , *I was watching TV* and … , *I was doing some work* and … , etc.
- *Just before* – act out the whole situation or show the time you wanted to leave (10:00) and the time your Mum phoned (9:59).
- *I overslept* – draw attention to *I woke up late*. Explain: *I usually get up at 8, but by mistake I got up at 9.* You could elicit reasons: *my alarm clock didn't work, I went to bed very late last night*, etc.

As a class discuss which are good reasons and which are bad. Tell students that next time they are late for class, you want them to say: *Sorry I'm late,* and then explain why!

Finally, ask students to read the conversation and to quickly practise having similar conversations in pairs.

7 Pronunciation /l/

If you can, use some correction of the pronunciation of /l/ from the previous activity to lead into this activity. Alternatively, just tell the students they're going to do some work on pronunciation and their listening skills. Model the sound yourself or use the recording and photo on page 145 and ask students to repeat it. Explain the next task. Play the recording. Students can check their answers against the **Tapescript** on page 129 or you can just go through the answers by writing the words they heard on the board and drilling them.

Answers

let's, light, left, plans, plate, ill, shelf, call, felt, pull

Explain the next task. Play the recording. Pause at the end of each sentence to give students time to write. Ask students to compare their answers and then play the ten sentences once more. Let students then compare what they have written again, before you go through the answers on the board, playing each sentence once more and pausing after each one as you do so. Alternatively, students can just compare with the **Tapescript** on page 129.

Students then practise reading out the sentences in pairs. Go round and listen to their pronunciation, correcting and remodelling things for them if they need it. You may notice some students make the mistake of saying /r/ instead of /l/. Refer students back to the photos on page 145. The lips push out more for /r/ and the tongue doesn't touch the roof of the mouth.

Homework
You could tell the class to do **Unit 15** in the **Workbook** for homework, if you haven't done so already.

You could also ask them to translate the last few phone messages they have left or received into English. Tell them to use the **Tapescript** for **5 Listening** on page 129 to help them.

Collect the writing next lesson and correct it. Correct any mistakes with things already studied in class and give students better ways of saying new things that they're trying to say.

16 Are you OK?

Unit overview

General topics
Talking about how you are.
Family holidays.

Conversation
A conversation between a teacher and a student, who isn't feeling very well.

Reading
Family holidays

Language input
- Questions: *Do you want a … ? / Do you want to … ?*
- *Are you OK?: No, no really. I've got a headache.*
- Holiday activities: *going fishing, lying on the beach,* etc.
- Talking about injuries: *I hurt my arm playing football.*
- Pronunciation: intonation; sounding positive

Language strip

Ignore the **Language strip** to begin with and deal with the language as it comes up in various activities. Come back to it later as revision. Alternatively, tell students to learn the expressions for homework.

Lead in

Do one of the following:

- Ask students to look at the **Expressions Organiser** for **Units 13** and **14** on page 152. Ask students to translate the expressions in pairs, then check their ideas. Students can then test each other by saying a translation, acting it out or drawing a picture, while their partner guesses. To make this easier, you could let both students look at page 152.

- Test the students on the expressions in the **Language strip** on page 72. Give students two minutes to look at the **Language strip** and remember as much as they can. They can ask you questions during this time. Ask students to close their books, and put them into two teams. If you can, use L1 to test them on different expressions, draw them on the board, or act them out. The first person to call out the correct expression wins a point for their team.

Conversation

1 Using vocabulary: *Are you OK?*

Ask students to look at the cartoons. You could use these to elicit what the students think each person is saying and pre-teach some of the words. Explain that the students are going to learn to have these kinds of conversations.
Explain the task. Do the first conversation with the class and then ask students to do the rest individually or in pairs. After a few minutes, let students compare in pairs and then elicit the answers from the class, writing them on the board.

Answers
1. tired, home, coffee
2. sick, lie down, OK
3. a headache, an aspirin, a bit
4. cuts, an ambulance, fine
5. hungry, eat, get

Go through any new language. For example:

- *Are you OK?* – drill this. Encourage students to sound concerned! Point out the weak form of *are*.
- *A bit tired* means quite tired, but not <u>very</u> tired. *A bit* goes with negative meanings: *I'm a bit cold, I'm a bit hungry,* but NOT I'm a bit ~~happy~~, I'm ~~a bit well~~.
- *I'll be alright* – drill this, focusing on the linking between words.
- *I'm feeling a bit sick* means a bad feeling in your stomach. Maybe you want to *be sick.*
- *Lie down* – point back to the cartoon or act it out.
- *Headache* – drill /eɪk/. You could elicit other aches. (*backache / toothache / stomach-ache*).
- *An aspirin* – give equivalent (brand) name in students' language. Draw a pill. Drill it, pointing out it's only got two syllables.
- *For a bit* – for a short time. Give other examples: *I waited for a bit, but then I left. I'm only staying here for a bit – I need to go home soon.*
- *Cuts* – point to the cartoon and act. You could ask how you get a cut: *I fell over, I cut myself shaving,* etc.
- *On my way home* – while I walk / drive / cycle from here to my house.

Give students a few minutes to remember as much as they can from the conversations. Ask them to act them out, then ask them to cover the conversations and practise them, using the cartoons as a prompt.

2 Using grammar: *Do you want … ?*

Ask students to read the three examples from **1 Using vocabulary** and translate them. Check students understand the meaning of the last two sentences by asking: *So in the second question, who goes home? Me or you?* (You.) *And in the third question, who calls the ambulance? Me or you?* (Me.) In some languages, people say: *Do you want that I call an ambulance?* You may need to tell students that this is not how we say it in English – we just add *me / him / them* before the infinitive.

Ask students to do the matching exercise in pairs, as it is quite difficult. After a few minutes, elicit the answers from the class and write them on the board.

Answers
1. b, d, h and j   2. c, f, i and k   3. a, e, g and l

Go through any new language. For example:

- *Something for it* – you could refer to the **Real English** note at this point. You could draw a picture of pills / medicine / drink.

- *Fresh air* – draw attention to *go outside*. Fresh air is outside a building (even if it's a bit polluted!).
- *Cake* – draw a picture. You could point out the difference between *a cake* and *some cake* (*part* of a cake).
- *A plaster* – draw a picture of one. Ask why you might need one, (*you cut yourself*). They're also known as *Band-Aid* or *Elastoplast* – two brand names. This is more common in American English than British.

Have a quick discussion with the class about what people take for a cold. Help students out with new vocabulary / expressions and write some of these on the board.

3 Practice

Explain the task and have a couple of different conversations with different students to model it. Ask students to practise the conversations in pairs. You might need to give the class a few minutes to prepare.

An alternative to this is to cut up some pieces of paper. On one side, write a problem prompt: *tired / hungry / headache / cold / stomach-ache / just a few cuts*, etc. On the other side, write a *Do you want … ?* prompt: *have a rest / a glass of water / an aspirin*, etc. Give one card to each student. Ask them to stand up and find a partner. They hold up their card, so the other person can see one side. One student starts the conversation by asking *Are you OK?* using what's written on the card. The other student then holds up their card and they repeat the task. Students can then change cards and change partner.

Monitor and check for any mistakes, particularly any errors involving the language you've just taught.

4 Listening: *You're very quiet*

Explain the context and the task. Play the conversation once all the way through. Give students a minute or two to compare their answers in pairs. Elicit the answers from the class.

Answers
1. Yong isn't feeling very well. Yong has hurt his leg.
2. No, he just needs to get some fresh air. He hurt his leg dancing.

5 Listen again

Tell the class they are going to hear the conversation again and that this time you want them to listen and complete the conversation by writing the words they hear in the gaps. Tell them that all the gaps are single words.

Play the conversation and then give the students a minute to compare their ideas with a partner. You may want to elicit the answers immediately or you may want to play the conversation one more time and stop after each gap. Students then call out their answers. Write them on the board.

Answers
1. really   2. get   3. get   4. few   5. hurry   6. hurt
7. back

Go through any new language. For example:
- *You're very quiet* – you might say this to someone who normally talks and participates a lot in class. They're not normally quiet. We often say: *He's not himself / She's not herself today.*
- *You don't look very well* – add that maybe you *look very pale* – when you don't have any colour in your face.
- *Maybe you should* – point out the *maybe*. It's more polite. You could give / elicit other examples of things we might suggest to Yong: *Maybe you should go to the doctor's, Maybe you should take an aspirin*, etc.
- *Take your time* – you decide how long you go for – five minutes is OK, 10 minutes is OK, 20 minutes is OK.
- *There's no hurry* – if you hurry, you do things quickly. *There's no hurry / rush* means you don't need to do something quickly. I can wait.
- *I hurt it* – act hurting it and calling out in pain. Give other examples: *I hurt my finger*, etc.
- *Poor Yong!* We can also say *Poor you!* We say it when we feel sorry for someone.

Next, ask students to read out the conversation in pairs. They can change roles once they finish. As they do so, go round and listen to their pronunciation, correcting and remodelling things for them if they need it.

6 What have you done to your leg?

You could pre-teach the body vocabulary simply by pointing to a part of the body and saying the word. Get students to repeat it. Students then test each other in pairs – one points and the other says the word. You could also pre-teach the verbs by acting them out, saying the words and then getting students to copy your actions. They then work in pairs and test each other – one student says the words while their partner acts the words out. (For more details, see the **Introduction** on TPR on page 8.)

Alternatively, just ask students to read the words and either ask you about anything they don't know or use a dictionary. Then ask students to write five conversations using the ideas in pairs. As they're writing, go round and check that they've understood and are writing sensible conversations and are following the patterns in the substitution tables.

Ask the students to practise reading their conversations. As they do so, go round and listen to their pronunciation, correcting and remodelling things for them if they need it.

As a follow-up, ask them to memorise the conversations and / or try to continue each one, for example by saying *Poor you!* You could elicit other comments and questions you might add and write these on the board for further support.

7 Practice

Model this task by telling the class a true story about a time you hurt yourself. Again, try to elicit further comments or questions and write these on the board. Keep your model fairly short and use the structure you've just taught. If the model you give is too long and uses a lot of language you haven't taught, students may feel a bit intimidated! You may also want to give the class a few minutes to prepare. Finally get them to tell some other students their stories. Ask them to decide who hurt themselves the worst.

Round up with a couple of corrections or by reformulating into better English interesting things you heard students say. Correct any new language the students have produced on the board.

For homework, ask students to try to learn the twelve questions from **2 Using grammar** and then test them in the next lesson. Alternatively, you could ask them to try to remember as many conversations from **6 What have you done to your leg?** as they can and then test them next lesson.

Reading

If you are starting a new lesson, begin with a bit of revision. Ask students to try to repeat as much of the conversation in **6 What have you done to your leg?** on page 77 as they can from memory. Alternatively, put students in pairs and give them the three question starters from **2 Using grammar** on page 77. Give them 3 or 4 minutes to see how many possible endings they can remember and / or think of for each one. Round up by eliciting their ideas and correcting any mistakes you hear. You could also do an activity from **Unit 16** of the **Teacher's Resource Book**.

1 Using vocabulary: holiday activities

Ask students to read the list of activities and ask about any they don't understand. Go through any new language. For example:
- *Amusement arcades* – point to the first photo on the right. The whole building is an amusement arcade. You could elicit what you do there: *play on the fruit machines, win or lose money, play video games, etc.*
- *Cafés* – explain the difference with a bar. *A café* doesn't generally serve alcohol. Elicit what it does serve: *coffee, tea, etc.* You could remind students that *a coffee* is the drink – not the place.
- *Fishing* – act it out. Point out we *go* fishing.
- *Theme park* – point to the second photo on the right, the photo of the ride. Say this is *a ride*. In a theme park, there are lots of different rides. You could elicit famous ones.
- *The countryside* is outside the city: fields, mountains, etc. Could also revise *the scenery is amazing* from **Unit 10**.

Explain the task and ask students to do it individually. After two minutes, stop the class and tell a couple students your own opinions. Ask them to agree or disagree, using *Me too / Really? I think it's ... .* Point out the example conversations given. You could drill these responses. Next, ask students to discuss their opinions in pairs.

2 While you read

Explain the context and the task. Do the text as a listening, a reading or both, (see **Introduction** for procedure). When students have finished listening / reading, ask them to discuss the answers to the three questions in pairs for two minutes. Then elicit the answers from the class.

Answers
1. a campsite in Dorset / in the countryside / by the sea
2. a good time (we're having a lovely time)
3. going for long walks, to the beach, to museums

As you elicit the answer to **3**, draw attention to the pattern *spend time (somewhere) doing something* and refer students to the **Real English** note. You could ask for some other examples of things students have spent their time doing recently.

3 Speaking

Give students a minute to read the questions and to ask if there is anything they don't understand. Ask students to discuss the questions in pairs. You could start by first telling the students to ask you the questions. You could write up some new vocabulary on the board as you give your answers or do it all orally.

As students are talking, monitor and make yourself available to help students say new things. You can round up this task in the normal way or alternatively just move on to the next reading task as there is quite a lot of speaking practice later on in the unit.

4 While you read

Explain the context and the task. Do the text as a listening, a reading or both, (see **Introduction** for procedure). When students have finished listening / reading, ask them to discuss the answers to the three questions in pairs for two minutes. Then elicit the answers from the class.

Answers
1. No. (I'm so bored I want to die).
2. going to the beach, going to cafés and amusement arcades, meeting boys
3. going to the beach (though possibly not for the same reasons!)

You might need to gloss some of the following for individual students as they read:
- *I'm so bored I want to die!* – she's exaggerating! It just means she's really bored!
- *Made me go to* – I didn't want to do it, but I had no choice. Give other examples: *They made my clean my room, They made me wear stupid clothes,* etc!
- *Plates* – draw a picture of one.
- *Rubbish* – stupid things. You could give other examples: *That film was rubbish. That shop just sells rubbish!*
- *Swimsuit* – draw a picture. Explain how it's different from *a bikini* (two pieces).
- *His feet smell* – act out how you feel when someone's feet smell. Ask why they smell – *he doesn't wash them!*
- *I wish you were here* – when we go on holiday, we often write this on postcards to friends back home. Don't worry about the grammar yet, just explain it means *I miss you. I want to see you now.*

You could follow this up by writing the following words on the board: *lovely, long, fresh, little, interesting, bored, rubbish, new, embarrassing, annoying.*

Ask students to discuss what these words from the two texts were used to describe. Students discuss their ideas in pairs. Then elicit ideas from the class. Reformulate their ideas into better English and point out new collocations.

Answers

The countryside there is **lovely**.
They're going to go for a nice **long** walk.
It's good to be out in the **fresh** air.
Jenny and Michael are sleeping in the **little** tent.
The parents think the local museum was very **interesting**.
Jenny is so **bored**, she wants to die, because there's nothing to do there!
She thinks the museum is full of **rubbish**. She's not interested in it.
She wore her **new** swimsuit to the beach.
Her dad is wearing his walking clothes. She thinks he looks stupid. It's **embarrassing**!
Her younger brother is really **annoying**!

5 Using grammar: *What was it like?*

You could pre-teach these questions: draw pictures of a hotel, clouds / sun, a plate of food and some people. Tell the students you went on holiday to X [name of a town / city] recently. Ask students what questions they could ask to find out more about the holiday. Elicit these questions using the pictures. Make sure you elicit: *What was / were … like?* questions. However, if students ask other sensible questions, such as *Where did you stay?* or *How long did you go for?* accept these, too. Every time you elicit a question, drill it and give your answer when students repeat the question. From time to time, go over the questions you have already elicited by pointing to the pictures again. Finally, students can role-play the conversation. Student A answers and Student B asks the questions. Ask them to change roles when they finish. Monitor and check for mistakes, particularly any errors with the language you've just taught. Round up with a couple of corrections.

Alternatively, explain the language, perhaps translating the questions for the students and then ask them to match the questions individually. After a minute or two, elicit the answers from the class and write them on the board.

Answers

1. b.   2. f.   3. a.   4. e.   5. d.   6. c.

You might need to explain:
* *delicious*: very nice-tasting food. Note we don't say *very delicious*. We say *really delicious* or *absolutely delicious*.

As a follow-up, put students into pairs. Student A is Mike or Linda (the parents) and Student B is their friend Ray or Sheila. Student B asks the six questions. Student A gives answers true for Ray / Sheila. After they have done this, this they could change roles. Student B is Jenny and Student A is her friend Kate.

Monitor and check for mistakes, particularly any errors in the language you've just taught. Round up with a couple of corrections. One thing you might want to pick up on is how students respond to what their partners say and if they show interest.

You might want to do **7 Pronunciation** now, so students can use these responses before they practise again with their own stories.

6 Practice

Explain the task. You could also elicit other questions students might want to ask about holidays, if you didn't do so at the beginning of **5 Using grammar**. It's probably best if you get students to write the answers to the questions first. Monitor and check students are writing down sensible things. Help out by providing them with any new language they need.

Ask students to practise the conversations in pairs. Ask them to change partners once or twice, depending on the time available.

Monitor and check for mistakes, particularly with any errors in the language you've just taught. You could do some correction / teaching between the students changing partners.

Round up with a couple of corrections or by reformulating into better English interesting things you heard students say. Correct any new language the students have produced on the board.

7 Pronunciation: sounding positive

Tell the students they're going to do some work on pronunciation and their listening skills. Write up the following on the board:
It was OK. It was quite sunny and warm.
It was OK, but it was quite cold.

Ask which person is more positive. Tell them you can say *It was OK* in a different way to sound more positive. Ask students to try to say the two sentences, then play the recording of the two different ways or model it yourself. The first has a higher pitch and the second has a lower pitch and falls away.

Play the recording of the six short sentences and ask students to repeat them. Encourage them to sound positive!

As a follow-up, students could write short 2-line conversations using the sentences and then practise them in pairs. As they do so, go round and listen to their pronunciation, correcting and remodelling things for them if they need it.

Homework
You could tell the class to do **Unit 16** in the **Workbook** for homework, if you haven't done so already.

You could also ask them to think about the last holiday they went on. Ask them to write an e-mail / letter to a friend from the place they went on holiday to. Tell them to use the two texts on pages 78–9 to help them.

Collect the writing next lesson and correct it. Correct any mistakes with things already studied in class and give students better ways of saying new things that they're trying to say.

17 Are you ready to order?

Unit overview

General topic
Talking about food.

Conversation
Two people in a restaurant decide what to order.

Reading
Food memories

Language input
• Food: *meat, seafood, vegetables*, etc.
• Describing food: *It's a kind of seafood*, etc.
• Ordering in restaurants: *I'll have the chicken, please.*
• Useful expressions when having dinner at a friend's house: *I'm full, Thank you, It was great.*
• Pronunciation: consonant sound: /w/
• Pronunciation: linking words naturally.

Language strip
Ignore the **Language strip** to begin with and deal with the language as it comes up in various activities. Come back to it later as revision. Alternatively, ask students to learn the expressions for homework.

Lead in
Do one of the following:
• Put students in pairs and ask them to try to repeat the five conversations from **1 Using vocabulary** on page 76, using only the pictures as prompts.
• Ask students to repeat **6 Practice**, page 79 with a different partner. Round up with a couple of corrections or by correcting and writing any new language the students have produced on the board.
• Do one of the **Teacher's Resource Book** activities from **Unit 16**.
• Test the students on the expressions in the **Language strip** on page 76. Give students two minutes to look at the **Language strip** and remember as much as they can. They can ask you questions during this time. Ask students to close their books then put them into two teams. If you can, use LI to test them on different expressions. Alternatively, draw them or act them out. The first person to call out the correct expression wins a point for their team.

1 Using vocabulary: food

A good way to lead in to the lesson is to do a short speaking activity connected to food. Write some questions on the board or on a handout for students to discuss in pairs. For example:
When was the last time you went to a restaurant? What was it like?
Do you like cooking? What kind of things do you cook?
Who usually does the cooking in your house?
What time do you usually have dinner?

Give students a few minutes to chat about the questions. As they do so, go round and monitor. Round up with a couple of corrections or by reformulating into better English interesting things you heard students say. Correct any new language the students have produced on the board. Tell the class that in this unit they're going to learn how to have better conversations about food.

Explain the task. Do the first couple of words in the box with the class and then ask students to do the task in pairs, using their dictionaries if necessary. Point out that some of the words are also illustrated on the right.

Elicit the answers from the class and write them on the board. Drill the words as you do so and ask students to mark the stress where appropriate.

Answers	
meat	chicken, lamb, pork
vegetables	carrots, potatoes
seafood	squid, mussels, prawns
fruit	oranges, watermelon
other	cheese, pasta, nuts, rice

You could follow-up by getting students to add one more word to each list, but note that this is done again at the end of **3 Practice**. Ask students to discuss which foods they don't like. Make sure they use the two sentence starters given. You could also ask if there are any they really love. You may want to do this as a fairly quick class discussion. If you can translate, there is no need to restrict yourselves to the foods in the activity.

2 It's a kind of...

This activity is a test of the words just taught and a way of presenting the useful expressions: *What's ... ?* and *It's a kind of ... ?* which we often use when discussing restaurant menus. With this is mind, ask students to cover the words in **1 Conversation** and to then do the matching individually. After a minute or two, let students compare in pairs and then elicit the answers from the class and write them on the board.

Answers					
I. d.	2. a.	3. b.	4. f.	5. c.	6. e.

Go through any new language. For example:
• *It's a kind of* – drill this. Point out the linking and weak forms of *a* and *of*.
• *What's / what are* – it's best to avoid talking about countable and uncountable nouns to explain this. Most uncountable nouns can be used as countables in certain situations anyway, and at this point it's better to keep things simple. Simply elicit / point out that *cabbage / pork / watermelon* are usually used in the singular, while the others are more commonly plural.
• With *lots of seeds* – point to the picture. You could elicit other seeds we eat, if these are common in the country you're in.

- *Chickpeas* – translate if you want to, but make it clear that the structures here help them to ask about food when they might not have a dictionary!
- *They're round* – draw the shape. You could elicit / give *square* and maybe *oval* or *egg-shaped*.

3 Practice

Divide the students into pairs. Explain the task. Make sure they look at the correct pages. The idea here is to practise the expressions in red, so if you are in a monolingual class, turn this into a guessing game where students have to guess the name in their own language. If Student A doesn't know the word after the first exchange, they could ask: *What does it look like?* Student B should explain as well as possible. You will probably need to demonstrate this.

In a multi-lingual class, let students look at each other's pictures at the end of the task and then they can write down the actual words in their own language. Monitor and check for mistakes, particularly any errors with the language you've just taught. You could correct it on the spot, if you like.

As a follow-up, ask students to find the name of another kind of fruit, meat, cheese, fish and nut. They should just write down ONE word for each category. Ask students to write their words on a clean sheet of paper. They can then compare their papers in pairs and see if they have the same. They can ask each other: *What's ... ?* and can either answer using L1 translations or, in a multilingual group, use: *It's a kind of ...* and a description.

Ask each pair to join another to make a group and repeat the task. You could then get each 4 to make a group of 8, if you want. To round up deal with any new vocabulary that came up to describe food.

4 Listening: *What would you like?*

Explain the context and task. You could find out if anyone has eaten Portuguese food and if they know what these things are. Play the conversation once all the way through. Give students a minute or two to compare their answers in pairs. Round up what they have and if the whole group between them can provide the answers, don't play the conversation again unless the class really wants you to. If they only have some of the answers, play the conversation again.

> **Answers**
> 1. Requeijão is a kind of (soft, white) cheese.
> 2. Crème de camarão is a kind of (seafood) soup.
> 3. Cabrito asado is goat (a kind of red meat).
> 4. Frango no churrasco is (spicy) chicken.

Kathrin has crème de camarão (for a starter) and frango no churrasco with vegetables for her main course.

Good students may add the language in brackets, but don't expect them to.

5 Listen again

Tell the class they are going to hear the conversation again and that this time you want them to listen and complete the conversation by writing the words they hear in the gaps. Tell them they might need to write one or more words in the gaps. Play the conversation and then give the students a minute to compare their ideas with a partner.

You may want to elicit the answers immediately or you may want to play the conversation one more time and stop after each gap. Students then call out their answers. Write them on the board.

> **Answers**
> 1. Quite a lot
> 2. a kind of
> 3. sounds
> 4. recommend
> 5. prefer
> 6. I love it
> 7. would you like
> 8. I don't drink

Go through any new language. For example:

- *Especially in the summer* – ask if Rui goes more in the winter or the summer? (Summer.) You could give other examples: *I love reading, especially novels. I find it difficult to get up in the morning, especially on a Monday!*
- *Soft cheese* – act / draw spreading it. Give / elicit examples of *soft cheese*. Ask for the opposite (hard).
- *I'll have that for a starter* – point out to the way we order, *I'll have ...* . Give students examples of how to continue: *I'll have the fish, I'll have the chicken, I'll have the roasted vegetables.* You could refer students to the **Real English** note at this point.
- *Starter / main course / desert* – explain that British restaurants usually offer three courses. A small *starter*; a big dish, usually meat or fish; a *main course* – and something sweet at the end – *dessert*. Drill *dessert* and mark the stress. You could also look at *main* which means the biggest / most important and give / explain other collocations, (*main road, main building, main office, main meal*). You could ask students when they have their main meal of the day and what they have to eat.
- *Can you recommend anything?* means *Can you tell me what things you think are good?* Give other examples: *I want to buy a dictionary. Can you recommend one? I want to go to Britain. Can you recommend anywhere to visit?* etc.
- *Red meat* – give examples. Elicit the other kind – *white meat*.
- *If you like ... you should try ...* – draw attention to the pattern. Show how you can change it. *If you like cheese, you should try the requeijão. If you like sweet things, you should try the ice cream.* You could give students prompts and get them to finish the sentence with their own examples: *If you like red meat you should try ... , If you like seafood, you should try ... , If you're vegetarian, you should try ... ,* etc.
- *Spicy* – draw a chilli. Give / elicit examples of spicy food.
- *Hot* means the same as *spicy*, but it can also mean the opposite of *cold*.
- *I don't drink* means you don't drink alcohol at all. You could elicit reasons, *I don't like it, It's against my religion,* etc.

- *Sparkling* – draw a bottle with some bubbles, make the sound of opening it.
- *Still* – no bubbles. You could also draw a tap and elicit *tap water*. You could ask students which they prefer and why.

Next, ask students to read out the conversation in pairs. They change roles once they finish. As they do so, go round and listen to their pronunciation, correcting and remodelling things for them if they need it.

6 Speaking

Check students understand the words in the box. Ask students to discuss the questions in pairs or small groups. Monitor and help out with any new language students might want to say. You could round up in the usual way by dealing with some corrections or new language, or if you are short of time, just move on to the next activity.

7 Restaurant questions

Explain the task. Ask students to do the matching individually and then compare in pairs. Elicit the answers from the class and write them on the board.

Answers
1. e.   2. d.   3. b.   4. c.   5. a.

Go through any new language. For example:
- *I'll have* – drill this, making sure students use the contraction. You can also drill the questions drawing attention to how *Would you* is often pronounced as /wʊdʒə/, (see the **Real English note** on page 85 for more information).
- *Red or white* – you could also give / elicit *rosé* and *sparkling* wine.
- *Fried chicken* – act frying and say *with oil*. You could elicit other things that are typically *fried* (*fish, egg, onion*) and also other ways that chicken could be cooked (*roasted, grilled, barbecued*). Elicit other ways of cooking.

Model the conversation with one of the better students and then ask the students to have similar conversations in pairs. You could ask students to spend two minutes trying to memorise the questions and answers and then ask them to have the conversations again with books closed. Again, you can deal with some pronunciation errors or just move on to the main practice, the role-play.

8 Role play

Put the students into pairs. Explain their roles. If you are doing this with an Italian-speaking class, ask both A's and B's to look at page 160. Student B will have to use their own ideas to describe the food in English. There is also an alternative menu in the **Teacher's Resource Book**.

With a non-Italian class, ask the students to first look again at the conversation in **5 Listen again**. Ask them to underline and remember expressions that they could use in their role. With weaker students, let them write down the expressions on a piece of paper that they can look at while they're doing the role-play. Now ask each

student to look at the correct page. Again, give them a couple minutes to decide what they want to eat. Student A should also check the conversation and decide what they want to ask about; Student B should decide what they would recommend.

Now model the beginning of the task with one of the better students. Obviously, don't do too much, just enough to give them a little further support to start the task. Ask students to do the rest in pairs. Monitor and check for any mistakes, particularly any errors in the language you've just taught.

Round up by acting as a waiter and taking the orders from two or three pairs in the class. Finish with a couple of corrections or by reformulating into better English interesting things you heard students say. Correct any new language the students have produced on the board.

For homework, ask students to write their own conversation in a restaurant. Tell them they have a foreign friend who they are taking to a local place. Their friend doesn't know much about the local cuisine. Tell them to use the conversation in **5 Listen again** as a model and to try to use as much language as possible from pages 80 and 81.

Collect the conversations next lesson and read them. Correct any mistakes with language studied in class and give students better ways of saying new things that they're trying to say.
If you are starting a new class, begin with a bit of revision. Ask students repeat **8 Role play** on page 81 in the same pairs as they were when they first did it, but this time they should change roles. Alternatively, do an activity from **Unit 17** of the **Teacher's Resource Book**.

Reading

If you haven't done so already, ask students to read the **Language strip** on page 80 and ask you about anything they don't know or can't remember. Answer their questions. Then give them two more minutes to memorise as much as they can. Ask students to close their books. Put them in pairs and ask them to write down as much as they can remember. After 5 or so minutes, let students look back and see what they had forgotten.

You could point out that this is a good way of trying to revise any of the language they learn in class. It doesn't take long and they could spend ten minutes after the lesson doing this.

1 Speaking

Let students read the three questions and make sure they understand them. You might need to explain *bitter* – pull the face you pull when you eat a lemon / lime and ask for examples of bitter things. Before students begin, you might want to tell them your own answers to a couple of these questions.

Put students in pairs and give them a couple of minutes to chat about the questions. As they do so, go round and monitor. Round up with a couple of corrections or by reformulating into better English interesting things you heard students say. Correct any new language the students have produced on the board.

2 While you read

Explain the task. Do the text as a listening, a reading or both, (see **Introduction** for procedure). After students finish reading / listening, ask them to compare their ideas in pairs and to explain how they made their decisions. Elicit answers from the class and check the students reasons.

Answers

Ian has a bad food memory: the sausages were disgusting. He ate them all and then he was sick in his bed and in the bathroom. He can't even look at sausages now.

Jackie has a good food memory: her gran made the best apple pie she's ever tasted! It was sweet and light and warm.

Lee has a bad food memory: he never liked vegetables when he was young, but his parents made him eat them. He always left the meat till last.

Mary has a good food memory: she ordered snake by accident in a restaurant in Asia. She was shocked when they killed it, but it was really nice. It tasted like fish.

At this stage, don't deal with any unknown vocabulary. Wait until after the **Word check**.

Ask students to discuss if any of the stories remind them of people or stories they know. You could give them the sentence starter:
Lee's story reminds me of ...

Explain that if something reminds you of something else, it makes you remember it or think of it. Give some other examples: *I liked Tokyo. It reminded me of New York. / That's a funny story. It reminds me of something similar that once happened to me.* Students discuss in pairs or small groups. Monitor and help out with any new language students might want to say. You could round up in the usual way by dealing with some corrections or new language or if you are short of time, just move on to the next activity.

3 Word check

Tell the class you're going to look at some of the new language from the text. Ask them to try to complete **1–8** from memory, without looking at the text. After a few minutes, have students compare their answers in pairs. You could also tell them to go back to the text to check their ideas. Tell them to underline the expressions in the text. Then elicit the answers from the whole group, writing them on the board as you do so.

Answers

1. reminds   2. made   3. disgusting   4. sick
5. ever   6. as, as   7. made   8. like

As you go through the answers, drill pronunciation where relevant. Go through any new language.

For example:
- *What's it made from?* – you could ask what some dishes from the country you're in are made from. For example: *What's risotto made from?*
- *It's disgusting* – act out eating something and spitting it out. You could also act and give them: *It was so disgusting, I had to spit it out / I was sick.*
- *I was sick* – act it out! You could ask students when the last time they were sick was and why. Note that if students ask about *ill*, we use ill more generally – *I'm feeling a bit ill – I've got a cold. / He's ill. He's got a really bad headache.*
- *Ever* means any time in my life. Draw attention to the tense and give other examples: *The best book I've ever read, The best film I've ever ...* (elicit *seen*), *the best place I've ever ...* (elicit *been to*).
- *It's not as good as* – drill this, pointing out the linking, (it almost sounds like one word). Ask which is better – the food last night or the food in Turkish place last week. (The Turkish place.) Give other examples: *The weather here is OK, but it's not as good as in my country. / I like Lord of the Rings 2 but it's not as good as the first one.*
- *My mum made me eat it.* Ask: *Did I eat rice when I was young?* (Yes.) *Did I want to?* (No!) So why did I eat it? (*My mum made me.*) Ask: *So if I didn't eat the rice, I couldn't have any ...* (elicit *dessert / meat / sweets*). You could ask students if their parents ever made them eat anything they didn't want to.
- *Frogs' legs* – draw them.
- *Tasted like* – we use *like* with a noun. It means *similar to*. Give another example: *Snake tastes like fish.* Also show that with an adjective, we don't use *like*, *It tastes horrible / It tastes quite sweet.*

You could follow-up by getting students to write four or five sentences using *X isn't / aren't as good as Y.* You could model this task for the class by giving some examples yourself. As students write their sentences, go round and monitor and check that they've understood and are writing sensible endings down. Then get students up and ask them to share their ideas with a partner. Do they agree?

4 Using vocabulary: having dinner at a friend's house

Explain the task and the meaning of *host* and *guest*. Do the first two or three with the class. Ask the students to do the rest in pairs, using a dictionary. After a few minutes, elicit the answers from the class and write them on the board. Drill some of the expressions that students have difficulties saying. As you go through, you could also elicit / give typical responses to the questions or statements.

Answers

1. G.	4. H.	7. G.	10. G.	13. G.	16. G.
2. H.	5. G.	8. G.	11. G.	14. G.	17. G.
3. G.	6. H.	9. H.	12. H.	15. H.	18. H.

Go through any new language. For example:
- *Let me take your coat* – act this out.
- *That smells delicious* – act this out. Give examples of other things that smell delicious. Point out we use an adjective after smells – *smells good / strange / terrible,* etc.
- *Non-alcoholic* means with no alcohol in. Give / elicit examples.
- *I'm fine* means I don't want any more, I'm full.
- *I'm full* – act it out. You could also give *I couldn't eat another thing!*
- *I should go. It's getting late,* means it's late in the evening. I think it's a good idea for me to leave now.

Now ask each student to choose the eight expressions they like the most. Ask them to compare their choices with a partner. Did they choose the same ones?

As a class, ask students to tell you if there are any of the sentences they wouldn't say in their country and why not. If they take a present, what do they take?

You could do the translation task in class if you want, or leave it and move on to the writing.

5 Writing

Explain the task. Ask students to work in pairs. You could ask different pairs to write different conversations – one pair for the conversation for when the guest arrives, another for the beginning of the meal, another for the end of the meal and another for when the guest leaves.

As students are writing, go round and help them with new vocabulary and correct any errors. Make sure they are using some of the new expressions, but are also adding extra things as they need as well. Students could practise reading their conversations in pairs or perform them for another pair of students. If you have access to a video camera or tape machine, you could even record the students and play the recordings back to the class, perhaps using them for pronunciation correction or for teaching new language. Alternatively, you may prefer to set this activity for homework.

6 Pronunciation: /w/

Tell the students they're going to do some work on pronunciation and their listening skills. Model the sound yourself or use the recording and the photos on page 145. Get students to repeat the sound and then the words in the box. The important part is getting the starting point for the lips which is similar to that for /uː/. If students say something similar to a /g/ sound, draw attention to the fact that the tongue doesn't touch the roof of the mouth, but is loose. If they say something like a /v/ sound, draw attention to the way the teeth touch the lips for /v/ unlike the position for /w/.

Explain the next task. Play the six sentences, which students should write down. Play them once, give students a chance to compare their ideas in pairs and then play them again, stopping after each one to elicit the group's ideas. Finally, look at the answers on page 130. If you want, drill these sentences too or get students to repeat them in pairs.

7 Pronunciation: linking

Explain the idea of linking. Note that with these expressions, students may hear an intrusive /w/. We often use a sound approaching a /w/ when linking words which end and begin in vowels. However, you do not need to mention this unless students ask you about it. Just concentrate on getting the students to say each example as if it was one word. As before, you can model these sentences yourself or use the recording if you prefer.

Homework
You could tell the class to do **Unit 16** in the **Workbook** for homework, if you haven't done so already.

You could also ask students to write a paragraph or two about food memories they have. Tell them to use as much new language as they can and to re-read the texts on page 83 before they start writing.

Collect the writing next lesson and correct it. Correct any mistakes with things already studied in class and give students better ways of saying new things that they're trying to say.

18 Do you sell ...?

Unit overview

General topic
Shops and shopping.

Conversation
Four different conversations in which people ask for things in shops.

Reading
I work in a shop

Language input
- Sections of a department store: *toiletries, shoe department*, etc.
- Useful words in shops: *the till, the top shelf*, etc.
- Things shop assistants say: *Would you like a bag? Next, please*.
- Pronunciation: consonant sounds: /tʃ/ and /dʒ/
- *Have to: I have to wear a uniform at work. I hate it!*
- Jobs in shops: *I'm a cashier. I'm a security guard*.

Language strip
Ignore the **Language strip** to begin with and deal with the language as it comes up in various activities. Come back to it later as revision. Alternatively, ask students to learn the expressions for homework.

Lead in
Do one of the following:
- Ask students to re-read the 18 expressions in **4 Using vocabulary**, page 82. If they have forgotten any, they can ask you about them. Then put students in pairs and ask them to role-play a conversation between a guest arriving at a friend's house and the host. Ask them to use as many of the expressions from the exercise as they can, but to use other language as well. Round up with a couple of corrections or by correcting and writing any new language the students have produced on the board.
- Ask students to look at the **Expressions Organiser** for **Units 15** and **16** on page 153. Ask students to translate the expressions in pairs, then check their ideas. Students can then test each other by saying a translation, acting it out or drawing a picture, while their partner guesses. To make this easier, let both students look at page 153.
- Do one of the **Teacher's Resource Book** activities from **Unit 17**.
- Test the students on the expressions in the **Language strip** on page 80. Give students two minutes to look at the **Language strip** and remember as much as they can. They can ask you questions during this time. Ask students to close their books then put them into two teams. If you can, use L1 to test them on different expressions, draw them on the board, or act them out. The first person to call out the correct expression wins a point for their team.

Conversation

1 Speaking

Explain the task. Let students read the questions and answers and make sure they understand them. You might need to explain that *all the time* just means a lot – 3 or 4 times a week, perhaps. You could ask for things students do all the time. You might also need to explain what a department store is. Tell the class it's a big shop that sells lots of different kinds of things such as clothes, furniture, TVs, etc. Elicit local examples.

Put students in groups of 3 or 4 to chat about the questions. This is a short lead-in task, so you don't need to spend a long time on it or do much feedback. However, if you are short of time, you might just want to get students to ask you the questions. Answer them truthfully and ask if anyone else in the class is like you.

2 Using vocabulary: parts of a department store

Pre-tech the vocabulary. Draw a picture of each thing on the board or have them prepared on sheets of paper. For each picture, elicit / give the word and drill it. Draw / show the next picture and repeat the procedure, going back to the words you have already presented from time to time.

Explain the task. Ask students to do it in pairs and to use their dictionaries if necessary. Elicit the answers from the class and write them on the board. As you do so, elicit other things you might buy in each department.

Answers
1. e.   2. a.   3. g.   4. d.   5. c.   6. b.   7. f.

Other things you might buy in each department include:
- *Cosmetics* – make-up, perfume, etc.
- *Ladieswear* – women's clothes: dress, skirt, tights, etc.
- *Menswear* – men's clothes: suit, tie, trousers, etc.
- *Toiletries* – things you use in the bathroom: soap, shaving foam, razors, deodorants, etc.
- *The Shoe Department* – shoes, boots, etc.
- *The Sports Department* – shorts, football shirts; sports equipment – footballs, rackets, frisbees, etc.
- *The Stationary Department* – paper, pens, pencils, exercise books, staplers, etc.

Ask students to briefly discuss the last time they bought these things and where. Monitor and help with any new language, if necessary. Round up with a couple of corrections or by reformulating into better English interesting things you heard students say. Correct any new language the students have produced on the board.

3 Using vocabulary: parts of the shop

Explain the task. Do the first one with the students. Ask them to do the rest in pairs, using a dictionary, if necessary. Elicit the answers from the class. You will have to hold up the book clearly for students to see, unless you have access to an OHP, in which case copy the page onto a transparency.

> **Answers**
>
> 1. the lift   7. the ground floor
> 2. the escalator   8. the basement
> 3. the second floor   9. the top shelf
> 4. the stairs   10. the bottom shelf
> 5. the main entrance   11. the aisle
> 6. the first floor   12. the till

Go through any new language. For example:

* *The aisle* – drill this. It's pronounced /aɪl/. You could ask / explain where else you find an aisle, (church, cinema, plane). You could ask students if they prefer *an aisle or a window seat* on the plane and why.
* *The bottom shelf* – elicit *top* and *middle shelf*. Check the plural – *shelves*. You could elicit verbs which go with shelf.
* *The main entrance* – elicit the meaning and other examples of how to use *main*, (*main road, main exit, main course, main office*, etc.) as this came up in the previous unit.

The main aim of this activity is to pre-teach some of the language that appears in the listening and to build towards **7 Role play**. There's no need for any further practice at this stage.

4 Listening: *Do you sell swimsuits?*

Tell students they are going to listen to four conversations in shops and department stores. Each customer is trying to find something they want to buy. They will all use some of the language already studied in the unit. Tell the class to listen and to answer the two questions about each conversation.

Play the conversations once all the way through. Give students a minute or two to compare their answers in pairs. Round up the answers and if the whole group between them can provide the answers, don't play the conversation again, unless the class really wants you to. If they only have some of the answers, play the conversation again.

> **Answers**
>
> **Conversation 1:** He wants a swimsuit and it's in the Sports Department on the fourth floor.
> **Conversation 2:** He wants a toothbrush. It's on the bottom shelf in the next aisle.
> **Conversation 3:** She wants batteries. She needs to go to an electronics shop round the corner (Maplins).
> **Conversation 4:** He wants the toilets, which are on the second floor.

5 Listen again

Tell the class they are going to hear the four conversations again and that this time you want them to listen and complete the sentences with one or two words. Play the conversations and then give the students a minute to compare their ideas with a partner. You may want to elicit the answers immediately or you may want to play the conversations one more time and stop after each gap. Students then call out their answers. Write them on the board.

Alternatively, just let students read the **Tapescript** on pages 130–1 as they listen a final time and check their own answers.

> **Answers**
>
> 1. out of   3. b. turn, the shop
> 2. a. next, bottom   4. a. in here
> 2. b. show   4. b. come off
> 2. c. stupid   4. c. signs
> 3. a. corner   4. d. welcome

Go through any new language. For example:

* *Come out of the lift* – point out the verb. You can also *take the lift*.
* *That was stupid of me* – you can say this when you *make a* (stupid) *mistake*. You could show other possibilities – *That was kind of him. That was nice of her.*
* *Come off the escalator* – point out the verb and contrast it with *come out of the shop / lift / building*.
* *You're welcome* is what you say when someone thanks you. You can also say: *That's OK* and *No problem*.

6 Speaking

If you are short of time, you might want to skip this activity and move on to **7 Role play**, which practises more of the language that has been presented so far in this unit.

If you do the activity, ask students to read the three questions first and check they understand everything. Refer students to the **Real English** note at the top of page 85 on *cash back*.

Put students in groups of 3 or 4 to chat about the questions. You don't need to spend a long time on this or do much feedback.

7 Role play

Before you begin this activity, you might want to let students read the words in the box. Answer any questions they have about new language. Draw, act out or translate any objects they don't understand.

Put the students into pairs. Student A should write down three of the objects from the box. A then asks B: *Excuse me. Do you sell … ?* and B replies with the directions. Demonstrate the task with a couple of students. Take the part of Student B as this is more demanding and students will benefit from the model and support.

Ask students to do the task in pairs. Monitor and check for mistakes, particularly any errors in the language you've just taught. When most pairs have finished, tell students to swap roles.

Round up with a couple of corrections and teach any new language which may have come up.

With weaker groups, you may need to give students the chance to prepare what they would say as the shop assistant, (Student B role). This means setting up the role play in a different way: ask all the students to each write down three of the things in the box on a piece of paper or prepare a role card with three things to buy for each student and hand them out. They should then imagine they are shop assistants in a department store. They should write down on another piece of paper what department you find these things in and how to get there. They should try to use some of the language they have studied so far in the unit. Monitor and check students have understood and are writing sensible things.

Next, ask students to swap the pieces of paper with the names of the things on them. One student then asks: *Excuse me. Do you sell … ?* while the other student replies using the directions they have written. Round up the activity as above.

8 | Using vocabulary: things shop assistants say

Explain the task. Do the first one with the class as a model. Ask students to do the rest individually and then compare what they have in pairs. If you don't want to write everything on the board, make sure you drill all the sentences so that students get the right answers.

> **Answers**
> 1. Next please.
> 2. That's 28 pounds altogether.
> 3. Would you like any cash back?
> 4. Could you sign there, please?
> 5. Would you like a bag?
> 6. Would you like me to wrap it?
> 7. Have you got anything smaller?
> 8. I don't have any five-pound notes.
> 9. Do you need anything else?
> 10. Have a nice day.

As you elicit the answers, you could also elicit / give typical answers to any of the questions. Go through any new language. For example:

- *Altogether* – ask: *Did they buy one thing or more than one thing?* (More.) *Altogether* means *in total* here.
- *Cash back* – refer students to the **Real English** note, if you didn't do so earlier.
- *Sign here* – demonstrate signing. Ask when you need to sign, (when you *pay by credit card* on *the receipt*).
- *Wrap it* – act this out. You could ask why you would wrap something. (It's a present for someone.)
- *Have you got anything smaller?* – you need to check what the *assistant* is talking about here. Students may think it's a shirt or some piece of clothing. Here they're talking about a £50 note or £20 note. The assistant may not have enough change, if the price is low.
- *Notes* – show the class some paper money and elicit *coin* by showing students one.

Ask students to write a conversation using the expressions. Explain that they can't use all the expressions. Students can work in pairs or on their own. As they're writing, go round and check that they've understood and are writing sensible conversations. Correct any mistakes you see and help out with any new language they need. Finally, ask students to practise their conversations in pairs. Alternatively, if you are pressed for time, ask the class to do the writing activity for homework.

9 | Pronunciation /tʃ/ and /dʒ/

Model the sounds yourself – or use the recording and pictures on page 145 as a model. Ask students to repeat the sounds. The difference between the two sounds comes from using your voice for /dʒ/. You can feel this by touching your throat. You also expel more air with /tʃ/. If you put your hand in front of your face, you should be able to feel more air when you say /tʃ/ than when you say /dʒ/. You can show these techniques to students as well as using the photos and diagrams on page 145.

Explain the next task. Students should say the words to each other in pairs and decide which don't have a /tʃ/ sound. Play the recording so they can check. Then repeat the activity for /dʒ/. For both tasks, elicit the answers and write them on the board.

At the end, draw attention to the **Real English** note.

> **Answers**
>
> The words which DON'T have a /tʃ/ sound are: school, stomach, headache
>
> The words which DON'T have a /dʒ/ sound are: ago, bigger, lager (a kind of yellow beer)

Explain the last task. Play the recording of the six sentences. Pause at the end of each sentence to give students time to write. Ask students to compare their answers in pairs and then play the six sentences one more time.

Let students compare again before you elicit the answers and write them on the board: play each sentence and pause after each. Alternatively, just let students compare their ideas with the **Tapescript** on page 131.

Ask students to practise saying the sentences to each other. Monitor for any problems of pronunciation and correct.

For homework, either set the task of writing a conversation in a shop, as suggested above or else simply ask students to remember as much of the language from this lesson as they can, as they will need to use it again at the start of the next lesson.

Reading

If you are starting a new lesson, begin with a bit of revision. Ask students to try to repeat as much of the conversation in **8 Using vocabulary** on page 85 as they can from memory. You could also do an activity from **Unit 18** of the **Teacher's Resource Book**.

1 Using vocabulary: jobs in shops

This activity pre-teaches some of the vocabulary in the reading text. Explain the task and ask students to do it in pairs or individually. Elicit the answers from the class and write them on the board.

> **Answers**
>
> 1. d. 2. a. 3. e. 4. b. 5. c.

Go through any new language. For example:

*   A *cashier* is the person who sits and takes your shopping and tells you how much it costs. Act out what cashiers do.
*   *Security guard / stealing things* – act out stealing. Ask where you see security guards, (usually on the door).
*   *I'm in charge of ten people* – *I'm in charge* means *I tell these people what to do. If they have a problem, they come to me. I'm responsible for them.* Give examples – *I'm in charge of the shop / the department / four people.* Ask if any of the students is in charge of anyone / anything.

2 Speaking

You could discuss these questions with the class or ask students to discuss them in small groups. You could start off by answering the questions yourself as a model. Give students 4 or 5 minutes to talk. Monitor and help students with any new language. They may have to talk about different jobs and different kinds of jobs. Round up with a couple of corrections or by reformulating into better English interesting things you heard students say. Correct any new language the students have produced on the board.

3 While you read

Explain the task. Do the text as a listening, a reading or both, (see **Introduction** for procedure). When students have finished listening / reading, ask them to discuss the answers to the three questions in pairs for two minutes. Then elicit the answers from the class.

> **Answers**
>
> 1. Kelvin is a security guard in a big department store. Lina runs her own bookshop. Janice is a cashier in a big supermarket. Jeremy is a buyer for the Menswear department in a big department store.
>
> 2. Kelvin likes chasing people who've stolen things. Lina likes working for herself and not having anyone telling her what to do. Janice likes the people she works with and the boss is OK too. Jeremy travels all over the world, which he enjoys. He flies business class and stays in the best hotels.
>
> 3. Kelvin finds his job a bit boring sometimes – just standing around, watching people. Lina finds her job stressful and sometimes she has to work very long hours. Janice said the money isn't very good and she has to work Saturdays, which isn't much fun. Jeremy has to work long hours and his partner doesn't like him going away so much.

Ask the class who they think has the best / worst job. Again, help out with new language students may want to use to explain why they (don't) like certain jobs.

At this stage, don't deal with any unknown vocabulary. Wait until after the **Word check**.

4 Word check

Tell the class you're going to look at some of the new language from the text. Do the first one with them and then ask them to try to complete **2–10** using the words in the box, all of which are from the text. Students can refer back to the text if they want to. Let them compare their ideas in pairs and then elicit the answers from the whole group, writing them on the board as you do so.

> **Answers**
>
> 1. earn   2. employ   3. boring   4. fun   5. go off
> 6. run   7. bored   8. stressful   9. rest   10. steal

Go through any new language. For example:

*   You *earn* money from a job. Give examples: *I earn £30,000 a year. I don't earn very much money. I only earn eight euros an hour.* You could ask students who earns the most / least of the people they know.
*   If you have a company, you *employ* people. This means you pay them money to work for you. They are sometimes called *employees*. If students work for a company or organisation, you could ask how many people the company *employs*.
*   *Not much fun* – refer to the **Real English** note on the right.
*   *My alarm clock didn't go off* – it didn't ring, (act out ringing). Alarms usually *go off*. Give / elicit other examples of things that *go off* – car alarm, fire alarm, etc.
*   *Run a restaurant* – if you *run* something, you are the owner or boss / manager. Elicit other examples of things you *run* – a hotel, your own business, etc.
*   *Complain* – give examples and act out someone complaining. *We went to a restaurant and we waited one hour for the food so I complained to the manager about it.* People complain *about* things, (*I complained about the bad service*) and *to* people, (*I complained to my teacher / the manager about it*).
*   *Stressful* – act out looking stressed. Say *The job is stressful*, *I get stressed out*. Ask students which jobs they think are stressful or if they ever *get stressed out* and why.
*   *Shouted* – act it out.

5 Using grammar: *have to*

Write the following sentences on the board:
I have to stand near the door and watch people.
I have to work long hours.

Ask the students who said these things in the text and how they felt about this part of the job. (Kelvin said the first and he doesn't like it. It's boring. Jeremy said the second sentence and he says it's a bad thing.) Ask students: *If it's boring and if it's a bad thing why do they do it*' (They must. They don't have a choice – it's part of the job). Underline and say: *I have to do it*. It means I have no choice.

Ask students to read the other examples and then explain the task. Do the first one with the students and then ask them to do the rest. Elicit the answers and drill the *have to* expressions. Also, repeat the questions: *Do I like working on Saturdays?* (No.) and *Can I choose not to work on Saturdays?*

Answers		
1. have to work	2. have to wear	3. have to clean
4. have to travel	5. have to help	6. have to take

You might want to explain what a *uniform* is – the same clothes everybody wears for a job. Elicit examples of people who wear uniforms: policemen, soldiers, people who work in McDonalds, etc.

6 Practice

Let students choose one of the jobs from the text or put students in groups of 4 and allocate one job to each student. Elicit the common questions we ask about jobs that students learnt in **Unit 3**. Let them look at **Unit 3** if they've forgotten, or write the following questions on the board:

What do you do?

Where do you work?

Do you enjoy it?

Is it a good place to work?

Do you like the people you work with?

Is it far from your house to where you work?

Explain the task. You might want to give students a couple of minutes to prepare. Tell them that if they can't find the answers to every question in the text, it's OK to invent their own. Then put students in pairs / groups of 4 to have the conversations. Students could change partners once or twice before finishing the task.

Monitor and check for mistakes, particularly any errors in the language you've just taught. Round up with a couple of corrections and teach anything new you heard students trying to say. To follow-up, students could talk about their own jobs.

Homework

You could tell the class to do **Unit 17** in the **Workbook** for homework, if you haven't done so already.

You could also ask them to write a paragraph about their job or about the job of someone they know. Tell them to use the texts on pages 86 and the language from this unit to help them. Collect the writing next lesson and correct it

Correct any mistakes with things already studied in class and give students better ways of saying new things that they're trying to say.

Review: Units 13–18

Activities **1–5** could be set as homework or done as a short test. If you do them as a test, it's best to give students 15–20 minutes to complete them.

You could also do these activities as a slightly more relaxed revision lesson. You can introduce tasks quite simply by saying: *Now we're going to revise some questions / vocabulary / grammar we've looked at before* and then explain the tasks. Students can do the tasks in pairs or individually. When you elicit the answers to each activity, you can ask questions about the language and re-teach any words and expressions students have problems with. After each activity, there is a suggested follow-up that you could do as a way of breaking up the lesson a little.

1 Questions and answers

> **Answers**
>
> 1. d.   2. a.   3. c.   4. e.   5. b.   6. g.   7. h.   8. i.
> 9. j.   10. f.

Ask students to memorise the answers and then test each other. Student A says the question; Student B closes the book and says the answer.

Alternatively, get Student A to ask Student B the same questions, but Student B should give a different answer. You may need to model this. Get the student to ask you two or three questions and give new replies. You could round up by writing on the board some of the new answers students produced.

2 What was it like?

> **Answers**
>
> 1. holiday   2. town   3. hotel   4. food   5. weather

You could ask students to role-play a conversation about someone's holiday, using these questions. The responses could be real or you could ask students to invent a holiday where everything was great or everything was awful!

3 Grammar: verb patterns

You could lead into this by writing the following on the board:
I'd like ... to Australia some day.
I can't ... English very well.
I love ... to the cinema.

Elicit the missing words (*to go, speak, going*) from the class. Students may get the words right, but the form wrong. Point out the different forms and make it clear that there is no reason why we use one form rather than the other in each case. Students need to learn the patterns. Ask students to read the introduction and then write their own sentence endings. As they're writing, go

round and check that they've understood and are writing sensible endings down. You could ask students to walk around and to compare what they have written. They could agree with each other using: *Me too / Me neither.*

Next, ask students to do the next task. Elicit the answers from the class and write them on the board.

> **Answers**
>
> The correct forms are:
> 1. go   6. lying
> 2. to visit   7. work
> 3. lift, help   8. to wrap
> 4. playing   9. going
> 5. to meet, say 10. stay

4 Verbs (1)

> **Answers**
>
> 1. shuts   2. turned (it) down   3. get (it) off
> 4. got divorced   5. forgot   6. had   7. hurt   8. employ

Ask students to discuss the questions in pairs or small groups. You might want to add some more questions of your own such as: *When was the last time you felt ill? What did you do? Do you know anyone who's had a very short marriage? How long was it? Did they get divorced? Why?* etc.

Round up with a couple of corrections or by reformulating into better English interesting things you heard students say. Correct any new language the students have produced on the board.

5 Verbs (2)

> **Answers**
>
> 1. you to the station   6. your suitcase
> 2. that for me   7. you some water
> 3. my leg   8. on the weather
> 4. my wallet   9. the taxi driver
> 5. nice   10. it's OK

You could follow this up by asking students to memorise the verbs and collocations. Student A says the verb and Student B closes the book and says the collocation.

You could also elicit one more collocation for each verb. Students could do this in pairs and use dictionaries, alternatively do it as a class.

You could also write some personalised questions for the students to discuss in pairs such as: *What kind of car do you drive? Have you broken anything recently? What? How?* etc.

Round up as above.

93

6 Look back and check

If you have repeated these tasks as a form of revision / warmer in a previous lesson, you may choose to skip this activity.

Let students look back at both activities and decide which one they want to do. Take a vote on which one they prefer or do both. Give students time to read and ask you questions about the language before they do the speaking task again.

Round up as above.

7 What can you remember?

If you have re-elicited these texts as a form of revision / warmer in a previous lesson, you may want to skip this activity.

You could do this activity orally if you like, instead of getting students to write notes. Students will remember quite a lot about the *content* of a text, but often will not remember the exact expressions or collocations. Try to remind students of these as you go through the answers. For example:
Student: Lina have bookshop.
Teacher: Yes, OK. Lina runs her own bookshop.

An alternative way of doing this is to replay the recording of one or both of the texts, depending on the time you have available.

8 Vocabulary builder: useful things

This page aims to revise and expand on vocabulary, in this case, useful things.

Explain the task and ask students to work in pairs. After a few minutes, elicit the answers from the class and drill the words where appropriate (saucepan, envelope, scissors, needle and thread). You could also ask why you might need these things. You could write up some of the language that students need as they try to answer this question, e.g. tie my parcel up, sew a button back on, staple these bits of paper together, etc.

Answers
1. bowl
2. envelope
3. chopsticks
5. fork
6. folder
8. hammer
10. needle and thread
14. saucepan
15. scissors
18. stamps

9 Listening: What *are you doing this weekend?*

Do this listening as you would do a normal listening. Explain the context and the task. Make sure students cover the conversation the first time they hear it. Ask students to compare their ideas in pairs. As they do so, go round and check to see how they're doing. Depending on how much they've got, either elicit the answers from the class or play the recording a second time and then do so.

Answers
1. Jake is going back to Britain on Saturday. His flight leaves at 7 in the morning. Jake needs to pack sometime before he leaves.
2. He and Ruby decide to go out tonight – to the Three Lions pub! They are going to ask some of their friends to see if they want to come out too.

Tell the class they are going to hear the conversation again and that this time you want them to listen and complete the conversation by writing the words they hear in the gaps. Tell them they might need to write two, three or four words in the gaps. Play the conversation and then give the students a minute to compare their ideas with a partner. You may want to elicit the answers immediately or you may want to play the conversation one more time and stop after each gap. Students then call out their answers. Write them on the board.

Answers
1. a few weeks
2. what time's
3. need to get
4. leave your house
5. early morning flights
6. any plans
7. I'm not going
8. Let's go
9. if that's OK

Ask students to discuss the questions in small groups or as a class. Round up as above.

10 Pronunciation: the letter 'i'

This activity looks at the relationship between spelling and sound. Use the recording or just model the sounds and words yourself and ask students to repeat them. Explain the task. Do this as a race – ask students to do this in pairs and see which pair finishes first. Stop the task when the first pair finishes. Let the students read out their route. If they give a wrong answer, let another pair try to finish the route. The pair with the correct route are the winners!

Answers
light mobile spicy sign flight bicycle exciting
lie kind decided exercise bright tidy

11 Collocations

This collocation exercise also uses the grid of words from **10 Pronunciation**. The idea is to find a different route by completing each pair of expressions with one word from the grid. You could do this as a race with students working in pairs or threes in the same way as **10 Pronunciation** above. Do the first two as a class.

Answers
1. light
2. wish
3. minute
4. skirt
5. disgusting
6. lift
7. kind
8. missed
9. hit
10. sick
11. tidy

As this is revision, there's no real need to go over the language here. However, after students have got the answers, ask if anyone has any questions.

19 Sorry I can't come

Unit overview

General topic

Talking about things you can't / couldn't do.

Conversation

Three conversations in which people apologize for missing things.

Reading

Why can't I drive?

Language input

- Useful expressions for cancelling plans: *I have to go to the dentist's.*
- Pronunciation: stressed sounds in sentences.
- Using *couldn't* and *had to* to apologise: *Sorry I couldn't come last night. I had to work late.*
- More expressions for missing things: *I had a really bad headache.*
- Things you couldn't do and why: *I couldn't see the band. They were too far away.*
- Pronunciation: consonant sound: /h/

Language strip

Ignore the **Language strip** to begin with and deal with the language as it comes up in various activities. Come back to it later as revision. Alternatively, tell students to learn the expressions for homework.

Lead in

Do one of the following:

- Ask students to look back through their notes from the last few weeks. They should note down two words or expressions for which they can't remember the meaning. Students then get up and walk round the room to see if anyone else can explain the words to them. Monitor to check students are giving correct definitions and help out when necessary. At the end of the task, explain any words that the students have forgotten and go over some of the other common problems again, eliciting collocations where possible.
- Ask students to look at the **Expressions Organiser** for **Units 17** and **18** on page 154. Ask students to translate the expressions in pairs then check their ideas. Students can then test each other by saying a translation, acting it out or drawing a picture, while their partner guesses. To make this easier, let both students look at page 154.
- Test the students on the expressions in the **Language strip** on page 84. Give students two minutes to look at the **Language strip** and remember as much as they can. They can ask you questions during this time. Ask students to close their books, then put them into two teams. If you can, use L1 to test them on different expressions, draw them on the board, or act them out. The first person to call out the correct expression wins a point for their team.

Conversation

1 Using vocabulary: cancelling your plans

A good way to lead in to the lesson is to ask students to look at the photo at the top of page 92 and discuss with the class what the relationship between the two people in the photo is and what they might be saying to each other. Help out with any new vocabulary.

You could pre-teach some of the language in this activity by telling the class you can't teach them next lesson. In pairs, students then use L1 to brainstorm reasons why not. Translate or correct students' language, making sure you include some of the ideas from **1–5**. Alternatively, try to elicit some of the reasons using pictures of a dentist, of someone moving house, or visiting someone in hospital, etc.

Tell the class they are going to learn how to apologise and to give reasons for not doing something. Explain the task. Ask students to complete the task individually. Ask them to check in pairs before eliciting the answers from the class and writing them on the board.

Answers

1. come + collect   2. come + go   3. help + work
4. drive + visit   5. come + going

Go through any new language. For example:

- *Can't / have to* – as you go through, ask concept questions: *When's the tennis / the meeting? Is it possible for me to play / go?* (*No, I can't.*) *Why not? Do I want to collect my sister / go to the dentist?* (*No, but I have to.*)
- *Collect my younger sister* – go to the school and take her home. Give / ask for other places you might collect someone from: *Can you collect me from the airport / from the station, I have to collect the kids from a party,* etc. You could also give the students *pick up* as a common synonym.
- *Toothache* – act it out and give / ask for other 'aches'.
- *I'm going on holiday* – it's a good idea to ask why we DON'T say *I have to go on holiday* – because it's a nice thing to do; we want to do it.

2 Practice

Give students a couple of minutes to memorise the conversations. There is quite a lot of text, but much of each conversation is exactly the same. Model the task by covering the conversations, but letting students see the box with the pairs of words at the top of **1 Conversation**. Have a conversation with one of the stronger students using the words in the box.

Ask students to practise the five conversations in pairs. As they do so, go round and listen to their pronunciation, correcting and remodelling things for them if they need it. After 2 or 3 minutes, ask students to change roles and repeat the conversations.

If you have time, you could then either ask the class for ideas about any other reasons why they sometimes cancel plans or else give them a few minutes to brainstorm ideas in pairs. Elicit ideas from the group and write them on the board, reformulating them into better English as you do so. For example:

Student: Help friend in shop.
Teacher: Oh, OK. You mean it's your friend's shop?
Student: Yes.
Teacher: Right. Yes, so [writing on board and speaking]
           I have to help out in a friend's shop. Any more
           reasons?

Students could then change partners and repeat the first A and B parts of each conversation, using some of these new reasons. Again, round up with a couple of corrections or by correcting any new language the students have produced on the board.

3 Listening: *Sorry, I couldn't come*

Tell the class you're going to play them three different conversations and that in each one they will hear people apologizing for missing something. Tell them to listen and to try to write down what each person couldn't do, when it was and why they couldn't do it.

Play the conversations once all the way through. Give students a minute or two to compare their answers in pairs. Round up what they have and if the whole group between them can provide the answers, don't play the conversations again. If they only have a few of the answers, play the conversations again, pausing after each one.

Answers

1. In Conversation 1, he couldn't go to the airport
    to pick his friend up.
    In Conversation 2, she couldn't come to class.
    In Conversation 3, she couldn't go out for dinner
    with her friend.
2. In Conversation 1, it was this morning.
    In Conversation 2, it was last Friday.
    In Conversation 3, it was last night.
3. In Conversation 1, he had to go to the hospital to
    visit his grandfather. (He's quite ill. It was the first
    time he could visit him.)
    In Conversation 2, she was ill.
    In Conversation 3, she had to work late. (She's got
    an important meeting this Friday and had to get
    ready for it).

4 Listen again

Tell the class they are going to hear Conversation 3 again, between two women, Molly and Karen. This time you want them to listen and complete the conversation by writing the words they hear in the gaps. Tell them they might need to write 2, 3 or 4 words in the gaps. Play the conversation and then give the students a minute to compare their ideas with a partner. You may want to elicit the answers immediately or you may want to play the conversation one more time and stop after each gap. Students then call out their answers. Write them on the board.

Answers

1. on Friday   2. Never mind   3. I'd like that
4. It was great   5. a good time

Go through any new language. For example:

- We use *never mind* to tell someone not to worry or feel bad. Give another example: *The bank was closed. Oh well, never mind. We can come back tomorrow.*
- *Get ready for it* means *prepare*. You could ask what you do to *get ready* for a meeting. Also give *get ready to go out, get ready to go on holiday* and ask what you do. We often ask: *Are you ready?*
- *Some other time* – at some time in the future that's good for both us. When someone cancels plans, we often say: *Oh well. Maybe some other time.*
- *Traditional* English food – *traditional* is what people always did in the past and so still do now. You could give examples of traditional food in the country you're in. Give also *traditional music* and *traditional dress* and ask for / give examples.
- *Let me know* means *tell me*. Give examples: *Can you let me know when you find out, Let me know when he arrives,* etc.

5 Pronunciation: stressed sounds in sentences

Read out the short explanation and ask students to say the five sentences to themselves. Play the recording or model the sentences yourself and then ask students to repeat them again, paying particular attention to stressing the sounds in capital letters and pausing where there are spaces between groups of words.

Next, ask students to read out the conversation from **4 Listen again** in pairs. They can change roles once they finish. As they do so, go round and listen to their pronunciation, correcting and remodelling things for them if they need it.

6 Using grammar: *Sorry I couldn't come*

Write the following on the board:
Sorry, I can't meet you next week. I have to go away on business.
Sorry, I ... last week. I ... on business.

Ask how you could re-write the first sentence to talk about the past. Elicit / give *couldn't meet you* and *had to go away*.

Ask students to read the other examples and then ask them to re-write the other sentences in the same way. Elicit the answers from the class and drill the sentences with the new forms (*couldn't* and *had to*). There should be no other real problems with the vocabulary, but students might get confused about the fact that the answers in **1** and **2** use *come*, whilst in **3** and **4** they use *go*. It's best not to try to explain this. Just tell students that's the way people say it and accept *come* for **3** and **4** if you want to. It's not 'wrong' to use *come here* and there's no real rule explaining why, but it just doesn't sound 100% right!

Answers
1. couldn't come to your party, had to work.
2. couldn't come to class, had to look after my dad, was ill.
3. couldn't go shopping with you, had to go to the bank.
4. couldn't go to the cinema with you, had to collect a friend from the station.

7 Practice

Explain the task and ask students to read the model conversation. Rather than dividing pairs into A and B, divide them into 'future' and 'past'. The future person cancels plans in the future and the past person apologizes for missing things in the past! Model the task with one of the better students. Make sure you have several turns and change what you're cancelling each time. Tell students they should do the same and ask them to continue for as long as they can without repeating an excuse. As they do so, go round and check for mistakes, particularly with any errors in the language you've just taught. Round up with a couple of corrections.

8 Using vocabulary: more reasons for missing things

Tell the students they're going to learn some more vocabulary for explaining why they couldn't come to things. Explain the task and ask students to work in pairs. After 2 or 3 minutes, elicit the answers from the class and write them on the board.

Answers
1. problems 2. appointment 3. meeting
4. bad day 5. headache 6. accident

Go through any new language. For example:
- When you want to see a doctor or a dentist, you have to phone and arrange the time. You *make an appointment*. Sometimes they're *fully booked – they don't have time* for you. You could draw an appointments diary on the board to illustrate this.
- *Had a bad day* – you could ask why: *I had too much work to do, I had to deal with a lot of complaints*, etc. and you could also give *had a bad week / time*.
- *An accident* – point to the picture at the bottom of the page. You could elicit the responses and questions you might give after someone tells you they've had an accident: *You're joking! Oh no! Are you all right? Was the car badly damaged? What happened?* etc.

As a follow-up, role-play the accident conversation in pairs. One person reads out **6** and the other responds using the questions above. They try to continue the conversation as best they can, using L1 if they need to. Round up with a couple of corrections or by reformulating into better English things you heard students say. Correct on the board anything new you heard students produce.

Ask students to discuss the final question. Give an example of your own as a model. You might need to give the class a couple of minutes to prepare. Then ask them to tell a partner their story. Monitor and check for mistakes, particularly any errors in the language you've

just taught. Round up with a couple of corrections or interesting things students said. Also, teach anything new you heard students trying to say.

For homework, ask students to write the accident conversation they had with their partner in **8 Using vocabulary**. They could compare the conversations they have written in pairs at the start of the next lesson and see if they can find any mistakes in their partner's writing.

Collect the conversations and correct them. Correct any mistakes with things already studied in class and give students better ways of saying new things that they're trying to say.

Alternatively, ask students to try to learn the conversation from **4 Listen again** and then test them in the next lesson.

Reading

If you are starting a new lesson, begin with a bit of revision. Ask students to try to repeat as much of the conversation in **4 Listen again** on page 92 as they can from memory.

Alternatively, ask students to role-play all six conversations from **8 Using vocabulary** on page 93. In each case, students should try to continue the conversations. You could elicit some typical responses and questions before they start or let students have a go straightaway, allowing them to make some use of L1 if they want to. Monitor and make a note of any new language students try to say. Round up by teaching it and writing it on the board. Get students to repeat the conversations using the new language. You could also do an activity from **Unit 19** of the **Teacher's Resource Book**.

Finally, ask students to look at the **Language strip** on page 92, if you haven't done so already, and ask them to underline all the expressions that came up in the previous lesson. Do they know what the others mean? Help the students with any they don't know.

1 Before you read

Tell the students they're going to read a text called *Why can't I drive?* but first you're going to check the meaning of some language from the text. Ask students to do the matching task on their own, or you could even do it quickly with the class.

Answers
1. c. 2. a. 3. e. 4. d. 5. b.

Go through any new language. For example:
- *Fail* – you can also fail an exam. Ask what % you might get if you fail, (probably anything under 50%). You could also ask what you have to do if you *fail a test – repeat the course* and / or *re-take the test*.
- *Calm down* – act this out and drill. Ask for ways to calm down.

Now ask students to work in pairs or as a class to think of how these words might be used in the text. What's the story? There will be a variety of answers. The point of this activity is not to guess correctly, but rather to check understanding of the words just looked at and to generate some interest in the text. Elicit a few ideas from the class and then say: *OK. We'll see if you were right.*

2 While you read

Explain the task. Do the text as a listening, a reading or both, (see **Introduction** for procedure).

Go through any new language first. For example:

*   *Problems on the line* – draw a train line and say: *Maybe there's an animal on the line or a tree or something like that.*
*   *I know from past experience* – I know because it's happened to me before. This is a fixed expression.
*   *Simpler* – easier.
*   *Park the car* – act it out or draw it. You could also teach *find a parking space / find a place to park / a car park.*
*   *The speed limit* is the fastest you are allowed to drive. Elicit local examples. Teach: *I went over the speed limit.*
*   *Badly damaged* – draw a badly damaged car! You could also explain that sometimes *houses are badly damaged in storms.*

When most students have finished reading, ask them to cover the text and to work with a partner to see if they can remember how the underlined words in **I Before you read** were actually used. Next, let them look back at the text and underline / check the expressions.

> **Answers**
>
> It's half an hour late. / The train is actually an hour late.
> Every time I fail my test / I've failed my test five times now.
> I left my house at eleven.
> I was quite nervous / I was very nervous / I was really nervous.
> It took me 5 minutes just to start the car.

As a follow-up, ask students how many times the writer failed his test and why. You could do this with the class or put students into pairs.

Before you do the next activity, ask students if they have any other questions about the text.

3 Speaking

Ask students to read the questions first and check they understand them. There shouldn't be a problem as this is all language that has come up before, but students may need reminding of some things. Explain the task. Ask students to discuss the questions in pairs or small groups. Monitor and help out with any new vocabulary. Round up in the usual way.

4 Using grammar: *I couldn't do it*

You could lead into this task by asking student to find examples of *couldn't* in the text. You could ask them to translate these and / or ask concept questions about them: *Is it talking about the past or the present here?* (The past.) *Did he park the car? Why not?* (He couldn't – he was too nervous.) so *he couldn't* – it was impossible for him.

Alternatively, simply tell students they're going to look at some other examples of *couldn't*. Explain the task. Do the first one with the class to model it, then ask students to try **2–10** on their own. After 4 or 5 minutes, ask students to compare their answers in pairs. Then elicit the answers from the class and write them on the board. Drill the *couldn't* expressions as you go through the answers.

> **Answers**
>
> I. d.   2. a.   3. c.   4. e.   5. b.   6. h.   7. j.   8. g.
> 9. f.   10. i.

Go through any new language. For example:

*   *Parking space* – draw an example. Elicit the place where there are lots of spaces to park, (*a car park*).
*   *Scary* – act looking scared. Make it clear that the film is *scary* but I *was scared.* You could elicit other things that are scary. If anyone asks, it's basically the same as *frightening.*
*   *Blood* – draw or act out cutting yourself and blood coming out. Drill it.
*   *Exhausted* – very, very tired. Drill it. Elicit examples of why you might sometimes be exhausted.
*   *The band* – a music group. Elicit examples. Ask some students who their favourite band is – prepare to be disappointed! You may need to explain how *bands* are different from *orchestras.*
*   *Standing in front of me* – demonstrate by doing it! Act out the whole situation.

5 Practice

As a follow-up, ask students to memorise the *couldn't* expressions. Then put the students into pairs. Student A says the situation and Student B says the *couldn't* expression with the book closed.

Explain the first task and brainstorm some ideas with the class. Then ask students to do the rest in pairs. As they're writing, go round and check that they've understood and are writing sensible endings down. Next, ask each pair to join another pair to see if they have the same endings or not. You could then ask each group to compare with another group.

Deal with any common problems or any particularly inventive endings before students do the final speaking task.

Explain the final task and give one or two examples yourself as a model. You might need to give the class a few minutes to prepare. Ask one student to tell you one of the things they have written and try to add some follow-up responses or ask some questions to continue the conversation. Then ask them to tell different students things they couldn't do and try to continue the conversations. Ask students to change partners two or three times. Round up in the usual way.

6 | Pronunciation: /h/

Tell the students they're going to do some work on pronunciation. Play the recording and ask students to repeat the sounds with /h/. We make the sound /h/ by blowing out a little more air when we say the vowel sound which follows it. Students may have problems with the vowel sounds as much as the /h/ in which case you might need to help them by referring to the photos and diagrams on page 144.

Now explain the next task and play the recording. After you have played all ten, ask students to compare their answers and then say the words they chose back to you to check. This is another opportunity to correct pronunciation if necessary.

Explain the next task. Play the recording. Pause at the end of each sentence to give students time to write. Ask students to compare their answers and then play the eight sentences once more. Let students then compare what they have written again, before you go through the answers on the board, playing each sentence once more and pausing after each one as you do so. Alternatively, students can just compare with the **Tapescript** on page 132.

Answers

1.	has	6.	air
2.	his	7.	heart
3.	I'm	8.	old
4.	hand	9.	ear
5.	open	10.	hate

Students then practise reading out the sentences in pairs. As they do so, go round and listen to their pronunciation, correcting and remodelling things for them if they need it.

If students have no problems with this sound, you might want to only do the final dictation task.

Homework

You could tell the class to do **Unit 18** in the **Workbook** for homework, if you haven't done so already.

You could also ask students to write a paragraph or two about either their driving test(s) – if they've taken one, or something they can't do, but would like to and why they've never learned. Tell them to use as much new language from this unit as they can.

Collect the writing next lesson and correct it. Correct any mistakes with things already studied in class and give students better ways of saying new things that they're trying to say.

Unit overview

General topic
Playing and watching sport.

Conversation
Three conversations between people who meet on holiday. One person invites the other to join them in their plans for later.

Reading
Sporting success, sporting failure

Language input
- Useful expressions for talking about sport: *I go cycling all the time.*
- Sports, places and equipment: *running, tennis court, football boots*, etc.
- Questions about the future using *going to*: *Where are you going to meet?*
- Talking about teams: *Arsenal are top of the league.*
- Pronunciation: connected speech

Language strip
Ignore the **Language strip** to begin with and deal with the language as it comes up in various activities. Come back to it later as revision. Alternatively, tell students to learn the expressions for homework.

Lead in
Do one of the following:
- Ask students to look back at **4 Using Grammar** on page 95. Give the class two minutes to memorise the sentences. Then put the students into pairs. Student A should read out the situations in **1–5**, while Student B closes his/her book and tries to repeat the things the people couldn't do. Students then swap roles.
- Put students in pairs and ask them to try to repeat the 5 conversations from **1 Conversation** on page 92, but this time using only the words in the box as prompts. To make it easier, give them a couple minutes to re-read the conversations first.
- Do one of the **Teacher's Resource Book** activities from **Unit 19**.
- Test the students on the expressions in the **Language strip** on page 92. Give students two minutes to look at the **Language strip** and remember as much as they can. They can ask you questions during this time. Ask students to close their books, then put them into two teams. If you can, use L1 to test them on different expressions, draw them on the board, or act them out. The first person to call out the correct expression wins a point for their team.

Conversation

1 Speaking

A good way to lead in to the lesson is to split the class into 2 to 4 groups, depending on the size of the class. Give them two minutes to write down as many sports in English as they can. They can use dictionaries if they want, but be strict on the time. The groups then swap papers. Find out which group has thought of the most sports. Write them on the board as the group tells you them and drill the words, checking for stress where relevant. Give one point for each sport correctly spelt. The winners are the group with the most points.

Ask students to read the 8 sentences first. Go through any new language. For example:
- *Go cycling, play golf, go to the gym* – the best way to deal with these is to act them out – or perhaps draw them. You could also point out the patterns *go + …-ing* (go cycling, running, swimming, jogging), and *play + ball games* (play football, tennis, rugby, golf). With good or interested classes, you could also elicit what you do in the gym: *go on the running machine, lift weights, go on the step machine*, etc.
- Point out that we say *on* Sunday, Monday, Friday, etc, but *at* the weekend and *in* the evening / morning.

Explain the task. Ask students to decide which sentences are true for them and tell a partner. You could model this for the class by giving your own true answers first, using as much of the language from this activity as you can and changing it slightly where necessary.

As students chat, monitor and help out with any new vocabulary. Round up in the usual way.

You could ask students to write some more similar sentences and then compare their ideas, but if you're short of time you might want to skip this task and move on.

2 Using vocabulary: sport, places and equipment

You might choose to pre-teach the words in this activity before doing the task. Draw a picture of each of the things in the box on the board or have some pictures prepared on sheets of paper. For each picture, elicit / give the word and drill it. Draw / show the next picture and repeat the procedure, going back to the words you have already presented from time to time.

Explain the task. Ask students to try it in pairs and to use their dictionaries if necessary. After a couple of minutes, elicit the answers from the class and write them on the board. As you do so, drill any of the words in the box that you think your students might have problems with.

Answers

1. trainers   2. racket   3. cycling   4. pool   5. boots
6. wetsuit   7. clubs

Go through any new language. For example:

- *Round the park / along the river* – draw a park and a river and draw arrows to show these ideas.
- *Trainers* are sports shoes; they are called *sneakers* in American English.
- *Shorts* – point to the tennis picture.
- The *court* is the place where you play tennis. Again, use the picture or draw a court on the board. You could add *basketball / badminton court*.
- *Racket* – point to the tennis picture. It's also spelt *racquet* – same pronunciation.
- A *pool* (swimming pool) – draw a picture or give a local example.
- *Trunks* – draw a picture. They are like shorts, but for swimming in. Men usually wear *trunks*, women wear *swimsuits*. Again, draw a picture.
- *Goggles* are like glasses, but for when you're swimming. Draw some!
- The *pitch* is the place where you play football. Draw one on the board – or ask a student to. You could add we also say *a rugby / cricket pitch*.
- *Windsurfing, windsurfer, wetsuit* – point to the picture on this page. You could add that you *go* windsurfing.
- A *lake* – draw one or ask for / give a local example.
- The *course* is the place where you play golf. Most are *18-hole courses*.
- *Clubs* – draw one or act out using one.

Ask the class which words they could use to describe the photos. Round up the answers quickly.

Answers

In the first picture, you can see a windsurfer windsurfing, wearing a wetsuit. In the second picture, there's a woman swimming. She's wearing a swimsuit and a swimming cap. In the third, there's a man playing tennis on a tennis court. He's holding his racket and is wearing shorts and trainers. You can see the ball as well. In the last picture, two men are (going) running / jogging. They're wearing shorts and trainers.

3 **Listening: *Why don't you come with us?***

Tell the class you're going to play them three different conversations. In each one, two people have met on holiday and one person invites the other to join them later on in the day. Tell them to listen and to match each conversation to one of the photos.

Play the conversations once all the way through. Give students a couple of minutes to compare their ideas in pairs and then elicit the answers from the class. As you do so, ask how they knew. Try to repeat some of the language from the conversations as you're rounding up.

Answers

Conversation 1: D
Conversation 2: B
Conversation 3: C

You might want to point out that *I like going swimming / running* means generally or usually, but that *I'm going for a swim / a run* means one swim or one run at one particular time.

Tell students they're going to hear the conversations again and that this time you want them to try to find out whether the people *accept the invitations* and why. This might be a good time to teach the opposite – *turn the invitation down*. Play the conversations all the way through again and give students a minute or two to compare their ideas in pairs. Elicit the answers from the whole group again, as above.

Answers

Conversation 1: She turns the invitation down. She hasn't got any trainers with her.
Conversation 2: He accepts the invitation. He's going to buy some trunks (from the sports shop – just round the corner).
Conversation 3: He accepts the invitation. He doesn't have a tennis racket, but someone else can lend him one.

4 **Listen again**

Tell the class they are going to hear Conversation 3 again, between Jess, a woman and Dario, a man. This time you want them to listen and complete the conversation by writing the words they hear in the gaps. Tell them they might need to write 1, 2 or 3 words in the gaps. With stronger classes, ask the students to read the conversation first and see if they remember or can guess the missing words. They then listen just to check their ideas.

Otherwise play the conversation and then give the students a minute to compare their ideas with a partner. You may want to elicit the answers immediately or play the conversation one more time and stop after each gap. Students then call out their answers. Write them on the board. As you do so, deal with any new / interesting language.

Answers

1. some tennis courts   2. playing   3. very good
4. a racket   5. Probably around   6. Let's say

Go through any new language. For example:

- *Like playing* – remind students of the *like + ...-ing* pattern.
- *All the time* just means a lot.
- *Back home* – in my country / home town. Refer students to the **Real English** note.
- *Me neither* is used to show you agree with a negative comment or statement. If this is a problem, give other examples:
  A: *I love tennis.*
  B: *Yes, me too.*
  A: *I'm not very good at maths.*
  B: *No, me neither.*

- *An extra player* – one more person to play. Give an example: *You've got 11 players, we've only got 10, so we need an extra player.* You could give other examples of the ways we use *extra* – *It was nil-nil (0–0) after 90 minutes, so we had extra time. / It's £10 to get in, but you have to pay extra for drinks.*
- *I'd love to, but ...* – point out we often turn down invitations using this structure. Give more examples: *Would you like to go out for dinner with me tonight? / I'd love to, but I'm busy, I'm afraid.*
- *Where shall I meet you?* means *Where is a good place to meet you?* or *Where do you want me to meet you?* Again, more examples are better than trying to explain the grammar here – *Where shall I put your stuff? Shall I open the champagne now? Shall we have some lunch now?*

Now ask students to look at the **Tapescript** on page 132. Put students in pairs and ask them to practise reading the conversation, paying particular attention to stressing the sounds in capital letters and pausing where there are spaces between groups of words. You could read out a couple of lines for them to model this or use the recording. Students can change roles when they have finished. Go round and listen to their pronunciation, correcting and remodelling things for them if they need it.

5 Useful expressions

Tell the students to translate 1–7 into their language and to write their translations in the book. If you share the same L1 as the class, check the translations or with weaker students simply tell them.

If any of the weaker students have problems translating any of the expressions, it may mean you need to explain them again or ask other students who share the same first language to help them.

If you have time, ask students to find examples of these expressions or similar ones in the **Tapescript**, (4 and 5 are found in every conversation).

If you haven't done so already, go through the **Real English** note.

6 Writing

Explain the task by telling students they're going to practise using this new language by writing similar conversations to the ones they heard in **3 Listening**. Put the students in pairs and tell them to choose one of the three conversations. Let students look at the **Tapescript** for support if they need to. Give them 6 or 7 minutes writing time. As they're writing, go round and check that they're writing sensible conversations. Correct where necessary.

You might want to deal with any common problems on the board when the students have finished. However, you may want to move on here, so ask students to either read out their conversations to another pair or else to memorise their conversations and then act them out. It's better to do this in fours (two pairs) than to ask each pair to perform in front of the class.

Here's a possible conversation for 1:
A: We're going to play football.
B: Oh really? Where are you going to play?
A: There's a pitch in the park about ten minutes from here.
B: Is there?
A: Yes. Do you like playing football?
B: Yes, I play two or three times a week back home.
A: Really? Well, why don't you come with us and have a game?
B: I'd love to, but I haven't got any boots with me.
A: That's OK. I can lend you some.
B: OK, great. What time are you going to play?
A: In about an hour. There'll be nine or ten of us, I think.
A: OK, sounds great. Shall I just meet you there?
B: Yes, that's fine. See you later.
A: See you. Bye.

2 and 3 will obviously follow a similar pattern. You could ask students to write the two other conversations for homework.

One way you could lead in to this activity is to write the following on the board:
Where _____ you _____ play?

7 Using grammar: questions about the future

Ask if students can remember the question they heard in the conversation. Elicit: *Where are you going to play?*

Remind the class that we use *going to + verb* to talk about things in the future we've already decided to do. Tell them they're going to learn some common questions using *going to*.

Explain the task. You might need to do the first one with the class as a model. After a couple of minutes, let students compare in pairs and then elicit the answers from the class. It might take too long to try to write all the answers on the board. If you don't, make sure you repeat each correct answer clearly, so that the class can check their ideas.

Answers
1. Where are you going to go?
2. What are you going to see?
3. Where are you going to meet?
4. What are you going to do?
5. Where are you going to stay?
6. What time are you going to leave?
7. Who are you going to play with?
8. How long are you going to go for?

Drill the questions yourself or use the recording. Point out the use of the weak forms of *are* and *to* – /ə/ and /tə/.

Some students may have heard songs in which *going to* is pronounced as *gonna*. This is common in both British and American English. If the class asks you about this, you might want to drill the questions again using this pronunciation too.

8 Practice

Put the students into pairs. Explain the task. You might need to model it with one of the better students in the class. Take the role of Student A yourself as this is the more demanding. Bear this in mind when assigning roles. You might want to give students a couple of minutes to prepare. With weaker classes, you could also ask them to write the 3-line conversations first and then try to memorise them.

Give students three or four minutes to practise. The pairs that finish first can change roles. Go round and monitor, checking for mistakes, particularly any errors in the language you've just taught. Round up with a couple of corrections.

For homework, ask students to write one or two more conversations like the one they wrote in **6 Writing**. They could compare the conversations they have written in pairs at the start of the next lesson and see if they can find any mistakes in their partner's writing. You could then collect the conversations and read them. Correct any mistakes with things already studied in class and give students better ways of saying new things that they're trying to say.

Alternatively, ask students to try to learn the conversation from **4 Listen again** and then test them in the next lesson.

Reading

If you are starting a new lesson, begin with a bit of revision. Ask students to try to repeat as much of the conversation in **4 Listen again** on page 97 as they can from memory. Alternatively, you could do an activity from **Unit 20** of the **Teacher's Resource Book**.

Finally, ask students to look at the **Language strip** on page 96, if you haven't done so already, and ask them to underline all the expressions that came up in the previous lesson. Do they know what the others mean? Help the students with any they don't know.

Using vocabulary: talking about teams

This activity is the one most focused on talking about sport in the whole unit, so if you have a class not particularly interested in team sports, you might want to skip this.

If you do decide to do the activity, you might need to begin by showing the class *the league table* and explaining what it is. Ask students to work in pairs and give them a few minutes to answer **1–10**. Elicit the answers from the class. You don't need to write the answers on the board, just make sure you say them clearly to the class.

Answers

1. Arsenal (pronounced /ɑːsnʌ/)
2. Tottenham (pronounced /tɒtnʌm/)
3. Ipswich Town
4. Everton
5. Middlesborough.
6. Arsenal
7. Southampton
8. Yes, Blackurn–Birmingham was a nil-nil draw.
9. Bolton lost two-nil / Fulham won two-nil.
10. No, they drew three-all.

Go through any new language. For example:
- *Lost / beat* – you lose, draw or win a match / league / cup, but you beat a team. You could give / ask for more examples: *Greece beat Portugal one–nil in the final. Brazil won the World Cup. My team lost 4–3.*
- *Nil–nil* – in football scores, we don't say *zero*. We say *nil*. In tennis, we say *love*.
- *A three–all draw* – this means the score was 3–3. We say *a one–all draw* or *they drew one-all, they drew two–all, it was a three–all draw*, etc. However, we don't say *a nil-all draw*. We say *a nil-nil draw* or *They drew nil–nil*. There's no reason for this. It's just the way it is!

You could discuss the two questions with the class or ask students to discuss them in small groups. Give students a couple minutes to talk. It's probably not worth doing much feedback here. Move on to the next activity.

2 While you read

Explain the task and give students a few minutes to read the article. You might need to explain *success* (doing something you planned to do very well), and *failure*, the opposite; not doing something you planned to do! Do the text as a listening, a reading or both, (see **Introduction** for procedure).

After students finish reading / listening, ask them to discuss their ideas in pairs for a couple of minutes. Then ask the class to share ideas. Ask students to explain how they made their decisions.

Answers

Andrew: failure – they were the worst team ever. They hardly ever won. Once, they lost 78–nil.
Ruben: success – he ran a marathon last year! He was so happy! It gave him a lot of confidence.
Carmina: success – she swam 5 kilometres in the sea! It took her a long time, but she did it!
Mikel: success – he beat his older brother.
Denise: success – she got to the top of a really high mountain. She felt great!
Sue: failure – she broke her leg skiing!
Paco: failure – they're playing really badly. They're fourth from bottom in the league. They only scored 58 points in their last game.

At this stage, don't deal with any unknown vocabulary. Wait until after the **Word check**.

3 Comprehension

In pairs, ask students to cover the text and say how the people used the numbers given. Go round and monitor for any errors. You could go through these on the board after they have finished. Alternatively, just elicit what the class can remember and reformulate this into better English, using as much of the actual language from the texts as you can. For example:

Teacher: *OK, so what about Andrew?*
Student: *His team lose 70 to nothing.*
Teacher: *Yes, OK. He was the captain of the school rugby team and **they once lost 78–nil.***

You could write the words in bold on the board or it might be quicker to ask students to finish by looking back at the text and underlining the expression using all of these numbers.

Go through any new language. For example:

* *I came 12,332nd out of 12,500* – it means 12 and a half thousand people *took part in / entered the race.* Ruben was the 12,332nd person to finish! Highlight the pattern and give some other examples: *I came ninth – out of ten people!* etc.
* *It took me* – remind students of the pattern, *It took me x amount of time.*
* *A 3000-metre mountain* – notice that here we don't say metres. This is because of the 'a'. It means we're using the number as an adjective. Give other examples – *a ten-minute walk, the million-dollar question.*
* *Scored 58 points* – in basketball, you *score points.* In football, you *score goals.* In baseball, you *score runs.*

4 Vocabulary check

Tell the class you're going to look at some of the new language from the text. Ask them to try to complete **1–8** from memory, without looking back at the text. After a few minutes, get students to compare their ideas in pairs. You could also tell them to go back and check their ideas. Tell them to underline the expressions. Then check the answers from the whole group, writing them on the board as you do so.

Answers

1. greatest   2. lost   3. at   4. took
5. confidence   6. beat   7. broke   8. scored

As you go through the answers, drill pronunciation where relevant. Go through any new language.
For example:

* A *hundred-metre race* – not a hundred-metres race.
* *I lost really badly* – ask the class what they think the score was.
* *It gave me a lot of confidence* – it made me feel good about myself. Give an example: *I spoke to an American last week and he understood me! It gave me a lot of confidence.* You could also give / ask for the opposite: *It knocked / damaged my confidence.*

5 Speaking

Ask students to read the questions first and check they understand them. There shouldn't be a problem as this is all language that has come up before, but students may need reminding of some things. Explain the task. Ask

students to discuss the questions in pairs or small groups. Monitor and help out with any new vocabulary. Round up in the usual way.

6 Pronunciation: connected speech

Again, if your students aren't particularly interested in sport, you might want to skip this activity.

Explain the context and the task. Play the ten sentences, which students write down. Play them once, give students a chance to compare their ideas and then play them again, perhaps stopping after each one to elicit the group's ideas. Finally, look at the answers on page 132. Explain one of the ways in which we link words together when we speak: if one word ends in a consonant and the next starts with a vowel, we link them together. You could use the phonetic transcriptions to make this point.

Drill the sentences or use the recording. Make sure students sound excited and make sure they link words together correctly.

Go through any new language. For example:

* *Come on United!* – if you're watching a football match and the team you want to win has *United* in their name, (Leeds United, Manchester United, Sheffield United, etc.), you shout this to encourage them! You could act it out, drill it and then give local versions – *Come on Spartak / Roma / Turkey,* etc.
* *Pass it!* – act out passing the ball from one player to another player.
* *Watch out!* – you shout when you can see another player coming up behind someone on your team.
* *That's a foul!* – act out fouling another player. The fans watching shout out *That's a foul!* You could also teach that usually you get a free kick (or sometimes a penalty) if someone *fouls* you.
* *Send him off!* – shouted at the referee after a bad foul. It means you want the referee to show the red card – to send the player from the pitch. If you want a yellow card to be shown, you can shout *Book him!*
* *It was out / in!* – point to *the line* on the tennis court on page 96 and act / draw a ball hitting just outside. One player (or *the umpire*) shouts *It was out!* The player who hit the ball shouts *It was in!*
* *Great shot* – shouted when someone tries to score a goal. Act it out.
* *Great save* – shouted at the goalkeeper after he stops the ball from going into the net. Again, act it out.

A short extension could be to ask students to cover the sentences and to use the phonetic symbols to recall **1–10.** They could do this in pairs.

Homework

You could tell the class to do **Unit 19** in the **Workbook** for homework, if you haven't done so already.

You could also ask them to write a couple of paragraphs about their greatest success and worst failure in sport or in life. Tell them to use the texts on page 99 and the language from this unit to help them. Collect the writing next lesson and correct it.

Correct any mistakes with things already studied in class and give students better ways of saying new things that they're trying to say.

Unit overview

General topic
Travelling and getting around.

Conversation
Two conversations in which people find out train information and plan a trip.

Reading
It's a small world

Language input
- Useful expressions for travelling: *You need to get a number 34.*
- Superlatives: *What's the best way to get to the airport?*
- Revision of comparatives: *I've travelled more than my parents.*
- Using *has got* to talk about changes: *Petrol has got more expensive.*
- Pronunciation: silent '*t*' at the end of words

Language strip
Ignore the **Language strip** to begin with and deal with the language as it comes up in various activities. Come back to it later as revision. Alternatively, tell students to learn the expressions for homework.

Lead in
Do one of the following:
- Ask students to look back at **3 Comprehension** on page 98. Put students into pairs and give them 4 or 5 minutes to re-tell as much of the stories from this unit as they can remember. Round up by eliciting ideas from the class and reformulating their ideas into better English, using the language from the text. (See the answers to this activity in the notes for **Unit 20**.)
- Put students in pairs and ask them to practise the three conversations from **6 Writing** on page 97, using the prompts. To help students, give them a couple minutes to re-read the conversation in **4 Listen again** first.
- Do one of the **Teacher's Resource Book** activities from **Unit 20**.
- Test the students on the expressions in the **Language strip** on page 96. Give students two minutes to look at the **Language strip** and remember as much as they can. They can ask you questions during this time. Ask students to close their books, then put them into two teams. If you can, use L1 to test them on different expressions, draw them on the board, or act them out. The first person to call out the correct expression wins a point for their team.

Conversation

1 Using vocabulary: travelling

One way you could lead in to this activity is to ask students to discuss how they get to school for each lesson. They can do this in pairs or as a class. Do they drive, take the bus or take the train? You could then ask them to say which buses / trains they get, where they get on / off, how much it costs, etc. You could even ask them to write down in L1 any conversations they have when buying tickets, etc. and then translate these into English. Help with the translations, correcting any errors with language already taught and giving students better ways of saying things they're not sure of yet.

Tell the class that in this lesson they're going to learn how to get around on trains and buses in English. Tell students they're going to read five different travel conversations and explain the task. You might want to do the first one as a class. After a few minutes, let students compare their ideas in pairs and then either elicit the answers from the class and write them on the board or else just play the recording so that students can check their answers themselves.

Answers

Conversation 1:	1. c.	2. b.	3. a.	
Conversation 2:	1. c.	2. a.	3. b.	4. d.
Conversation 3:	1. d.	2. c.	3. b.	4. a.
Conversation 4:	1. d.	2. a.	3. c.	4. b.
Conversation 5:	1. b.	2. a.	3. e.	4. d.	5. c.

Go through any new language. For example:
- *Does this bus go to … ?* – point out the structure. You could add *train / tram* as well as *bus* and ask for other endings using local places.
- *Tufnell Park* is an area in London.
- *Is this the right bus for … ?* means more or less the same as *Does this bus go to … ?*, but usually you ask the first question on the bus, the second one at the bus stop. Tell students not to worry if they get these mixed up. People will still understand them!
- *Can you tell me when to get off?* – it's probably best not to worry too much about explaining the grammar here (it's an indirect question), but to simply give some more examples: *Can you tell me where to change / how much it'll be / if need to book in advance?* etc.
- *I'd like a ticket to Bath, please* – this is the normal way to ask for tickets. If you say *I want*, it sounds a bit rude. Lots of younger people also often say, *Can I get a ticket to Bath, please?*
- *Single or return?* – draw a quick map and mark a couple of places in your country on it. Explain you're in one place and ask for a ticket to another. Draw one arrow there and say *a single ticket*. Draw two arrows, one there and one back, and say *a return*.
- *Returning today?* – you don't need to say *Are you returning today?* It's understood. It's quicker to leave it off!

- *When's the last train? / What time does it get in?* – if any students ask about the tense here, you could just quickly say we often ask about timetables using the present simple. Give one or two more examples: *What time do you finish work tomorrow? What time does the movie start?* If students don't ask about it, there's no need to mention it.
- *Get in* means the same as *arrive*, but is more common in spoken English. Give some more examples: *I didn't get in to Heathrow until 3 in the morning! What time does your bus get in?*

Next, ask students to read out the conversation in pairs. They can change roles once they finish. As they do so, go round and listen to their pronunciation, correcting and remodelling things for them if they need it. Do this with each pair rather than the whole glass, unless you hear some things everybody has trouble with. In that case, deal with it at the end of the activity as a class, by remodelling it and drilling it.

2 Practice

You might want to put students into new pairs for this activity or to simply skip it if you're a bit short of time. Ask students to rewrite the five conversations from **1 Using vocabulary**, but changing the place names and some of the information to suit the place you're in. As they're writing, go round and check that they've understood and are writing sensible things down. After a few minutes, ask students to read the conversations out and monitor as above.

With stronger classes, skip the writing part and simply put students in new pairs and ask them to read the five conversations again, but adding local information.

3 Listening: What day are you travelling?

Tell the class they are going to hear a telephone conversation: Harry is an American visiting his friend, Michael, in London. They're planning a trip to Scotland. Michael phones National Rail Enquiries to check times and prices. Tell the class to listen and to complete the table.

Play the conversation once all the way through. Give students a minute or two to compare their ideas in pairs and then elicit the answers from the class. Write them on the board.

Answers

The earliest train from London Kings Cross to Edinburgh arrives at ten past eleven (11.10). The last train back leaves Edinburgh at seven in the evening (19 hundred hours). Return tickets for this train are £94.50.
The earliest Saver Return from London to Edinburgh leaves at 10.15 in the morning and gets in to Edinburgh at 15.05 (five past three in the afternoon). That ticket costs £83.20 return.

Tell the class they are now going to hear Michael and Harry discussing this information. Ask the class to listen and find out what train they decide to take.

Play the conversation once all the way through.

Give students a minute or two to compare their ideas in pairs and then elicit the answer from the class. You probably don't need to write it on the board, just make sure the class hears it. As you're eliciting the answer, ask if the class heard why Harry and Michael decided this.

Answers

They decide to get the 6.15 from Kings Cross, the one that gets in to Edinburgh at ten past 11 in the morning. (The Saver Return takes quite a long time. They're going to lose half the day if they take it. The earlier train is only ten pounds more expensive.)

4 Listen again

Tell the class they are going to hear the telephone conversation again and that this time you want them to listen and complete the sentences by writing the words they hear in the gaps. There is only ONE word missing from each sentence. With stronger classes, ask the student to read the six sentences first and see if they remember or can guess the missing words. They then listen just to check their ideas. Otherwise play the phone conversation again and then give the students a minute to compare their ideas with a partner. You may want to elicit the answers immediately or you may want to play the conversation one more time and stop after each gap. Students then call out their answers. Write them on the board. As you do so, drill **1–6**.

Answers

1. help   2. check   3. station   4. travel   5. train   6. last

5 Role play

Explain the task and then put the class into pairs. Student A reads their role-play card on page 160 and Student B reads their on page 158. Give students three or four minutes to read their cards and ask any questions they may have. You might then want to let them read the **Tapescript** of the telephone conversation on page 133 and underline any expressions they think they will need to use.

Next, ask students to role-play the conversation the task in pairs. It's a good idea to put the pairs back to back, so they can't see each other's faces, like in a real phone conversation. You could start the activity by making the noise of a phone ringing. Monitor and check for mistakes, particularly any errors in the language you've just taught. When most pairs have finished, round up in the usual way.

You could then ask students to swap roles and have the conversation again, but this time using the language you've just worked through on the board.

With weaker classes, you may need to give students the chance to prepare for the role-play a bit more. You could ask students to write the phone conversation in pairs first and to then try to memorise it for the actual role-play.

6 Using grammar: superlatives

If you can, use some corrections from the last activity to lead into this one. In **5 Role play**, students may have said things like: *What's the more early train?* or *The most early train is …* . If they did, write this on the board and see if any students can correct it.

Another way you could lead in is to write the following on the board:
What's … train to Edinburgh?

Elicit the question students heard in the conversation. Elicit / give *What's the earliest train to Edinburgh?*

Alternatively, simply ask students to read the short explanation in the book and see if anyone has any questions. Explain the task and do the first one with the class. Get students to do the rest individually. Monitor and help with any problems. Elicit the answers from the class and write them on the board.

Answers
1. the cheapest   2. the biggest   3. the best
4. the earliest   5. the most difficult   6. the quickest

Go through any new language. For example:
- *Snobs* is the name of a restaurant.
- *BA* is short for British Airways. *Mod-air* isn't a real company; it's a made-up name.
- *Cardiff* is the capital city of Wales.

As you elicit the answer to **5**, ask the class how many syllables *difficult* has (three) and remind them that that's why we say *most difficult*, not ~~difficultest~~! All the other adjectives here have one or two syllables.

Ask students to read **Grammar Note G21** on page 141.

If you have time, ask students to read the conversations out in pairs. As they do so, go round and listen to their pronunciation, correcting and remodelling things for them if they need it. Make sure students are using the weak form of *the* /ðə/.

7 What's the best … ?

Tell students you're going to look at eight useful questions using the superlative form of *good – the best*. Explain the task and do the first one with the class to model it. Give students a few minutes and then let them compare their ideas in pairs. Elicit the answers from the class and either write them on the board or else simply make sure you repeat them clearly enough for everyone to hear. Drill each question as you come to it.

Answers
1. What's the best place to eat in town?
2. What's the best time to phone you?
3. What's the best place in town to stay?
4. What's the best time of year to visit?
5. What's the best place to go shopping?
6. What's the best university to study at?
7. What's the best way to get to your house?
8. What're the best places to visit while I'm here?

As you're eliciting the questions, you could also ask the class for possible answers to each one and write on the board anything they struggle with. For example:
Teacher: *And a possible answer to number 2?*
Student: *Some times from 6.*
Teacher: *Yes, OK.* (writing on the board) *Anytime after 6.*

Teacher: *And a possible answer to number 4?*
Student: *September, October. Not hot!*
Teacher: *Yes, OK.* (writing on board) *The autumn. It's not so hot then. The weather's nice and cool.*

Explain the role-play and put students into pairs. Monitor and check for mistakes, particularly any errors in the language you've just taught. When most pairs have finished, round up in the usual way.

You could then ask students to swap roles and have the conversation again, but this time, using the language you've just worked through on the board.

For homework, ask students to write a conversation like the one they had in **7 What's the best … ?** Tell them to try to add more information to their answers and to continue the conversation further if they can. They could compare the conversations they have written in pairs at the start of the next lesson and see if they can find any mistakes in their partner's writing. You could then collect the conversations and read them. Correct any mistakes with things already studied in class and give students better ways of saying new things that they're trying to say.

Reading

If you are starting a new lesson, begin with a bit of revision. Ask students to repeat the role-play at the end of **7 What's the best … ?** on page 101, but with a new partner. Alternatively, you could do an activity from **Unit 21** of the **Teacher's Resource Book**.

Finally, ask students to look at the **Language strip** on page 100, if you haven't done so already, and ask them to underline all the expressions that came up in the previous lesson. Do they know what the others mean? Help the students with any they don't know.

1 Speaking

This activity leads in to the reading by generating interest and giving students the chance to talk, but it also gives them more exposure to comparatives in use.

Explain the task. You might need to give your own answer for the first one to model the task. After a minute or two, put students in pairs to compare their choices. You could begin (or finish) the activity by telling the class your own choices and saying a bit about each one. This is a short lead-in task, so you don't need to spend a long time on it or do much feedback.

2 While you read

Explain the task. Do the text as a listening, a reading or both, (see **Introduction** for procedure). When students have finished listening / reading, ask them to discuss the answers to the two questions in pairs for two minutes. Then elicit the answers from the class.

Answers

1. People are complaining about the government's plans to expand Heathrow and Stanstead airports, (two of the biggest airports in London). They say the planes already make too much noise, they cause too much pollution and air travel is already too cheap and easy. They think the government should be making air travel more expensive and difficult instead!

You could point to the picture on the right-hand side of page 103 and explain these people are *on a demo* (or *demonstration*), *protesting against the plans*. You could also ask if anyone in the class has been on a demo and what they were protesting against.

2. The writer disagrees with them – and agrees with the government. The writer thinks it's good to travel as much as possible and enjoys going to different countries as cheaply as possible!

Go through any new language. For example:
- *Presented its plans* – the government makes plans for new laws and then presents (shows) *them to Parliament*. Parliament then decides if they want to *pass them* or not. Point out the stress – preSENT.
- *Complaining* – to say you're not happy about something. You could point out you complain *about* things and *to* people.
- *They cause a lot of pollution* – draw a factory with some big industrial chimneys and lots of smoke pouring out. You could also draw a pipe going into a nearby river and lots of stuff coming out of it.
- *Went abroad* – went to another country.
- *In fact* – we mainly use this in written English when we're going to mention something new and surprising.
- *Even* – it used here to emphasise and show you're surprised. You could give a couple more examples: *I can't swim at all, not even a little bit! He can't read, not even in his own language.*
- *Back then* – in the time you've just been talking about. Give another example: *I grew up in the 1980s and things were very different back then.*

- *Nowadays* means now, often used to contrast the past with now: *In the past, young people were more polite, but nowadays some kids are really rude.*
- You *check in at an airport or at a hotel* – tell them you've arrived, got your room key, etc.
- *It really is a small world* – this is a stronger way to say *It's a small world.*
- *It's a small world!* – this is a fixed expression we often use when we bump into someone we know in an unexpected place or when we find out that someone we're talking to knows a friend of ours. It means *Wow! What a coincidence!* Here, it also means that the world is getting smaller because we can travel so easily.

3 Speaking

You could discuss these questions with the class or ask students to discuss them in small groups. Give students a couple of minutes to read the questions and to think about / plan what they want to say. Let them use dictionaries or ask you if they need to. Next, give students a few minutes to discuss the questions. Round up in the usual way.

4 Using grammar: talking about changes

This activity looks at one particular use of the present perfect, but also allows students yet another opportunity to encounter comparatives in action as well. To lead in, write the following sentence from the text on the board:
Tickets have got a lot cheaper.

Underline the verb part in the sentence. Tell students they have studied this structure before and ask if they can remember its name, (the present perfect). Ask what time it's talking about, (from the past to now). Then ask if the class can remember the time expression that was used with it, *since my grandparents were young*. Tell the students that here *have got* has nothing to do with the other meaning of *have got* – *I've got 2 older sisters, He's got a new car*, etc.

Ask students to read the explanation and then explain the task. Do the first one with the students and then ask them to do the rest. After two or three minutes, let students compare their ideas in pairs and then elicit the answers and drill the present continuous sentences as you do so.

Answers

1. taller   2. cheaper   3. easier   4. more expensive
5. better   6. thinner

Go through any new language. For example:
- *He's grown* – ask what the 's means. (Has.) And ask the name of this structure. (Present perfect.) Ask why – it's talking about the time from the past to now.
- *More expensive* – you could ask why we say *more expensive* and not *expensiver* – because it's a 3-syllable adjective.
- *The food's so bad I never eat* – this is a common way of talking about cause and effect in spoken English. The first part of the sentence is the problem; the second the result. You could give more examples: *It was so cold I nearly died! I was so tired I fell asleep in the meeting!*

You could also ask students to underline the time expressions in the six expressions. Ask what the expressions are and then drill them. The expressions are: *over the last year, over the last couple of years, over the last few months, over the last few years, since I came to Ireland, since I came here*. Remind the class that we usually use the present perfect with these expressions.

5 | Practice

You could ask students to read **Grammar note** G22 on page 141 before they try this activity. Give students a few minutes to write. You might want to make this a bit easier by eliciting ideas for the first one from the class. As they're writing, go round and check that they've understood and are writing sensible endings down.

Then put students into pairs and give them a couple more minutes to compare their ideas. You don't need to spend a long time on feedback, but discuss any problems or common errors that you came across as you were monitoring.

6 | Pronunciation: silent 't'

To lead in, write on the board: *the worst place* and ask the class what happens to the pronunciation when they say the words together quickly. If no-one guesses correctly, refer them to the explanation.

Model the eight expressions yourself or use the recording as a model. Ask students to repeat the expressions. Make sure students aren't pronouncing the 't'. Remodel it for them if necessary. You could ask if students can see a connection between all the expressions here and then tell them that when one word ends in 't' and the next starts with a consonant, the 't' is often not pronounced.

Explain the last task. Play the recording of the eight sentences. Pause at the end of each sentence to give students time to write. Ask students to compare their answers in pairs and then play the eight sentences one more time.

Let students compare again before you elicit the answers and write them on the board. Play each sentence and pause after each as you do so. Alternatively, just let students compare their ideas with the **Tapescript** on page 133. Ask students to practise saying the sentences to each other. Monitor for any pronunciation problems and correct them.

Homework
You could tell the class to do **Unit 20** in the **Workbook** for homework, if you haven't done so already.

You could also ask them to write a couple of paragraphs about either how their lives are different from their grandparents or else about the way in which their country has changed over the last few years. Tell them to use the language from this lesson to help them.

Collect the writing next lesson and correct it. Correct any mistakes with things already studied in class and give students better ways of saying new things that they're trying to say.

Unit overview

General topic
Describing people

Conversation
Two telephone conversations about what people are like.

Reading
She's famous!

Language input
- Describing people: *She's really fit.*
- *What's he / she like? What's her husband like?*
- The past continuous: *I was staying in a hotel and he was staying there too.*
- Pronunciation: sentences stress and weak forms

Language strip
Ignore the **Language strip** to begin with and deal with the language as it comes up in various activities. Come back to it later as revision. Alternatively, tell students to learn the expressions for homework.

Lead in
Do one of the following:
- Put the class in pairs and ask them to write down as much as they can remember about the text on page 103, *It's a small world*. Round up all the ideas from your group and correct students' language, using as much of the language from the text as you can.
- In pairs, students see how many of the eight questions with the word *best* from **7 What's the best ... ?** on page 101 they can remember. After rounding up how much they remember, give them one minute to look back at the questions. They then ask these questions in pairs, giving new answers.
- Do one of the **Teacher's Resource Book** activities from **Unit 21**.
- Test the students on the expressions in the **Language strip** on page 100. Give students two minutes to look at the **Language strip** and remember as much as they can. They can ask you questions during this time. Ask students to close their books, then put them into two teams. If you can, use L1 to test them on different expressions, draw them on the board or act them out. The first person to call out the correct expression wins a point for their team.
- Ask students to look at the **Expressions Organiser** for **Units 19** and **20** on page 155. Ask students to translate the expressions in pairs then check their ideas. Students can then test each other by saying a translation, acting it out or drawing a picture, while their partner guesses. To make this easier, let both students look at page 155.

Conversation

1 | Using vocabulary: describing people

One way you could lead into this unit is to write on the board: *She's really nice, really friendly* and ask the class: *This is the answer, what's the question?* Students will probably say things like *How about her?* or *How is she?* Point out the unit title and tell the class it means *Tell me about her – what kind of person is she?* Don't try to explain the grammar. It's better here just to teach this question as a whole and to make sure students understand what it means. If you can, give an L1 translation of the whole question.

Tell the class that the first activity is going to help them answer this kind of question better.

Tell students to look at the six pictures, and drill the descriptions. As you drill each word, ask a few extra questions or give a bit of extra information to make sure students understand the words. For example: *So, if you're really fit, you do a lot of ... ?* (exercise). *And if you're boring, what kind of things do you talk about all the time? And if you're really funny, you're always making people ... ?* (laugh). *And you're good at telling ... ?* (jokes).

You could start (or finish) the speaking task by telling the class about someone you know who's like one of the people in the pictures. For each person you mention, try to add one or two comments saying a bit more about how the person is like this, as in the example given.
Put students in pairs and ask them to talk about anybody they know like these six people. Monitor and check for mistakes, particularly any errors in the language you've just taught. Round up in the usual way.

Explain the task and give students a minute or two to complete the first six sentences. Elicit the answers from the class and write them on the board. As you do so, deal with any new / interesting language.

Answers
1. fit   2. funny   3. creative   4. boring   5. shy
6. clever

Go through any new language. For example:
- *Cycles to work* – you might need to act this out. Ask the class: *So she gets to work by ... (bike / bicycle)?*
- *Tell really good jokes* – point out that you *tell* not *say* jokes. Ask what else you can *tell* – *lies, the truth, someone a story*, etc. Ask if anyone in the class is good at telling jokes. Maybe they could tell one now!
- *Shy* – if you want to, ask for / give the opposite here (*outgoing*).

Explain the next task and give students two or three minutes to complete **7–12**. Let them use dictionaries if they want to or ask you. Ask them to check in pairs before eliciting the answers from the class and writing them on the board. Drill the new adjectives as you write them up.

Answers

7. quiet   8. lazy   9. easy to talk to
10. interesting   11. strange   12. horrible

Go through any new language. For example:

* *Quiet* – this is negative. It means she doesn't talk a lot and is quite hard to talk to. You could teach the opposites, too – *very talkative / chatty / easy to talk to*.
* *Lazy* – act out a lazy person lounging round the house, doing nothing!
* *Easy to talk to* – she's good to talk to if I have problems or need advice. You could teach the opposite – *hard / difficult to talk to*.
* *Interesting* – ask for the opposite – *boring*.
* *Strange* – you could ask for other examples of what people do if they're *strange*. You could also teach a common synonym – *weird*.
* *My old boss* – refer students to the **Real English** note.
* *Horrible* – you could ask what bosses do if they're horrible: *shout at staff, get angry a lot, not pay you on time*, etc.

You could remind students that all 12 sentences are answers to *What's he / she like?* Ask if they noticed the word used to make both positive and negative adjectives stronger (*really*).

Give students a minute to choose which adjectives they think describe themselves and then let them compare with a partner to see if they agree. As a twist on this, put students in pairs and ask them to make two lists – words they think describe themselves and words that describe their partner. They can then compare lists! You could extend this by giving students a minute or two more to find two more adjectives in their dictionaries that they think describe themselves or other people in the class! Check their adjectives make sense and that students are using them in ways that sound appropriate to you.

2 | Using grammar: *What's she like?*

Tell students they're going to look at some more questions asking about people's personalities – asking what people are like. Give the class a minute to read the short explanation and example and to ask any questions if they want to. Explain the task and give the class a minute or two to do the matching exercise. Elicit the answers from the class and write them on the board. As you do so, you might want to ask students how they know. All of the language in this activity has been presented before, so it shouldn't pose too many problems.

Answers

1. d.   2. e.   3. c.   4. f.   5. b.   6. a.

Tell the class they're going to ask each other these six questions. Give them a couple of minutes to prepare. If you want to, let students ask you some of these questions first. Try to give honest answers. Give students a few minutes talking time and then round up in the usual way. You may need to write up things like this:
A: *My dad's d......, actually. He d....... last year.*
B: *Oh no! I'm so sorry to hear that.*

3 | Listening: *What's she like?*

Tell the class you're going to play them two different conversations and that in each one they will hear descriptions of what people are like. Tell them to listen and to try to write down who they're talking about in each conversation. You could also ask them to note down anything else they hear about the two people.

Play the conversations once all the way through. Give students a minute or two to compare their answers in pairs. Round up what they have and if the whole group between them can provide the answers, don't play the conversations again. If they only have a few of the answers, play the conversations again, pausing after each one.

Answers

1. Colin's telling Jim about his new neighbours.
2. Emily's telling her mum about her brother Jon's new girlfriend.

Ask if students can remember which adjectives from **1 Using vocabulary** each person uses. If the class can tell you most of the adjectives, move on, but if they're struggling, play the conversations again and ask the class to listen out for which adjectives are used. Elicit answers from the class and ask if students heard in what way (how) the people were like this. Don't expect all students to be able to answer this and reformulate anything they come up with.

Answers

Conversation 1: Colin's new neighbours are *horrible*. They're really noisy. They play really loud music at night! Colin can't sleep. They're also *not very easy to talk to*: when Colin complained about the noise, the father threatened to kill him! Colin's old neighbours were *strange*, but at least they were *quiet*!

Conversation 2: Emily's brother Jon has got a new girlfriend. She's very *interesting* and very *creative*: she works in an art gallery and she likes painting. Emily thinks her brother is really *boring*: he's not interested in art at all.

4 | Listen again

Tell the class they are going to hear Conversation 2 again, between Emily and her mum. This time you want them to listen and complete the conversation by writing the words they hear in the gaps. Tell them they might need to write 2, 3 or 4 words in the gaps. Play the conversation and then give the students a minute to compare their ideas with a partner. You may want to elicit the answers immediately or play the conversation one more time and stop after each gap. Students then call out their answers. Write them on the board. As you do so, deal with any new / interesting language.

Answers

1. It's me
2. how are things
3. a couple of
4. a new girlfriend
5. what's she like
6. very creative

Go through any new language. For example:

- *It's me* – this is the normal way of telling friends on the phone who's calling. Give some more examples: *Hello. / Oh hiya. It's me, Yukako.* In more formal calls, we often say: *This is Maria-Jesus Garcia.*
- *Dear* – older people often call people they love or are good friends *Dear*.
- *So how're things?* is another way of asking *How's it going?* Both expressions are a bit more informal than *How're you?* They're usually used by younger people to good friends.
- *He never tells me anything* – about his private life. Give some examples: *My son is 19 now and he has his own life. I don't know where he goes or who he sees. He never tells me anything*.

Now ask students to look at the **Tapescript** on page 133–4. Put students in pairs and ask them to practise reading the conversation, paying particular attention to stressing the sounds in capital letters and pausing where there are spaces between groups of words. You could read out a couple of lines for them to model this or use the recording. Students can change roles once they finish. Go round and listen to their pronunciation, correcting and remodelling things for them if they need it.

5 Practice

If you are short of time, set this writing activity for homework.

Alternatively, ask students to find a new partner and spend a couple of minutes choosing a conversation to write and underlining any language from Activities **1–4** that they'd like to use. Give students 6–8 minutes to write their conversations. As they're writing, go round and check that they've understood and are writing sensible things down. Help students formulate things they're trying to say.

You could ask students to swap their conversations and look for mistakes or round up by looking at a few common mistakes on the board and feeding in any new language students were looking for.

Put students into groups of four and ask them to read their conversations out. The other pair listening could respond afterwards using *He / She sounds … .*

For homework, ask students to write another telephone conversation like the one they wrote in **5 Practice**. To make this harder for the class, ask them to try to write their conversation without looking at the Coursebook. They could compare their conversations in pairs at the start of the next lesson and see if they can find any mistakes in their partner's writing. You could then collect the conversations and read them. Correct any mistakes with things already studied in class and give students better ways of saying new things that they're trying to say.

Reading

If you are starting a new lesson, begin with a bit of revision. Ask students to repeat the practice at the end of **2 Using grammar** on page 105, but with a new partner. Alternatively, do an activity from **Unit 22** of the **Teacher's Resource Book**.

Finally, ask students to look at the **Language strip** on page 104, if you haven't done so already, and ask them to underline all the expressions that came up in the previous lesson. Do they know what the others mean? Help the students with any they don't know.

1 Speaking

This activity leads in to the reading by generating interest and giving students the chance to talk. Give students a minute or two to read the questions and to ask any questions if they need to. Then put students in pairs and give them a further three or four minutes talking time. Round up in the usual way. It's probably a good idea to ask students if they know who any of the people in the pictures are: don't worry if they don't or if they get the wrong person! This is just an activity to generate interest.

2 While you read

Explain the task. Do the text as a listening, a reading or both, (see **Introduction** for procedure). When students have finished listening / reading, ask them to discuss the answers to the two questions in pairs for three or four minutes. Then elicit the answers from the class. Don't expect students to be able to repeat the whole stories without looking at the text, but try to get the basics of each story. Good classes may also come up with some of the ideas in brackets.

Answers

The person in the first picture is (the late) Princess Diana. Michael saw her once in a car. (He was driving through London when suddenly a big black car and lots of police cars came past, going the other way. Princess Di was in the back of the big black car.)

The person in the second picture is Michael Foot – he was a famous British politician. Andrew met him at Nottingham University. (He presented all the students with their degrees when they graduated. He shook his hand!)

The person in the third picture is Hidetoshi Nakata, a famous Japanese footballer. Shunsuke saw him in Oxford Street, London. (He was walking down the road and saw Nakata coming out of a shop.)

The person in the fourth picture is Ben Kingsley, a famous British actor. Isobel met him at a wedding. (He was a family friend of the bride.)

The person in the fifth picture is Craig. He didn't meet someone famous – he WAS famous for a few days! (He got stuck on a mountain in the Faroe Islands, a group of islands north of Scotland. His story got into the local paper.)

Ask the class which story they think is best and why. You may want to do a quick class vote.

3 Vocabulary focus

Explain the task and put the students in pairs. Give them a couple of minutes to read the words. Go through any new language. For example:

- *Shouted out* – act this out! Give examples of things you can shout out – the answer, someone's name, etc.
- *Real life* – not in films or on TV. Give another example: *He's great in all his films and I'm sure he's great in real life as well!*
- A *speech* – you *give a speech* on formal occasions. Ask for / give examples of when – wedding receptions, goodbye parties, etc.
- *Leader* – ask for / give examples of leaders of local political parties.
- A *crowd* – draw one.
- *Star* – a famous person, especially from TV, the movies or sports.
- An *Oscar* – a famous American award for the best film, best actor, etc.
- A *Bride* is the woman on the day she gets married. The man is called the *groom*.
- *Got stuck* – couldn't move / leave. Ask for / give examples of where people *get stuck*: in lifts, in traffic, in a tunnel, etc.
- *The front page* – of a newspaper. Ask what's usually *on the front / back page*.

Ask students to discuss how they think these words were used without looking at the text. As they do so, go round and listen and help out. When they've finished, ask students to check their ideas against the text. They might want to underline the parts of the text that give the answers. Then elicit the answers from the class. You don't need to write the answers on the board, but repeat the whole expressions.

Answers

Michael shouted out of his car window, 'Lady Di, I love you'!
Princess Diana looked better in real life than in photos.

Michael Foot was the leader of the Labour Party.
He gave a speech at Nottingham University.

Shunsuke saw a big crowd of people.
Hidetoshi Nakata was the biggest football star in Japan.

Ben Kingsley has won an Oscar.
He was a family friend of the bride.

Craig's knee got stuck between two rocks and he couldn't move.
His photo was on the front page of the national newspaper!

If you have time, ask the students to re-read the text and to ask you about any other language they're not sure of. If they have questions, try to answer them as best you can and give extra examples if possible.

4 Using grammar: past continuous

One way you could lead in to this activity is to write the following on the board:
I … down Oxford Street and I suddenly … a big crowd of people.

Tell students this is a sentence from Shunsuke's story. Ask if anyone can remember the missing words. If you want to, give them a clue and say they need to use the verbs see and *walk*, but to change the grammar. Elicit the answers and draw a timeline similar to that on page 107. Ask which action started first, the walking or the seeing, (the walking). Ask which action was the quick action, (the seeing). Tell the class the first verb form is called the past continuous and that they're going to look at how to use it.

Alternatively, ask students to read the examples and the short explanation in the book. Ask if anyone has any questions. Explain the task and do the first one with the class. Get students to do the rest individually. It's probably best to ask the class to try **2–10** all in one go. Monitor and help with any problems. After a few minutes, let students compare their ideas with a partner. Elicit the answers from the class and write them on the board. Drill the sentences as you do so, paying attention to the weak form of was /wəz/. It's also a good idea to reiterate the basic rule as you're going along by saying things like this:
Teacher: OK, so number 2?
Student: Was sitting.
Teacher: OK. Good. (Write it on the board.) *So, I sat down and then I was sitting and sitting and sitting and THEN he walked past – quite quickl. (Use the timeline to reinforce this concept.)*

Answers

1. were having
2. was sitting
3. was signing
4. was opening
5. was standing
6. was playing
7. was doing
8. was studying
9. was watching
10. was visiting

Go through any new language. For example:

- *Signing copies of his new book* – act this out. Ask what else you can sign – *cheques, till receipts, contracts*, etc.
- *Opening a new shop* – act out cutting a ribbon and say: *This shop is now open!* Ask if anyone famous has opened anything near where you are recently.
- *In a queue* – make sure you drill this /kjuː/, and explain it by acting or drawing. Ask where you usually get queues: *ticket offices, outside good restaurants / clubs*, etc.
- *I was out* – not at home.
- *Matlock* is a town in England.

Refer students to **Grammar note** G23 on page 141.

5 Practice

The first part of this activity is a relatively controlled practice context. Explain the task and tell students to work in pairs. Their examples don't have to be real. They can use their imagination. You could break the first part down into two sections and model the task by having the conversation with one of the better students first. For example:

Teacher: I met Michael Jordan once.
Student: Really? Where?
Teacher: I was working in a toy shop and he came in and bought some toys! OK, now you practise in pairs.

After two or three minutes, you could stop and deal with any grammar problems that you heard and then ask students to practise the second conversation, modelling it with a good student again if you want to. For example:

Teacher: I phoned you last night, but you didn't answer.
Student: Yes, sorry. I was sleeping!
Teacher: OK, now you practise.

You could discuss if anyone in the class has met anyone famous or put students into small groups to discuss this. Round up in the usual way.

6 Pronunciation: sentence stress and weak forms

Tell the students they're going to do some work on pronunciation and their listening skills. Explain what auxiliary verbs are by giving examples: I've never been there, I'm not hungry, etc. Let students read the explanation given and then drill the six sentences, either by modelling them yourself or else using the recording. Make sure students stress the sounds in capital letters and pause where there are spaces between groups of words. Correct and remodel things for them if they need it.

Explain the next task. Play the eight sentences, which students write down. Play them once, give students a chance to compare their ideas and then play them again, stopping after each one to elicit answers. Finally, look at the answers on page 134. If you want to, drill these sentences too or get students to repeat them in pairs.

Homework

You could tell the class to do **Unit 21** in the **Workbook** for homework, if you haven't done so already.

You could also ask them to write a paragraph about a time they saw / met a famous person. The stories don't have to be true, but it's always nice if some of them are! Tell them to use the texts on pages 106 and the language from this unit to help them.

Collect the writing next lesson and correct it. Correct any mistakes with things already studied in class and give students better ways of saying new things that they're trying to say.

Unit overview

General topic
Talking about houses and moving house.

Conversation
A woman visits at a friend's home for the first time.

Reading
Moving house

Language input
- Using *Could I ... ?* to ask for something: *Could I have one too?*
- Paying compliments: *What a lovely house! It's really big.*
- Describing your house: *It's got two bedrooms.*
- Describing the area you live in: *It's very central.*

Language strip
Ignore the **Language strip** to begin with and deal with the language as it comes up in various activities. Come back to it later as revision. Alternatively, tell students to learn the expressions for homework.

Lead in
Do one of the following:
- Get students to do one of the activities in Unit 22 of the **Teacher's Resource Book**.
- Test the students on the expressions in the **Language strip** on page 104. Give students two minutes to look at the **Language strip** and remember as much as they can. They can ask you questions during this time. Ask students to close their books, then put them into two teams. If you can, use L1 to test them on different expressions, draw them on the board or act them out. The first person to call out the correct expression wins a point for their team.
- Ask students to look at the **Expressions Organiser** for **Units 21** and **22** on page 156. Ask students to translate the expressions in pairs then check their ideas. Students can then test each other by saying a translation, acting it out or drawing a picture while their partner guesses. To make this easier, let both students look at page 156.
- Look back at **Review: Units 1–6**, page 34 and ask students to underline any vocabulary they've forgotten. Then ask students to repeat the conversation practice. This is a way of revising some of the house-related vocabulary that students have already met.

Conversation

1 | Listening: *Come in*

You may want to do a quick discussion as a lead-in to this task, if you haven't done any of the previous warmers. Ask students who has the nicest flat or house out of all the people they know. What do they like about it?

Explain the context and task. Play the conversation once all the way through. Give students a minute or two to compare their answers in pairs. Round up what they have and if the whole group between them can provide the answers, don't play the conversation again. If they only have a few of the answers, play the conversation again, pausing after each one.

> **Answers**
> 1. She thinks it's great and it's quite big.
> 2. She comments on a room and a painting.

2 | Listen again

Tell the class they are going to hear the conversation again and that this time you want them to listen and complete the conversation by writing the words they hear in the gaps. Tell them they might need to write 2, 3 or 4 words in the gaps. Play the conversation and then give the students a minute to compare their ideas with a partner. You may want to elicit the answers immediately or play the conversation one more time and stop after each gap. Students then call out their answers. Write them on the board. As you do so, deal with any new / interesting language.

> **Answers**
> | | |
> |---|---|
> | 1. take your coat | 5. very light |
> | 2. great flat | 6. I love |
> | 3. Almost a year | 7. could I have |
> | 4. sit down | 8. I won't be long |

Go through any new language. For example:
- *Come in* – act opening the door and gesturing *Come in* to someone.
- *Come through* – students may ask the difference with *Come in*. There is no big difference, but *Come in* is more usual at the door, and *come through* from the door (through the corridor) to a room.
- *What a great flat!* – draw attention to the pattern *What a + adjective + noun*. Give / elicit some more examples.
- *Gosh* – this is a way of showing surprise, like *Really?* Younger British people may say *God* or some other swear word instead. It's up to you whether you teach these to your students or not.
- *Very light* – the room has a big window. It gets a lot of sun. You could elicit the opposite (*very dark*).

113

- *Kettle* – draw a picture. You could ask: *What do you use it for?* and elicit / give *boil or heat water.* We often say *The kettle's boiled.* If students say *make tea* or *soup*, you might want to contrast it with *a teapot* or *saucepan.*
- *Recharge my mobile* – you could demonstrate if you have a mobile and then ask why you need to do it, (*the battery's low / dead*).
- *I won't be long* – *won't* means *will not.* We usually use *will* when we promise (not) to do something. Give other examples: *Can I borrow some money? I'll pay you back tomorrow. I'll be back by 6, I promise. I won't be late, I swear.*

As a follow-up, ask students to read the conversation to each other, although the lesson contains other reading aloud activities.

With stronger groups, you could ask them to practise the conversation, but every time someone asks a question the other student should give a different reply to the one in the text. For example:
F: Shall I take your coat?
G: No, it's OK. I'm fine for the moment.

You might want to get students to write the different answers in pairs first and then perform the new conversation to another pair of students.

3 | Using grammar: *Could I ... ?*

Write: *... use your phone?* on the board. Ask students if they remember how Gail asked the question in the conversation. Write: *Could I ...* on the board and drill the whole question. Tell the students they're going to look at some more examples of these questions and the kinds of conversations we use them in. Explain the task and ask students to do it in pairs. Elicit the answers from the class and write them on the board. As you do so, drill the questions and expressions.

Answers

1. have some tea
2. use your toilet
3. have some milk
4. use your phone
5. leave my bag somewhere

Explain the use of *will* for offers and promises. Ask students to decide if the examples are an offer, (*I'll put the kettle on / I'll put it in my room*) or a promise, (*I won't be long*). You could ask students to translate the sentences. Do they use the same tense in their language?

You could ask them to memorise the conversations for a few minutes and then ask students to do them again with their books closed.

4 | Practice

Write the following on the board:
A: have something / eat?
B: Yes. / I / make / a sandwich / if you like.
OR:
B: Yes. / some bread and things / cupboard.

Elicit the complete question: *Could I have something to eat?* and the choice of replies: *Yes, of course. I'll make you a sandwich, if you like. / Yes, of course. There's some bread and things in the cupboard.* Then ask students to write similar conversations with a partner using the ideas in the practice activity. As students write, go round and monitor and help out where necessary.

After a few minutes, get pairs to swap what they've written and check each other's writing for mistakes or simply check the answers by eliciting from the class.

Possible answers

1. A: Could I wash some my clothes?
   B: Yes, of course. I'll do it, if you like!
   A: Really? Thanks.
2. A: It's raining. Could I borrow an umbrella?
   B: Yes, of course. I'll go and get it.
   A: Thanks. I'll give it back to you tomorrow.
3. A: I haven't got any money. Could I borrow £10?
   B: Yes, of course.
   A: Thanks. I'll pay you back tomorrow.

Students then practise reading these conversations out in pairs. As they do so, go round and listen to their pronunciation, correcting and remodelling things for them if they need it.

As an extension, ask students to ask some other questions with *Could I ... ?* Students can reply in similar ways to the examples. Monitor and check for mistakes, particularly any errors in the language you've just taught. Round up in the usual way.

Refer students to **Grammar note** G24 on page 141.

5 | Speaking

Explain or translate what *compliment* means. Get students to discuss the questions in small groups or as a class. You could give your own answers first as a model.

This is a short lead-in task to the activities on complimenting people, so you don't need to give much feedback.

6 | Complimenting people

Ask the students what Fiona complimented Gail on in the conversation. Ask the students if they remember the three things that Fiona actually said. Elicit: *What a great flat, I love this painting* and *This is a very nice room.* Write them on the board. Tell the students to look at the other examples in the Coursebook. Point out the difference between the two *what* expressions: the second is before a plural noun and so doesn't have 'a'.

Explain the task. You could give examples by using two of the complimenting expressions you wrote on the board and asking the class to convert them into *What* sentences. Students can work individually or in pairs.

Play the recording for students so that students can check their answers. Tell them to notice the intonation. Either pause the recording after each 'What …' expression and ask students to repeat it or play the recording all the way through and then ask students to tell you the answers, correcting their pronunciation / intonation as they do so.

> **Answers**
>
> 1. What a great flat!
> 2. What a great kitchen!
> 3. What lovely shoes!
> 4. What a brilliant photo!
> 5. What a fantastic shirt!
> 6. What lovely flowers!

Before students practise in pairs, go through any new language. For example:
- *They really suit you* means they look good on you. You could give examples of clothes / colours / styles which suit you and don't suit you. Ask some students what suits / doesn't suit them.
- *Who took it?* – point out that you *take* a photo, not *make* one.
- *Where did you get it?* – *get* here means *buy*.

Ask students to practise the conversations in pairs. Monitor and correct any problems with pronunciation or with the language just taught. Students may not always have good replies. Let the students read the **Tapescript** on page 134 and listen to the recording again, if you like. They could then swap roles and try again.

7 Practice

Explain the task. Ask students to read the examples and see if there's anything they don't understand. You could brainstorm any other questions they might want to ask, *What make is it? Was it very expensive?* etc. and which things they would ask questions about.

Put students in pairs to practise the conversations. Monitor and check for mistakes, particularly any errors in the language you've just taught. Round up in the usual way.

For homework, ask students to write their own conversation like the one in **2 Listen again**. They could compare the conversations they have written in pairs at the start of the next lesson and see if they can find any mistakes in their partner's writing. You could then collect the conversations and read them. Correct any mistakes with things already studied in class and give students better ways of saying new things that they're trying to say.

Reading

If you are starting a new lesson, begin with a bit of revision. Ask students to repeat **4 Practice** on page 108, using the notes as a guide. Alternatively, do an activity from **Unit 23** of the **Teacher's Resource Book**.

Finally, ask students to look at the **Language strip** on page 108, if you haven't done so already and ask them to underline all the expressions that came up in the previous lesson. Do they know what the others mean? Help the students with any they don't know.

1 Using vocabulary: describing your house

Get the students to read the sentences and go through any new language. For example:
- *A spare* room is an extra room that you don't usually use. You can also have *a spare key* or *a spare pen*.
- *Huge* means very big.

> **Answers**
>
> A Sentences 2 (*front* garden) 4
> B Sentences 2 (through the window) 5
> C Sentences 2 (through the window) 6
> D Sentences 3 (through the window) 5, 11

Students may also argue for other sentences. You can be flexible about this. You could ask students to discuss which house they like most.

Ask students to decide individually which of the words and sentences they could use to describe their house or flat. Give them one or two minutes to do this. Then get students to ask each other the two questions.

Alternatively, get students to draw a plan of their house and then explain it. They should tell their partner what they like about the different rooms and what they don't like. Students could change partners once or twice. Whose house sounds the nicest?

2 Before you read

You could ask students to do this exercise in pairs or simply brainstorm ideas as a class. The aim of this task is both to lead in to the reading and to give you the chance to pre-teach some new language that may be useful for understanding the text. When students give their ideas, make sure you reformulate them into correct sentences.

3 While you read

Explain the task. Do the text as a listening, a reading or both, (see **Introduction** for procedure). When students have finished listening / reading, ask them to discuss the answers to the three questions in pairs for a few minutes. Then elicit the answers from the class.

> **Answers**
>
> 1. Luke and his partner, Mary, and their kids need a bigger place, so their children won't have to share a room.
> 2. It's bigger; it's got a spare room; it's got a small garden; it's in a nice area; it's convenient for the shops.
> 3. It's not very central; it's not very convenient for transport.

Before you move on to the role-play, ask the students if they have any other questions about the text.
Go through any new language. For example:
- *Central* means in or very near the city centre.
- *Convenient* means it's easy to get to or to use. It is near something. Give / elicit other examples: *convenient for the shops / work / the school*, etc.

Before you move on to the role-play, you could ask the students if they have any other questions about the text. You may need to explain:
- If you're *looking forward to* something you are going to do something in the future and you feel very happy and excited about it. Give a couple of examples: *I'm going to a party on Friday. I'm really looking forward it. I'm going to the dentist tomorrow. I'm not looking forward to it at all.*
- *Forever* means *all their lives*. Give some other examples: *I don't want to do this job forever.* Sometimes *forever* just means *a long time*. For example, *the traffic was terrible this morning. It took me forever to get to work.*
- *You're always welcome to stay / visit* – we'll be happy if you visit us. It doesn't matter when.

4 Role play (1)

You could introduce this task by writing on the board the following start to the conversation, or something similar (M = Mary and F = friend):
M: *Hello.*
F: *Hi Mary. It's me, ...*
M: *... ! Hi, how are you?*
F: *Great thanks. What about you?*
M: *OK, but I'm quite busy because we're going to move house next week.*
F: *...*

You could elicit the next line and then brainstorm some other questions you might ask if you were the friend. It's best not to have more than five questions. Keep the dialogue and questions you brainstormed on the board to re-use in **6 Role play (2)**. Now give students one or two minutes to find answers to the brainstormed questions in Luke's letter. If they can't find any, encourage them to invent the answer.

Put the students in pairs and ask them to practice the conversation. Go round the class and deal with any problems. One thing may be that the 'friend' doesn't use words like *Really?* or *Right* or *That sounds nice* to show interest in what Mary is saying. You could teach some of these and then ask the students to swap roles and repeat the task, this time showing more interest when they respond.

5 Using vocabulary: describing areas

You could lead into this by re-eliciting one of the good things about Mary and Luke's house in the text. When students say *convenient* you could ask for the opposite. Students may say *inconvenient*, which is not wrong, but we say *It's not very convenient.* more often. Explain the task and ask students to do it individually or in pairs. Elicit the answers from the class and write them on the board.

Answers
1. very convenient for the shops
2. very convenient for transport
3. very central
4. not very convenient for the shops
5. not very convenient for transport
6. not very central

Drill the *very / not very* expressions and point out some of the other language:
- *Round the corner* means *near here / there.*
- *The main square* means *the most important / the biggest. The main square* is usually in the centre of the city, where people might meet. Ideally, give examples from the place you live in.
- *It takes nearly an hour – nearly* means *almost.* Ask which means *nearly* – an hour, 55 minutes or 65 minutes?
- *Highgate* is an area in London.

6 Role play (2)

Use the conversation beginning and the questions you had on the board earlier from **4 Role play (1)**. Give students the role of A or B. Ask Student A to think where they're moving to and their own answers to the questions they thought of earlier. Ask Student B to memorise the questions and anything else they might want to say.

Give students a few minutes to do the role-play. Monitor and check for mistakes, particularly any errors in the language you've just taught. Round up in the usual way. Then ask students to swap roles and repeat the activity.

Homework
You could tell the class to do **Unit 22** in the **Workbook** for homework, if you haven't done so already.

You could also ask them to write a letter to a friend about a house they're going to move to. The letters don't have to be true, students can use their imagination and write about a place they'd like to move to. Tell them to use the letter on page 111 and the language from this unit to help them.

Collect the writing next lesson and correct it. Correct any mistakes with things already studied in class and give students better ways of saying new things that they're trying to say.

Unit overview

General topic
Celebrating

Conversations
Three different conversations in which people talk about their plans to celebrate good news.

Two people arrange to go out and celebrate some good news.

Reading
The big day

Language input
- Present continuous for the future: *I'm going out with some friends tonight.*
- Arranging to meet people: *Is 7 OK for you? I know the place you mean.*
- Pronunciation: sentence stress
- Relationships: *They were married for 35 years.*
- Making suggestions: *Why don't you buy her some flowers? How about some perfume?*

Language strip
Ignore the **Language strip** to begin with and deal with the language as it comes up in various activities. Come back to it later as revision. Alternatively, ask students to learn the expressions for homework.

Lead in
Do one of the following:
- Ask students to repeat the role-play in **6 Role play (2)**, page 111. Students can work with a new partner or reverse the roles they played last time. Give students one or two minutes planning time and ask them to try to use as much language from **Unit 23** as they can. Round up with a couple of corrections, or by correcting and writing any new language the students have produced on the board.
- Put the students in pairs and ask them to write down as much as they can remember about Luke's letter to his friend, Marcel, on page 111. Round up the ideas from the class and correct the student's language, using as much of the language from the text as you can.
- Do one of the **Teacher's Resource Book** activities from **Unit 23**.
- Test the students on the expressions in the **Language strip** on page 108. Give students two minutes to look at the **Language strip** and remember as much as they can. They can ask you questions during this time. Ask students to close their books, then put them into two teams. If you can, use L1 to test them on different expressions, or draw them on the board, or act them out. The first person to call out the correct expression wins a point for their team.

Conversation

1 Speaking

Tell the class that because it's nearly the end of the course, they might want to go out and celebrate soon! Explain we usually celebrate good news or special days like a birthday. Maybe we go out for dinner or go out for a drink. Put students in pairs and give them three minutes to note down as many different reasons for celebrating as they can think of. Tell them to look at the pictures on page 113 for some ideas. As they do so, monitor and check they are writing sensible ideas down. Elicit ideas from the class, reformulating them into better English where necessary and maybe writing some new vocabulary on the board. For example:

Student: Pass a driving license.

Teacher: Yes, OK. So I passed my driving test. Write this on the board. Any other reasons?

Next, ask students to read the two questions and the model answers and make sure they understand them. You might need to explain *went bowling* – act it out or draw a picture of some bowling pins and a bowling ball. Put students into pairs to chat about the questions for a few minutes. Round up in the usual way.

2 Listening: *Are you doing anything to celebrate?*

Tell students they are going to listen to three conversations in which people tell friends about their good news. Ask the class to listen and to answer the two questions about each conversation.

Play the conversations once all the way through. Give students a minute or two to compare their answers in pairs. Round up the answers, and if the whole group between them can provide the answers, don't play the conversations again. If they only have some of the answers, play the conversation again.

Answers

1. In conversation 1, he has got a new job (in a great school in Gateshead – it's in the north-east of England). In conversation 2, it's her birthday. She's 29. In conversation 3, he got his exam results this morning – he passed all his exams.
2. In conversation 1, they're going out to a bar in the town centre for a drink with some friends. In conversation 2, they're going out for dinner with a couple of friends (to a seafood place in Chinatown). In conversation 3, he's going to borrow his dad's car and meet some friends tonight. They're going to go up to the beach and have dinner. Then they might go to a disco.

Tell students they will have a chance to read the **Tapescript** of the conversations at a later stage and not to worry if they didn't understand every word, so long as they got the main ideas.

3 Using grammar: the present continuous for the future

Write the following sentences from the conversations on the board:

Are you doing anything to celebrate?
We're going to a seafood place in Chinatown.

Underline the structure in each sentence. Tell students they studied this structure in **Unit 12** and ask if they can remember its name. (The present continuous). Ask if it's talking about things happening at the moment. (No.) Then ask when is it talking about. (The future.) You could also ask: *So, is it talking about something you do on your own or something you've arranged to do with other people?* (An arrangement.)

Ask students to read the explanation and the other examples and then explain the task. Do the first one with the students and then ask them to do the rest. After a few minutes, let students compare their ideas in pairs and then elicit the answers, drilling the present continuous sentences as you do so.

> **Answers**
> 1. Are (you) doing, are going
> 2. Is (it still) raining
> 3. (I)'m looking
> 4. (We)'re meeting
> 5. (I)'m going, (I)'m, doing
> 6. (I)'m not feeling
> 7. (They)'re doing
> 8. are getting, are coming

Go through any new language. For example:

- *Going to Paris for the weekend* – if you go somewhere for the weekend, usually you leave on Friday night and come back on Sunday night. Ask if anyone has been anywhere for the weekend recently.
- *I'm afraid so* – here, it means it is raining. You could give another example: *Is your granddad going to be OK? I hope so.*
- *Some scissors* – act out using scissors or draw / point to some. Scissors are always plural, even if you're only talking about one; they're *some* or *a pair of scissors*. Drill it, pointing out the silent 'c'.
- *I'm doing something else tomorrow* – you could point out this is a good way of turning down an invitation you don't want to accept. Ask for other situations when you could use it.
- *The wedding* – when you *get married*, you have a *wedding*. It's the name of the celebration. Ask if anyone has been to any weddings recently. Whose? Was it *a big wedding* – with lots of people there – or *a small wedding*?

Next, tell students that 4 of the 8 sentences are about unfinished activities around now and 4 are about things people have arranged to do in the future. Give students a minute or two to decide which are which and ask them to compare their ideas with a partner.

Then elicit the answers from the class. As you do so, ask how students know and draw attention to time expressions like *tonight at 8 o'clock*, *tomorrow* and *next weekend*.

> **Answers**
> Talking about unfinished temporary activities around now: 2, 3, 6 and 7.
> Talking about things we've arranged to do in the future: 1, 4, 5 and 8.

Finish by asking students to read **Grammar note G25** on page 141.

4 Role play

Put the students into pairs. Tell students to read their role-play cards. Student A can choose one of the reasons for celebrating that you brainstormed at the start of the lesson. You might want to give students a few minutes to prepare and tell them to look back at Conversation 5 in **3 Using Grammar** to see one way of inviting someone. Demonstrate the task with a couple students. Take the part of Student A as this is more demanding and students will benefit from the model and support.

Ask students to do the task in pairs. Monitor and check for mistakes, particularly any errors in the language you've just taught. When most pairs have finished, stop the activity. Round up in the usual way.

Next, tell students they're going to do the role-play again, but that this time they'll change roles. First, however, ask them to look at the **Tapescript** on page 134 and underline any expressions in the three conversations that they'd like to use. You could provide some extra support by putting all the A's together and all the B's together before the second role-play and asking them to compare what they've underlined. Go round and check they've chosen useful, relevant expressions.

With stronger classes, tell students to memorise the expressions they want to use, while weaker students can simply read them from the book. As students do the role-play again, monitor and check for any mistakes, particularly any errors involving the language already looked at in this lesson.

5 Listening: *I'm just phoning to tell you about tonight*

Tell students they are going to hear the two people from Conversation 1 in **2 Listening** arranging their evening. You might want to ask what students can remember about the conversation – the new job in a great school in Gateshead, the plan to go out for a drink with some friends to celebrate and the invitation to join them. Tell them to listen and note down the answers to the two questions.

Play the conversation once all the way through. Give students a minute or two to compare their answers in pairs. Round up the answers and if the whole group between them can provide the answers, don't play the conversation again.

Answers

Stronger students may also have heard the extra information in brackets.

1. They're going to meet in a bar / pub called *The Social*. (It's in Black Prince Road, near the park. They're going to be in the upstairs bit).
2. They're going to meet at 8. (7 is suggested, but it's a bit early. He needs to go home and get changed first).

6 Vocabulary check

Tell students these nine sentences are all from the conversation and there is one word missing from each. Play the recording and give them a few minutes to try to complete the sentences individually before asking them to compare their ideas in pairs. It's best not to say if they're right or wrong yet.

Play the conversation again, either all the way through or else stopping after each gapped sentence. Elicit the correct answers from the class. Write them on the board. Alternatively, just let students read the **Tapescript** on page 135 as they listen a final time and thus check their own answers.

Answers

1. me, about   2. want   3. of, it   4. really, it
5. place   6. OK   7. bit, need   8. say   9. see

Go through any new language. For example:

*   *It's me* is the normal way to introduce yourself on the phone when you're calling a friend. You could also elicit / give other ways of starting phone calls: *Hello. / Hi. How're you? / Who's this? / It's me, Hugh*, etc.
*   *I'm just phoning to …* – point out we often use this sentence starter to explain the reason for our call. Give other examples of endings: *… see if you're OK / congratulate you on getting that job*, etc.
*   *We're thinking* means we haven't decided for sure yet, but this is our main idea.
*   *Again* – we often put *again* at the end of questions we think we should know the answer to. Give more examples – *Sorry, but what's your name again? Where do you live again?* etc.
*   *Get changed* – take these clothes off and put some different clothes on. Explain it's different from *get undressed*.
*   *Well, let's say* – give some other examples: *Shall we say 8 outside the station? Let's say six-thirty at my house, OK?*

7 Pronunciation: sentence stress

Tell students they're going to practise saying the conversation. Ask them to look at the **Tapescript** on page 135. Put students into pairs. Model the task for them by reading out the first couple of lines yourself, making sure you stress the sounds in capital letters and pause at each gap. Ask students to read the conversation. Monitor for any problems of pronunciation and correct. Listen particularly for stress, linking of words and intonation.

When students have finished, ask them to read the conversation silently to themselves whilst listening once more to the recording. They could then change roles and read it one final time.

For homework, ask students to write the conversation they had with their partner in **4 Role play**. Tell them to try to use as much of the language from this lesson as they can. They could compare the conversations they have written in pairs at the start of the next lesson and see if they can find any mistakes in their partner's writing.

Collect the conversations and read them. Correct any mistakes with things already studied in class and give students better ways of saying new things that they're trying to say. Alternatively, ask students to try to learn the conversation from **5 Listening** and **6 Vocabulary Check** and then test them in the next lesson.

Reading

If you are starting a new lesson, begin with a bit of revision. Ask students to try to repeat as much of the conversation from **5 Listening** and **6 Vocabulary Check** on page 113 as they can from memory. Alternatively, do an activity from **Unit 24** of the **Teacher's Resource Book**.

You could also ask students to repeat the role-play from **4 Role play** on page 113, but this time to walk around and have several different conversations with different students. They can choose to repeat one piece of good news and arrange to meet people in one place or they can change the good news and the place / time to meet for each new partner. Round up in the usual way.

1 Using vocabulary: relationships

One way you could lead in to this activity is to ask the class how many of them are married / have boyfriends or girlfriends. (Obviously, you need to be sure that your class won't mind you asking this kind of personal question before you do so.) Ask how long they've been together and how they met. If you haven't taught it already, this is also a good time to introduce the polite expression, *if you don't mind me asking?* If you can, let students use their own L1 when answering and translate what they're saying into English for them. You could write a few new things on the board for them.

You could also lead in to this activity by telling the class your own answers to the questions. Students generally tend to have a healthy interest in their teacher's private life!

Tell students that in this lesson they're going to learn how to have better conversations about relationships. Explain the first task. You might need to elicit / give the first answer as a model. Give students two or three minutes to try it individually. Let students compare their ideas, if you have time, before eliciting the answers from the class and write them on the board.

Answers

g. 1.   b. 2.   d. 3.   c. 4.   f. 5.   a. 6.   e. 7.

Students could argue that maybe *they had children* before *they got married*! Accept this if they do!

Go through any new language. For example:
- *Started going out together* – became boyfriend and girlfriend. If any of the students have a boyfriend or girlfriend, ask them: *How long've you two been going out together?*
- *Grew up* – live from when you are a child to when you're an adult. Give extra collocations: *I grew up in the countryside / in the 1990s*, etc. You could ask students where they / their parents grew up.
- *Left home* – moved out of their parents house into a place of their own. You could also teach, *I still live at home* (with my parents). You could ask how many of the class still live at home and when the rest left home.
- *A dance* – like an old-fashioned disco. Maybe the men asked the women to dance – for one or two songs.

Next, ask the class to cover **a–g** and to try to complete the story in the box by adding the correct missing words; one word in each gap. You might want to let weaker students look at **a–g** if they need to. After a few minutes, let students compare in pairs. Elicit the answers from the class and write them on the board. Drill any new or problematic language as you do so.

> **Answers**
>
> 1. met   2. going   3. got   4. had   5. grew   6. left
> 7. were   8. died

Go through any new language. For example:
- *Over 60 years ago* means more than 60, so maybe 62 or 63 or 64 years ago.
- To *start a family* means to have children.
- Anymore – in the past we did, but now we don't. Give other examples: *I smoked for 15 years, but I don't anymore. I stopped a few years ago*, etc.
- *Sadly* is used to introduce sad, depressing news: *Sadly, I won't be teaching you next term. Sadly, he died last year.*

2 Practice

You could discuss these questions with the class or ask students to discuss them in small groups. You could start off by talking about a few couples you know as a model. Give students a few minutes to prepare. Let them use dictionaries, or ask you if they need to. Tell them to think about how they're going to use some of the language from **1 Using vocabulary** and give them any new language they're looking for, maybe write some of it on the board. Next, give students a few minutes to tell each other about the couples they know. Round up in the usual way.

3 Before you read

Tell the class they're going to read an article about two weddings in Britain. First, discuss the three questions. It might be best to do this with the class, especially if the students are quite young and don't have much experience of going to weddings. This is a short lead-in task, so you don't need to spend a long time on it or do much feedback. However, if students have problems trying to say things in English, help them and write the new language on the board, ideally in whole sentences. If you are short of time, you might just want to get students to ask you the questions. Answer them truthfully, if possible.

4 While you read

Explain the task. If you have some students who have never been to a wedding, tell them not to worry and to simply put exclamation marks next to anything that surprises them.

Go through any new language. For example:
- *Get divorced* – act out throwing a wedding ring away and make a snapping movement with your hands. It's the opposite of getting married. Point out that married *couples get divorced*, but *marriages end in divorce*.
- *Spend £11,000 on their wedding* – point out the preposition: spend money *on* things.
- *Big days* – wedding days. If someone tells you they're getting married, you can ask: *When's the big day?*
- *A very traditional wedding* – in Britain, this means *a church wedding* where *the bride wears white* and is usually *given away by her father*. Point to the picture.
- *It was worth it* – it was expensive, but it was a good use of money. Give the opposite: *It was a waste of money.*
- *A suit / a big Rolls Royce* – point to the picture.
- *A castle* – draw a picture of ask for / give local examples.
- *Gave a long speech* – act out giving a speech. Ask when else people give speeches – at formal dinners, retirement parties, etc. Make sure they don't get it confused with *giving presentations* at school or work.
- *Got a bit drunk* – act it out. She drank too much alcohol!
- *They always happen* – these things are normal at weddings in Britain!
- *A registry office* – in Britain, you can have a religious wedding in a church or a non-religious wedding in a registry office. You could ask if things are the same in the students' countries.
- *Close families* – brothers and sisters and parents, but not all the aunts and uncles and cousins.
- *Shared the cost* means they paid 50%, we paid 50%. Elicit other things you can share – *food, a room, a book*, etc.
- *Hired* – paid to use it for a short period of time. Ask for / give other things you can hire – *bikes for a day, a guide*, etc.
- *DJ-ed* – refer students to the **Real English** note on page 115.

Do the text as a listening, a reading or both, (see **Introduction** for procedure).

5 After you read

Explain the task and refer students to the examples given. You might want to model the task first by giving one or two examples of things that were the same / different to weddings you've been to and things that surprised you. Make sure you use the sentence starters given.

Give students four or five minutes to compare their ideas. Round up by asking if anything in the texts really surprised anyone and why.

6 Speaking

Ask students to read the questions first and check they understand them. There shouldn't be a problem as this is all language that has come up before, through students may need reminding of some things. Explain the task. Ask students to discuss the questions in pairs or small groups. Monitor and help out with any new vocabulary. Round up in the usual way.

7 Using grammar: making suggestions

You could lead in to this activity by telling the class a friend of yours is getting married soon and you want to buy them a present, but don't know what to get. Have they got any suggestions? Students will probably call out single words such as plates or perfume or maybe even money. Write these on the board and try to elicit the missing grammar. You could add extra prompts like this:

Why ... you just give her some money?

How ... some perfume?

If you can't elicit the missing words, simply give them and refer students to the task. Explain it and give students two minutes to do the matching. Let them have one more minute to compare with a partner and then elicit the answers from the class and write them on the board.

> **Answers**
>
> 1. d.   2. c.   3. e.   4. a.   5. b.

Go through any new language. For example:

- *Give my mum for her birthday* – highlight the pattern here. Give examples: *My dad gave me this for Xmas. I gave her a great book for her birthday.*
- *You look good in that* – you can add: *It really suits you.* You could ask a few students what kind of clothes / colours they look good in.
- *It's a bit older* – if we don't know if the baby is a boy or a girl, we often say *it*. If someone is pregnant, we often ask: *When's it due?*
- *I don't know ...* – highligt the endings and add some more to show the pattern, *I don't ... know where he lives. / ... how old she is / ... what he's doing now / ... why she married him, etc.*

Point out that after *How about* there's a noun, but after *Why don't you*, there's a verb.

Tell the class they're going to listen to the five questions and answers, but that in each they'll hear the response to the suggestion. The first speaker in each conversation will say if they think the suggestion good or not. Ask students to decide which speakers like the suggestion and which don't.

Play the conversations once all the way through. Give students a minute or two to compare their answers in pairs. Play the conversations once more, stopping after each one. Ask if the speaker likes the suggestions or not and how they know. As you elicit the answers, write on the board some of the expressions used in the responses to the suggestions.

> **Answers**
>
> **Conversation 1:** Doesn't like the suggestion. Their mum doesn't really like perfume. She never wears it. (Point out *you wear perfume, you don't use it.*)
> **Conversation 2:** Likes the suggestion. Says, *Yes, OK. Maybe I'll do that.*
> **Conversation 3:** Doesn't like the suggestion. Says, *I don't really want to. I'm not a very good cook.*
> **Conversation 4:** Likes the suggestion. Says, *Yes, that's a good idea. Thanks. I'll do that.*
> **Conversation 5:** Likes the suggestion, but says, *It's too expensive. I don't want to spend that much money.*

Ask students to read **Grammar note** G26 on page 142.

Finally, put students into pairs. Student A reads out the problems in 1–5. Student B makes an alternative suggestion to those heard on the recording, using *Why don't you* and *How about*. Student A then responds to the suggestions, saying if they like them or not. To make this easier for students, get them to write the five conversations first in pairs. They could then memorise the conversations and try to repeat them without looking. Round up in the usual way.

To extend this activity, get students to swap roles or to write their own individual problems. They can walk around and talk to some different students, getting different advice. Round up by asking who gave the best advice to a few problems.

Homework

As this is the last unit in the book, tell students to make sure they finish the **Workbook**. You could refer them to the **Grammar Organiser** at the back of the Workbook, if you haven't already done so and encourage them to translate the expressions in it.

Tell students that the best way to prepare for **Pre-Intermediate Innovations** is to use their L1 translations to help them remember all the expressions in both the **Grammar Organiser** and the **Expressions Organiser**. Remind them of how they can use the L1 translations to try to re-elicit the whole English expressions.

Review: Units 19–24

Activities 1–5 could be set as homework or done as a short test. If you do them as a test, it's best to give students 15–20 minutes to do them.

You could also do these activities as a slightly more relaxed revision lesson. You can introduce tasks quite simply by saying: *Now we're going to revise some questions / vocabulary / grammar we've looked at before* and then explain the tasks. Students can do the tasks in pairs or individually as you wish. When you elicit the answers to each activity, you can ask questions about the language and re-teach any words and expressions students have problems with. After each activity, there is a suggested follow-up that you could do as a way of breaking up the lesson a little. They all provide some opportunities for speaking.

1 Grammar: continuous forms

Answers

The present continuous: meeting, doing, feeling
The past continuous: staying, looking, saying

1. are (you) doing, 'm meeting, 'm going
2. wasn't listening
3. 's not feeling
4. was working
5. was watching
6. Is (it still) raining

Ask students to discuss the questions in pairs or groups of three. Monitor and help out with any new language. Round up with a couple of corrections or interesting things students said. Also, teach anything new you heard students trying to say.

2 Describing changes

Answers

1. more expensive   2. taller   3. better   4. fatter
5. easier   6. cheaper

Ask students to discuss the questions as a whole group or in pairs. If students are in pairs, monitor and round up in the usual way.

3 I couldn't

Answers

1. b.   2. f.   3. a.   4. e.   5. c.   6. d.

Explain the next task. As students are writing, go round and check that they've understood and are writing sensible things down. Correct what they've written, where necessary. Ask students to discuss the final questions. Monitor and round up as before.

4 Questions

Answers

1. d.   2. a.   3. f.   4. b.   5. e.   6. c.

Before doing the next part, ask students to memorise the answers and to then test each other. Student A says the question; student B closes the book and says the answer.

Answers

1. Do you like sport?
2. Do you like playing tennis?
3. What are your parents like?
4. What's the best place to eat in town?
5. What's the best way to get to your house?
6. What's the best time to phone you?

Get the students to ask and answer the questions in pairs.

5 Verbs

Answers

1. took   2. spent   3. got   4. lent   5. caused
6. failed

As a follow-up, write one or two personalised questions on the board for students to discuss. For example:
What's the most money you've ever spent? What on?
Have you ever lent something to someone and then they didn't give you it back?

Round up by re-telling any interesting things you heard to the class.

6 Look back and check

If you have repeated these tasks as a form of revision / warmer in a previous lesson, you may want to skip this activity.

Let students look back at both activities and decide which one they want to do. Take a vote on which one they prefer or do both. Give students time to read and ask you questions about the language before they do the speaking task again. Round up in the usual way.

7 What can you remember?

You could do this activity orally if you like, instead of getting students to write notes. Students will remember quite a lot about the *content* of a text, but often will not remember the exact expressions or collocations. Try to remind students of these as you go through the answers. For example:

Student: Andrew know politician.
Teacher: Yes, OK. Andrew met a politician.

An alternative way of doing this is to replay the recording of one or both of the texts, depending on the time you have available.

8 Vocabulary builder: food and cooking

This page aims to revise and expand on vocabulary, in this case ways of preparing food.

Ask students to discuss the questions. Tell the students your own answers to the questions first to model the task and draw students' attention to the pictures and words on the right to help them. Monitor and help out with any new language. Round up with a couple of corrections or interesting things students said. Also, teach anything new you heard students trying to say.

Ask students to use their dictionaries to think of answers to the next six questions. Then ask them to discuss the questions in small groups. Do they all agree? Again, model this by giving your own ideas first. Where students don't share a common language, encourage the students to describe any new foods they want to talk about: *It's a kind of vegetable, etc.* Round up as before.

9 Listening: *I like your flat*

Do this listening as you would do a normal listening. Explain the context and the task. Make sure students cover the conversation the first time they hear it. Ask students to compare their ideas in pairs. As they do so, go round and check to see how they've done. Depending on how much they've got, either elicit the answers from the class or play the recording a second time and then do so.

Answers

There is no fixed answer to the first task. It's up to you how much you want students to get. However, as a guide, it's best for students to have understood the following before moving on to the next task:
The flat's lovely. John's been there for 3 months. It's got a huge bedroom. The kitchen's got a nice table in it.

Tell the class they are going to hear the conversation again and that this time you want them to listen and complete the conversation by writing the words they hear in the gaps. Tell them they might need to write two, three or four words in the gaps. Play the conversation and then give the students a minute to compare their ideas with a partner. You may want to elicit the answers immediately or you may want to play the conversation one more time and stop after each gap. Students then call out their answers. Write them on the board. As you do so, deal with any new / interesting language.

Answers

1. It's really nice
2. What would you like?
3. There you are
4. how long've you
5. It's huge
6. did you get it
7. How long've you
8. on the left

Ask students to discuss the questions in small groups or as a class. Round up as above.

10 Pronunciation: the letter 'e'

This activity looks at the relationship between spelling and sound. Use the recording or model the sounds and words yourself and ask students to repeat them. Explain the task. Do this as a race – ask students to do this in pairs and see which pair finishes first. Stop the task when the first pair finishes. Let the students read out their route. If they give a wrong answer, stop them and let another pair try to finish the route. The pair with the correct route is the winner!

Answers

collect   dentist's   get   let   tennis   extra   lend   best   friendly   celebrate   central   wedding   kettle

11 Collocations

The collocation exercise also uses the grid of words from **10 Pronunciation**. The idea is to find a different route by completing each pair of expressions with one word from the grid. You could do this as a race with students working in pairs or threes in the same way as **10 Pronunciation** above. Do the first two as a class.

Answers

1. collect
2. great
3. heart
4. there
5. government
6. return
7. kitchen
8. extra
9. early
10. celebrate
11. league
12. wedding
13. kettle

As this is revision, there's no need to go over the language here. However, after students have got the answers, ask if anyone has any questions.

You could re-use the grid now or at another time. Read out some sentences in 1–11 below, but say *blank* (or *whistle* or *hum*) instead of saying the word in the grid. Students listen and try to follow the route by deciding the missing word.

1. I _____ stamps. I've got hundreds.
2. I've got an appointment at the _____ tomorrow?
3. I'm just going to the shop to _____ some milk.
4. Our teacher doesn't _____ us eat or drink in the class.
5. Did you watch the _____ yesterday?
6. I've got an _____ racket I can lend you.
7. I've got to get up really _____ tomorrow.
8. I think I might go to the doctor. I've got a horrible _____ache.
9. Thanks for the present. I _____ like it.
10. I'm too short to be any good at _____ , but I enjoy watching it.
11. Can you make the tea? The _____'s boiled!

Notes

Notes

Notes